Currents of Change in English Language Teaching

Edited by Richard Rossner
and Rod Bolitho

Oxford University Press

Oxford University Press
Walton Street, Oxford OX2 6DP

Oxford New York Toronto
Delhi Bombay Calcutta Madras Karachi
Petaling Jaya Singapore Hong Kong Tokyo
Nairobi Dar es Salaam Cape Town
Melbourne Auckland

and associated companies in
Berlin Ibadan

OXFORD and OXFORD ENGLISH
are trade marks of Oxford University Press

ISBN 0 19 437010 0

© Oxford University Press 1990

First published 1990
Second impression 1990

All rights reserved. No part of this publication may be reproduced, stored in a retrieval system, or transmitted, in any form or by any means, electronic, mechanical, photocopying, recording, or otherwise, without the prior permission of Oxford University Press.

This book is sold subject to the condition that it shall not, by way of trade or otherwise, be lent, re-sold, hired out or otherwise circulated without the publisher's prior consent in any form of binding or cover other than that which it is published and without a similar condition including this condition being imposed on the subsequent purchaser.

The authors and publisher would like to thank the following for permission to reproduce the material below:

Cambridge University Press for 'Table 2: Selected ELT activities' from Meaning into Words (1984), Doff et al.

Longman for 'Figure 1: A discourse chain' from The Communicative Teaching of English (1981), C. Candlin (ed.)

Typeset by Pentacor PLC, High Wycombe, Bucks

Printed in Hong Kong

Contents

Introduction   1

Section One **The role and purpose of ELT**   5

  John Rogers: 'The world for sick proper'   7
  Gerry Abbott: Should we start digging new holes?   15
  Cem and Margaret Alptekin: The question of culture:
    EFL teaching in non-English-speaking countries   21
  Luke Prodromou: English as cultural action   27
  Harry Krasnick: Images of ELT   40

Section Two **The communicative era: second decade**   47

  Jack C. Richards: Communicative needs in foreign
    language learning   48
  Li Xiaoju: In defence of the communicative approach   59
  Michael Swan: A critical look at the communicative
    approach   73
  H. G. Widdowson: Against dogma: A reply to Michael
    Swan   99
  Péter Medgyes: Queries from a communicative teacher   103
  Pit Corder: Talking shop: Pit Corder on language
    teaching and applied linguistics   110

Section Three **Issues in methodology and teacher training**   119

  Alan Maley: New lamps for old: realism and surrealism
    in foreign language teaching   120
  R. L. Allwright: What do we want teaching materials
    for?   131
  Robert O'Neill: Why use textbooks?   148
  Iain MacWilliam: Video and language comprehension   157
  Anita Wenden: Helping language learners think about
    learning   161
  Caleb Gattegno: Talking shop: A conversation with
    Caleb Gattegno, inventor of the Silent Way   175

Contents

David King: Counselling for teachers	182
Rob Nolasco and Lois Arthur: You try doing it with a class of forty!	188
Esther Ramani: Theorizing from the classroom	196
Jeremy Harmer: Balancing activities: a unit-planning game	208
Graham Carter and Howard Thomas: 'Dear Brown Eyes': Experiential learning in a project-orientated approach	215
Rod Ellis: Activities and procedures for teacher training	226

Conclusion 236

Appendices 241

  Bibliography 241

  A chronology of recent events and publications 252

  Contributors 255

  Topic index to volumes 36–42 261

Acknowledgements 268

Introduction

Papers published in professional or academic journals have an uncertain future. Most are read when they appear with varying degrees of thoroughness by subscribers and in libraries. Some are dismissed as ephemera or exotica; others are noted for later reference; a few find fame because they are considered 'landmarks', 'seminal', or controversial; one or two live on for years in the mainstream of the profession; but the majority fall victim to the march of time.

The English language teaching (ELT) profession is no exception to this rule. There is little enough time in any teacher's life to glance at—let alone absorb—the multitude of items that appear in the various national and international organs of the profession, and most of what is written—however poignant and inspired—slips quietly into oblivion. This is an inevitable feature of periodical (and newspaper) writing, and is no reflection on the well-honed efforts of contributors or the judgement of editors (who often have to reject five or ten times as many papers as are published). ELT is also an area of teaching that has undergone massive quantitative and qualitative development over recent years, so there is more to write about, and there are more potential readers than ever before.

This collection is an attempt to pause in order to allow further scrutiny of a cross-section of papers that appeared in the *ELT Journal* between 1982 and 1988. This was an interesting and challenging time to be editors of *ELTJ* because the more tentative and exploratory phase in the development of the 'communicative approach' was ending in Britain and there was an attempt to consolidate, call into question, and explore the ramifications of the various pedagogical and linguistic shifts of emphasis that had occurred. *ELT Journal* is a key publication in the profession as it is truly international in the contributions it accepts and the readership it obtains (it is read in more than 100 countries), although its roots lie in Britain. Founded in 1946 on the initiative of the British Council, the *Journal* has always striven to highlight through its contents the links between 'theory' and 'practice', and to respect the necessarily different priorities for the development of ELT in different countries around the world. The current Statement of Aims puts it like this:

> ... the *Journal* is concerned with the fundamental practical factors that have influenced the profession, as well as the theoretical issues that are relevant to it. It seeks to bridge the

gap between the everyday concerns of teachers in their classrooms and the various disciplines . . . that may offer significant insights.

The papers collected in this volume are, we feel, particularly good examples of this policy in action. It is probably too early to regard any of them as 'seminal', and that is not the main reason for selecting them for second publication. Rather, our criteria have been based on a desire to offer through typical contributions to the *Journal* a feel for the currents of change that were swirling through ELT. Sometimes trends and changes emerge gradually over a period of years. The main advantage of a retrospective collection of this nature is that it provides the reader with an opportunity to survey some of these trends with the benefit of hindsight, rather than in the heat of the moment. As the period in question—the early 1980s—was one of reassessment and increasing awareness of the complex implications of the communicative 'revolution', the currents were not uniform in direction, depth, geographical distribution, or durability. This is a feature that we have tried to capture in this selection.

1981 marked the beginning of the second decade of the communicative era in language teaching—and for some the first of the post-communicative era. The previous ten years had seen lively debate and activity surrounding the development of basic principles and tools, confined at first to the narrow borders of Western Europe. Fanned by the enthusiasm of teachers for these developments, and by the commercial drive of publishers, the communicative message spread fast, if unevenly, particularly among those around the world with international contacts and the financial resources to explore communicative 'products'. Among practitioners who came into direct contact with the communicative movement, the enthusiasm generated was remarkable: here was an approach—or rather a set of approaches—that seemed to offer more relevant, interesting, and humane language-learning experiences for learners, and that suggested broader, more fulfilling roles for teachers through more varied and motivating materials.

By 1981, while the currents were still reaching some places and sectors for the first time, those in the profession who were now familiar with communicative practices were analysing and reconsidering some of the issues in the light of experience. The three sections of this book—'The Role and Purpose of ELT', 'The Communicative Era: Second Decade', and 'Issues in Methodology and Teaching Training'—group together under these headings some of the best papers written for the *ELT Journal* in that period. The papers, like those that appear every quarter in the *Journal*, come from a variety of places and sectors of the profession. Some adopt the perspective of native-speakers of English in English-speaking countries, while others—native-speakers and non-native speakers—consider the issues on the basis of experience in environments where English is used only for certain purposes or very little.

We have made explicit our own framework for considering these disparate but complementary contributions in the hope that this will help readers to see the collection as a more or less coherent whole. Thus, each section begins with our own brief introduction, and short linking pieces provide (we hope) an unobtrusive bridge from one item to the next. At the end of the collection we tie together the various strands we have identified in the items, and we pose some questions which may be relevant to the immediate future development of ELT. We also suggest a few other readings, and, as a context for the communicative movement itself, we offer a chronological summary of some of the major developments and publications of the last fifty years. In addition, we have included a Topic Index which spans all the subject areas covered in *ELTJ*, volumes 36–42.

We are aware that a collection like this leaves plenty to be said, not least because it draws on a fixed period in ELT history. Our hope is that it will provide a useful resource for practising teachers and those in training, as they work through these and other matters. We also hope that it may stimulate more writing about ELT of a similar kind, and we urge anyone with thoughtful points to make and experiences to share to offer their work to the *ELT Journal* and the other periodicals which provide a forum for professional exchange, so that the dynamic exemplified in this collection can continue unabated. For, if one thing is clear from these writings, it is that there are no magic formulae or easy answers, and much thinking, writing, and experimenting remains to be done.

SECTION ONE

The role and purpose of ELT

These days English language teaching (ELT) is big business. An 'international' language is a logical requirement in an era of worldwide information-sharing and commercial exchange. For better or worse, the role has fallen to English. The result is that its status in education systems and settings is an extraordinary one. From an early age, vast numbers of people and their parents have looked on English as being one of the most useful subjects in the curriculum. Core subjects like maths, science, and the mother tongue, are usually quite rightly given more time than the first foreign language, but for many pupils and students, it is harder to understand the future relevance of any of these than to foresee the practical usefulness of English. In adult education, much greater numbers of students spend time on English than on other languages and 'modern' subjects, such as computing or technology. Many of them invest substantial sums of money in tuition and materials for learning English—an expense that would have been confined to the well-off enthusiast only twenty or thirty years ago.

The fact that so many are involved in learning English does not, of course, mean that all is wonderfully well in the classrooms. Many learners, young and old, quickly become disillusioned because of inappropriate or stultifying methods and materials. Moreover, at school level there is some doubt about the credentials of English (or any other foreign language) as a full-blown subject. For example, how much time should be spent on matters relating to literature and culture? How much time should be spent comparing the mother tongue and the foreign language, and how much on simply 'practising' the foreign language in realistic ways, the main priority for most learners? These and other questions make curriculum development for foreign language teaching a complicated matter in which educational beliefs come up against 'market forces' in unexpected ways.

This huge expansion in ELT worldwide has given extraordinary responsibilities to those who contribute to the development of teaching and learning programmes, methodology, and materials. Methodologists, materials writers, and publishers in ELT now find themselves working in an international arena that is unique in the history of education. In particular, for publishers the temptation to offer 'products' that have universal appeal and can generate large profits in the worldwide marketplace has proved irresistible. Try as some British and American publishers may, in the commercial world it is hard to pay proper heed to the various requirements of different groups of learners in widely differing cultural, socio-economic, and political contexts. Nor is it possible for writers working in Britain or the U.S.A. to step aside from their own cultural context and language-teaching background, heavily influenced as it may be by liberal 'western' educational thinking, and to take on board the educational and language-learning priorities of radically different communities of learners. So it may (and has) come about that teachers whose mother tongue is not English and who have not visited an English-speaking country find themselves using approaches that run counter to their own experiences as learners and their training as teachers, and using materials which look seductive but are partially incomprehensible and/or irrelevant. For learners want to be able to use English for whatever purpose *they* wish, and this may have nothing to do with the culture of the English-speaking world.

These and related issues that touch on the relationship between more developed and less developed countries, and the responsibilities of the former in this relationship, are ably addressed in the first paper in this collection, 'The world for sick proper' by John Rogers and in Gerry Abbott's response, which follows it. Rogers' central question relates to the ethics of any education system that raises false hopes among a majority of those within it. Worse still, in Rogers' view, are the hopes that are raised for an approximation to a way of life that would be inappropriate and damaging. In some senses, English is cast in the role of a sinister seducer, and those teaching ELT in developing countries are seen merely as agents in the global socio-economic conspiracy. It would, in Rogers' view, be far better and far less wasteful to leave the teaching of English until tertiary level. By that time, the 'natural selection' that operates within educational systems will have defined the small group who might benefit from learning English.

Abbott's view, however, is that the fault—if there is one—lies with whole educational systems including those in the industrialized world. Formal education as currently organized promises much more than it can deliver and leaves 'consumers' poorly equipped to improve on—or even cope adequately with—the disappointing reality that most face. For foreign experts in ELT to query national decisions to include English in the secondary or even primary curriculum is impertinent. All that can be done is to attempt to make the teaching as relevant and effective as possible so that a maximum number of consumers can benefit if the opportunity later presents itself.

'The world for sick proper'

John Rogers

In a short story by Paul Theroux, *The Flower of Malaya*, one of the characters is a young American woman:

> ... She was a teacher ... She taught English, most of them do, never asking themselves what happens when a half-starved world is mumbling in heavily-accented English, 'I want—'.

Shortly after I read this, I read the June 1979 issue of the *New Internationalist*, 'Children's Voices', in which seventy children from five continents talk about their lives and their hopes for the future. Quite a few of these children, from West and East Africa, the West Indies and India, Pakistan and Bangladesh, spoke in their own varieties of English. Here is what some of them said, or 'mumbl[ed] in heavily-accented English':

—Kweku (9), Accra, Ghana:
> My work is that I sell chewing gum around the Orion Circle at cinema time ... My mother died before they born me. My father nobody know ... I sleep in the far night at 2.00 a.m. sometimes 3.00 a.m. morning time. I no have sleeping house. I sleep at the lorry petrol station ... The world for sick proper. I want 1979 to have no war and no children born like I am ... I want 1979 to bring house for us and water for village people to drink. Don't take photo of me. I don't want white man see me dirty.

—Keshar (9), Nagpur, India:
> I am looking through all this rubbish every day. It is my work ... I look for glass, paper, old iron things, plastic sandals ... I don't like this work. You work in sun all day. You get dirty. You get sick easy ... I would like to go to school. I like to see small girls going to school with books and slate ... I would like to have a house and two sets of clothes ...

—Vinton (14), Kingston, Jamaica:
> I want to go back to school and get myself a trade. I learn welding, woodwork, and learn to fix electrics. You have some boys and they get trade, but they follow their friends. They go robbin' and the police kill them. Them idiots. If I get a trade, I cool ... In twenty years' time I wish I'm in nice job with my wife and children and house, you know ...

—Wambgu (12), Nairobi, Kenya:
I left school because I failed and I have no money. I want a job nicely. Every day I look for work. Mainly I work with cars. Look at my clothes. I am a dirty boy because I am a mechanic. I am the spanner boy. I only get 5 shillings a day. I try to save it. But I need the money for smoking.

—Kenyatta (14), Kenya:
... The [boy] at school will get to be a manager and have a big car. The [boy] at home will just become a thief and a robber ... If you don't know English they will say that you are a useless man and they won't do what you tell them. I want to be a manager and then they will just bring my letters and I will put my signature there. I will give many orders to others, and I will warn those ones who are lazy or drunk. And if they don't agree with me, I will sack them ...

—Fibi (15), Kenya:
At school we used tribal language. When we moved to Nairobi my English is not enough for school. I am sad because I used to do well and now you can see I am not a person who is educated.

And so on.

Has English helped these children and the countries they are trying to survive in, or has it in some way been part of the cause of their miserable existence? Is it ethical to go on teaching English to so many children, and so encourage them to believe that it will automatically entitle them to a better job, an office job, a manager's job with a big car, a house and two sets of clothes, a 'better' life? Have we omitted to ask ourselves what happens when this 'half-starved world' mumbles, 'I want—', in English?

The rest of this article attempts a brief examination of what English teaching (and learning) might be responsible for and what some future options might be. It is of course very tentative and, I trust, very provocative. I would very much like to start a discussion of the question and hope that readers will respond, for or against, with feeling.

At the outset I should perhaps make it clear that my attack—for it is an attack—is not directed at the teaching of English to migrants or immigrants who come to live in an English-speaking country and who do not speak English, although even here I would prefer to see facilitation rather than intervention. It is, rather, directed at the often indiscriminate teaching of English in countries where it is a second or a foreign language and where a knowledge of English is regarded as a passport to a 'better' job. In these countries English is also considered essential as a means of international communication and as the means for acquiring access to 'Western' technology, science and, finally, 'Western-style development and progress'. (I make no apologies for the liberal use of quotation marks. These words have been over-used to such an extent that they are now almost meaningless and need drastic redefining.)

Several questions are begged. It may well be that in some countries there are a number of attractive, well-paid jobs for which a knowledge of English is essential. How many such jobs are there? How many English learners are there in schools? Do they all want these jobs? Are there enough jobs of this kind for all those who want them? If there aren't, and if there are unlikely to be enough, isn't it dishonest, even immoral, for the schools and the systems that run them to pretend that learning English *is* a passport or entry visa to a so-called better future? An example from Kiribati suggests that any secondary school English programme that doesn't warn its customers about 'progress', in the form of the microchip/ word processor revolution, isn't fulfilling its obligations. One Kiribati commercial company installed an IBM machine that resulted in the 'redundancy' of a number of office workers who, at school, believed that competence in English would guarantee a permanent office job. Perhaps their secondary school English textbook should have included the lexical items, 'redundancy' and 'multi-national companies'. Let me quote another young Kenyan office hopeful, Faith (13), from Masailand:

> My best subject is English. I try very hard to learn it well. It is the fashionable language nowadays. You can't work in an office without it. How can you get a job if you just say 'Nintaka Kaze' in Swahili? I will start by sweeping the office and after that I will move up to be a secretary . . . When I am working I will find jobs for people of my family and tribe. I am the one who studied, the lucky one, so I shall help . . .

All our Dip.TESL (Diploma in the Teaching of English as a Second Language) course members at the English Language Institute in Wellington tell us that one of the reasons their students learn English is that English is essential as a means of international communication. When we ask these same course members how many of their students can realistically expect ever to meet native-speakers of English, or indeed non-native speakers who use English as a second or third or foreign language, or how many of them *will* need English for communication purposes, the replies suggest that only a very, very small percentage will need English for that purpose.

Related to this, of course, is the necessity for some tertiary level students to be able to read English-language texts and, if they study overseas, to be able to understand the English of lecturers and tutors and to be able to make themselves understood in seminars and tutorials. But what do the figures tell us? In Tonga, to take an example from the South Pacific, only two per cent of secondary school leavers actually need English for higher education overseas. In March 1980, I was told by the then Senior Education Officer for Curriculum in the Tongan Ministry of Education that the number of Tongans studying overseas was decreasing. Also in March 1980, I was told by the Director of Education in Western Samoa that 0.08 per cent of school leavers need English for higher studies overseas or scholarships. He added that between 15 and 18 per cent of school leavers needed English for government or private company jobs in Western Samoa itself. This need, the need for scholarship students to be able to study through the medium of English, is often quoted as a justification of the learning of English by *all* secondary students. It would be interesting to know the figures for all the countries that continue to insist that *all* secondary students, if not primary pupils, must learn English.

The third question that is begged is the implication that English is the most, or at least one of the most, important means for acquiring access to Western technology, science and, through this, to Western-style development and progress. Apart from the question of the desirability of Western-style 'progress', there is the assumption that progress or development can come only through the medium of English. There is now abundant evidence to show that many worthwhile improvements in traditional cultures are being made where local people are consulted not instructed, that beneficial changes are being implemented without the imposition of Western solutions. The Food and Agricultural Organization bulletins, *Ideas and Action*, are full of examples of successful development programmes that do not rely on the importation of Western ideas and approaches. As Edward F. Douglass says, in 'The discovery of commonness—essential for cross-cultural dialogue' (*Ideas and Action* 112, 1976/5):

> No warnings are offered to the people of the developing countries about the intrinsic problems of Western life: alienation, poverty amidst vast wealth, and the constrictions of urban life. Traditional peoples are not cautioned about the loss of family ties and security, the ulcerous pace of life and the psychological dislocations from the basic truths of traditional life. Yet these changes represent, in part, the price of adopting the Western notion of modernity.

The programmes that took the trouble in the first place to see why African farmers, for example, farmed the way they did have proved to be the most successful.

As an illuminating aside on the role of language in development, in *Ideas and Action* 115, 1977/2, there is an article by Dohol Chandra Soni, 'The spoken and unspoken word in rural communication', which points out that even a country's standard and uniform language may be a barrier to development. In India, particularly in the four states of Bihar, Uttar Pradesh, Rajasthan, and Madhya Pradesh, the standard and uniform type of Hindi is used as the medium of communication between the programme agents and the programme targets. But the programme participants, mostly unschooled adults, have strongly-formed speech habits in the locally spoken dialects. The so-called educators do not 'step down' to the local spoken languages. They expect the programme-target people to change their deeply ingrained adult speech habits and adopt the uniform standard Hindi as a pre-condition of becoming literate, educated and developed. To quote Mr Soni:

> This is indirectly to discourage the people, to tell them that their speech habits are incapable of literacy, education, and development. As soon as the educator talks and teaches in Hindi, he SILENTLY or in an unspoken manner imprints upon the minds of the people that their own spoken language (which is a part of their personality) is incapable of becoming the medium of education. And since the man cannot make a distinction between himself and his speech habit, he cannot have the necessary self-confidence for becoming literate, educated, and developed when his spoken language is not made the medium of his literacy, his education and his development.

Similarly, an insistence on the need for English as the vehicle for development and progress might well be counter-productive.

It might be argued that English itself it neutral and does not necessarily bring anything else with it, no alien values, but, like Hindi in the example quoted above, the very fact of using it, relying on it, does have implications. One is reminded of Paulo Freire, in *Pedagogy of the Oppressed*:

> There is no such thing as a neutral educational process. Education either functions as an instrument which is used to facilitate the integration of the younger generation into the logic of the present system and bring about conformity to it or it becomes the 'practice of freedom', the means by which men and women deal critically and creatively with reality and discover how to participate in the transformation of their world.

One reason for my mistrust of the use of English as a means of access to change and improvement is that in the countries of Asia, Africa, and the Pacific where I have seen English taught, its function has too often been the first function Freire describes above, and too rarely the second.

Whatever we may think about the advisability or desirability of teaching English to so many learners, a lot of English *is* being taught and a lot of textbook writers (and publishers) are making money out of this English teaching. One wonders, though, how much English is *learnt*. On a recent tour through Polynesia, for example, I was repeatedly told by secondary school teachers that children came to the secondary schools after their primary course 'unable to read English, unable to write English, and unable to understand spoken English'. These teachers complained that they 'had to start all over again'. At the University of the South Pacific, in Suva, Fiji, I was told that average first-year students, some from these same Polynesian secondary schools, know the meanings of about 7,500 common English words. 'Amongst those words known by less that two-thirds of students were 'frequent', 'anxiously', explanation', 'diligent' and 'radical'. These Pacific Islands students have an English reading vocabulary comparable to that of New Zealand thirteen-year-olds on the same tests. The results for the Listening Comprehension Tests were even lower' (Elley 1980).

English is, of course, a second language for these students, but they have to study through the medium of English and they are expected to be able to handle textbooks written for native speakers of English. As Elley goes on to say in the same report:

> After six years of primary school instruction, large numbers of pupils are reading with insufficient competence to cope with the expected reading tasks of the classroom. Throughout high school the problem becomes more serious, despite a severe drop-out rate and a series of selective examinations. By the time they reach university, the surviving students are still struggling with what must be largely meaningless English prose in their texts and reading assignments. By their own admission, many students are out of their depth, in coping with English as a second language.

Similar situations exist in many other countries. In Ethiopia we found (Rogers 1969) that after ten years' English learning, including six years with English as the medium of instruction for all secondary school subjects except Amharic, the national language, first-year university students needed to go right back to the beginning again in English. And these were the persistent, hard-working survivors of a dauntingly flattened educational pyramid-cum-obstacle course. Very few of them could read English passages written within a 2,000 word vocabulary at a speed of 100 words per minute. Very few could write a correct sentence in English. Thai and Indonesian university students often cannot cope with university textbooks written in English. We have found that some of these same students' English teachers, at the English Language Institute in Wellington, through no fault of their own, cannot read university level texts. And their written and spoken English is often poor. What hope have their students? Why go on teaching English if it's taught and learned badly?

Why are attempts made to teach English to so many students who are never going to need it? In Ethiopia's Third Five-Year Plan (1968–73) the projected drop-out figures were astounding. 70,000 children were to be in Grade 3 for the year 1968/9. (Grade 3 is where English teaching begins.) 10,000 of these children were expected to drop out after Grade 3. By the time this intake reached Grade 7, in 1972, there were expected to be only 38,100 survivors. In other words, 31,900 children were expected to drop out between Grade 3 and Grade 7. Yet they were all being taught English. What were they going to do with their pathetic scraps of English? English became the medium of instruction at Grade 7. 17,900 children were expected to drop out at the end of Grade 6. They would have been learning English for four years because they would need it for junior secondary classes. Was it fair to give so many children the idea that they would be going on to secondary schools, perhaps even to university?

Quite apart from the dubious ethics of raising so many false hopes, is no concern ever shown about the cost-effectiveness of such language-teaching programmes? I know of only one attempt to encourage cost-effectiveness studies in the teaching of foreign languages—in a paper by Peter Strevens, 'Where Has All The Money Gone?' (Strevens 1969). L. A. Hill (in 1978) suggested that English might better be taught at the tertiary level, the way Anglo-Saxon, Old Icelandic, Classical Arabic, Persian, Science German, and Science Russian are taught. As Hill says,

> Then [at the tertiary level] the best brains will have been selected out; students will have reached an age when they can make use of reason in their language learning; they will no longer be so afraid of making fools of themselves . . .

He lists further advantages, related to the points I have been trying to make about student numbers and teacher quality:

> [English] could be taught only to those students who were going to use it, so we would need fewer teachers and could choose the best available; the enormous wastage rate at school level (vast numbers of students failing to reach a level where they could make any meaningful use of the language; or never using the language after they have finished their studies) could be cut down considerably; and both the teachers and the students would be happier because the latter would be learning the language because they really wanted to. The course could concentrate heavily on the reading skill, since that is the most useful one to most students starting at this level.

As far as I can determine, this very sensible proposal provoked no comment or discussion. If it was read, it was ignored or forgotten. But imagine my delight when, in March 1980, the Senior Education Officer for Curriculum in the Tongan Ministry of Education said she would like to see English teaching discontinued in the primary schools, Tongan used as the medium of instruction in secondary schools, and a major effort directed at the teaching of Tongan. She advocated the teaching of English, technical and scientific English principally, to those groups of students, often 'mature' students, who need it for specialized studies overseas. She described one of her department's most successful ESP (English for Specific Purposes) projects, the teaching of English to groups of elderly ladies in Tongan villages who sell their handicrafts to tourists. In other parts of the world also, ESP courses seem to be proving very successful. The consumers are highly motivated, the instructors know very clearly what is required and such courses seem to avoid becoming EFNPP courses (English For No Particular Purpose: Coffey 1978), like so many school courses.

I realize, as do L. A. Hill and the Tongan Senior Education Officer (Curriculum), that any such decision will be very unpopular, to say the least, with parents, government officials, and members of parliament. As Hill puts it,

> ... in many countries parents insist on their children all learning a foreign language, because they believe that it will help them to get a good job; so if it is taught only to tertiary students, parents whose children do not reach that level will cause trouble to their members of parliament, the Minister of Education, etc.

(I like that 'etc.'.) Hill doesn't suggest a way to overcome this resistance; nor does the Tongan education official; nor do I.

However, by an interesting coincidence, or perhaps as yet another example of serendipity, a 1980 BBC TV documentary, and the book it was based on (Glasser 1977), describe a similar situation, happening almost in reverse in Europe. The book and the documentary describe a small southern Italian village, San Giorgio, where parents were very anxious to get higher education for their children. The young people realize that their parents, 'by sending them in for higher education ... have already made a choice on their behalf to send them away [from San Giorgio] simply because there is no chance whatsoever for [them] to get a job as an engineer, a doctor, an accountant, a lawyer and so on, in a tiny place like this. So by the very fact of education they are being made into exiles from fairly early childhood.'

English teaching was not, of course, the reason for the exiling of the young in San Giorgio. But their parents' desire for higher education *was*. In other countries parents' insistence on their children learning English has a similar origin and might well have similar effects.

> In the early 1960s, the Italian Government raised the school-leaving age to 16 and made it easy for nearly everyone to proceed to the state universities. Today, of Italy's two million unemployed, half have a university or similar qualification. There are also two million job vacancies, but they are not the sort of jobs that [San Giorgio's] parents hoped for as a reward for their 'sacrificio'—the sacrifice they made to get them a good education. (BBC TV script 1980)

According to Glasser, who has been involved in development in various countries for fifteen years, what we (developers? agents of change? English-teachers?) have been doing

> is to impose upon people a series of very violent emotional changes as the price of achieving industrialization and technological change. And this realization is such an emotional shock to them that you get a violent explosion in that society which leads to misery, cruelty and all those other things which we now (1980) see in Iran and Kampuchea ...

I don't feel that I have reached any conclusions. I think I have asked some questions that are not perhaps asked when countries embark on or modify English teaching programmes. I have suggested one or two alternative approaches to the problems of English teaching, alternative approaches which might reduce the frustration and inadequacy felt by planners, administrators, teachers, and 'consumers'.

The questions and approaches I have outlined are one of the results of my English teaching experiences in Europe, Asia, Africa, and the South Pacific, experiences that have left me with many doubts, a great deal of unease, and a growing realization that more of the same might not be the answer. Edward de Bono in *The Use of Lateral Thinking* (1967) has a very apt metaphor about the digging of holes and deepening and enlarging existing holes instead of deciding to dig new ones:

> It is not possible to dig a hole in a different place by digging the same hole deeper ... If the hole is in the wrong place, then no amount of improvement is going to put it in the right place. No matter how obvious this may seem to every digger, it is still easier to go on digging in the same hole than to start all over again in a new place ... The disinclination to abandon a half-dug hole is partly a reluctance to abandon the investment of effort that has gone into the hole without seeing some return. It is also easier to go on doing the same thing rather than wonder what else to do: there is strong practical commitment to it ... Yet great new ideas and great scientific advances have often come about through people ignoring the hole that is in progress and starting a new one ...

Perhaps ELT/ESL/EFL/TESOL 'experts' should consider climbing out of their current ELT holes and should start looking for sites for more useful, more productive holes, even though, as de Bono says, 'experts are not usually the first to leap out of the hole that accords them their expert status, to start digging elsewhere.'

(*Originally published in Volume 36/3, 1982*)

Should we start digging new holes?

Gerry Abbott

John Rogers' heartwarming article 'The world for sick proper' is the sort that demands a response. I found myself agreeing with the tenor of the argument, with the insistence on the need to ponder deeply upon the significance of English language teaching for the individual, especially the young learner. And yet there are some 'buts' that have to be expressed in any debate upon the issues that Rogers raises. One purpose of this article is to contradict some of his tentative arguments; the other is to support his implied championship of mother-tongue education, whether in poor underdeveloped countries or rich and perhaps overdeveloped ones.

Reasons for going on teaching English

Rogers first asks whether English has helped the sort of children whose views he quotes, or whether in some way it has contributed to their misery. But it is his second question which has to be answered first: 'Is it ethical', he asks, 'to go on teaching English to so many children, and so encourage them to believe that it will entitle them to ... a "better" life?' This question is couched in terms designed to elicit the answer 'No'. It also assumes that in giving the answer expected, we will be coming to some kind of policy-making decision. But of course we are the wrong people to ask. (I assume that Rogers is addressing teachers, teacher-trainers, so-called 'experts' in ELT and so on.) A decision in Colombo that English is to be a national language is one that I can challenge, as an academic exercise; but it is not one that I can change. A decision that English is to be retained as the medium of schooling in Uganda is one that the Ugandan government must make, not the foreign ELT expert. The establishment of a role for English in *any* country is a part of that country's national education policy, and is quite rightly effected with little or no reference to outside expertise; expatriates who hold advisory positions soon become aware of how seldom their advice is sought, let alone heeded. On this subject, the first chapter ('The adviser and his dubious role') of Curle (1966) should be made compulsory reading for all would-be experts.

When governments decree that English is to be taught, it is possible that the language might, in various areas for various reasons and in various ways, be taught badly. In these cases, the ELT outsider's job is to try to help to improve the teaching, not to try to erase English from the curriculum against the wishes of the government. Rogers' question is 'Why go on teaching English if it's taught and learned badly?' The answer is, 'Because that's the law, that's why.' Besides, we do not abolish school subjects merely because most students fail to master them. Recent investigations have found that large numbers of first-year secondary schoolchildren in Britain have learned very little of the arithmetic taught in primary schools, but no-one dreams of suggesting that we should therefore delete arithmetic from the primary curriculum.

Students who 'won't need English'

Another question posed not only by Rogers but also by many of the teachers I have worked with in various parts of the world asks why 'attempts are made to teach English to so many students who are never going to need it'. It is not the statistical accuracy but the assumed omniscience in this question that is dangerous. It is true that very few of the secondary students in a country like Ethiopia (and many others) will ever need to use English; but which ones are they? In the primary school or in first-year classes in the secondary school, prediction is hazardous. Since a compulsory English course is part of a system of compulsory education designed by a government to give (or appear to give) equal opportunity to all, who can say which particular children should be prevented from learning English? And at what stage can such a judgement be passed?

As an outsider one can of course try, as I once did in Thailand, and Rogers (1969) later did in Ethiopia, to persuade the decision-makers that English was not important enough to be on a particular curriculum. But in general, I believe that one has to be very careful to take into account the broad educational principle of equality of opportunity before offering such advice. Take, for instance, a territory where a knowledge of English is—whether we like it or not—considered an asset on the employment market, and where a large number of youngsters leave school after completing a compulsory period of primary education. Many of them leave school not because they want to but because there are too few secondary school places available. To delete English from the primary curriculum would be to make these young people even less employable. I know that many of them don't find reasonable employment anyway; but *some* of them do, and *sometimes* this is *partly* because they know *some* English.

Or take a very different case—the teaching of a foreign language in British secondary schools. I happen to believe that one very desirable educational opportunity is that of viewing aspects of life through the filter of a foreign language, and that we should therefore make this chance available to all our children. It has to be admitted that, for a variety of reasons (e.g. poor learner-motivation and poor teacher-performance in classes of wide ability range), the output of successful language-learners is low. But that does not mean that the children have gained nothing of value from the course. The teaching of French to primary schoolchildren in Britain is a case in point: the children's later performance in French may not be significantly better than that of their secondary school peers who have not done any primary French, but their attitudes may have changed for the better (see Burstall 1975) and this may be no mean achievement. Nevertheless, low foreign language achievement in schools has spurred the modern language teaching profession, first in the USA and now in Europe, to attempt 'individualization'.

Another recent move is towards 'compact courses', which provide intensive study over a brief period, instead of the usual handful of lessons per week over a period of several years. Now, there is no doubt a lot to be said in favour of such a policy. But the tendency will almost certainly be to start such courses later than the current ones; and of course, if compact courses were held after the age of sixteen, then all those who leave school at that age would be prevented from participating in them. FIPLV (the Fédération Internationale des Professeurs de Langues Vivantes) assures us (1982) that the aim 'is neither to reduce the time available, nor to lower standards, nor to narrow the focus'. We are also probably safe in assuming that no drastic delay such as I have just described is envisaged. But there are governments that might well be tempted to carry out a little social engineering by, for example, ensuring that access to English is reserved for the children of a social or even racial *élite*, the children who (by reason of wealth, influence, sponsorship or whatever) reach the later stages of the school system. Without having to use a delaying mechanism, the Residential Schools of mainland Malaysia carry out this sort of racial preferment, in that they continue to prepare selected Malays for Cambridge English examinations with a view to subsequent higher education in other countries using the medium of English, while the non-selective schools catering for all races prepare students for exams not accepted as valid for university entrance in those countries.

English and education

Let us return to Rogers' argument. Most of his observations are on aspects of English-medium education, rather than the learning of English as a foreign language; and I think it is fair to say that he tends to blame English where he should be blaming education; indeed, Rogers half admits this. No doubt it is a pity that Western education systems, along with their values and aims, were implanted or imported into countries (not all of them parts of former Western empires, remember) which could well devise more suitable ones for themselves. No doubt people such as Rogers and myself are disenchanted by the fruits of 'progress' that our own education systems have borne. And no doubt we are saddened when we see our own educational and social mistakes being re-enacted, sometimes as if to a script by some Third World Kafka. But could we outsiders really do any better in the circumstances? It is vital to avoid the paternalism that sometimes accompanies true concern: our own disenchantment with the product of our labours must not lead us to forbid the components to others who want them, or to interfere with the assembly of them. There is, after all, a good chance that others will make a better job of assembling them than we did. Again, if a nation's system of schooling is used 'to facilitate the integration of the younger generation into the logic of the present system' (Freire 1972), we may deplore its function; but we must not attach any special blame to English simply because it happens to be the nationally-appointed medium of instruction. Education has the same function in Tanzania, where Kiswahili has replaced English as the medium, and in Thailand, where the vehicle of learning is and always has been Thai.

What Rogers calls 'the dubious ethics of raising so many false hopes' probably applies to every education system in the world; with over three million unemployed in Britain at the moment, it certainly applies to ours.

And as he says, it is higher education of the kind currently offered, as much as anything else, which helps to alienate the young from their parents, including me from mine. It is the systems that are at fault, and perhaps what the world needs most is governments willing to re-design their educational ladders so as to help their young citizens to climb up different rungs towards more appropriate objectives, so that as adults they will contribute more effectively to the national well-being. Or perhaps young Kweku was right: it is the *world* that is 'for sick proper'.

The importance of the mother tongue

So far, I have concentrated on denying the guilt that Rogers attaches to the teaching of English as a second language in Asia and Africa. I want now to look at the alternative or parallel possibility: the teaching and use of the mother tongue (MT) in education.

I am convinced that wherever it is possible to start schooling and to achieve literacy in the MT it should be attempted. Fortunately, the catchment areas of the world's primary schools, even in multilingual nations, often lie within one language area, and the teachers are often 'locals'—or at least able to function socially in the local language. Nevertheless, there are often reasons why even children entering school for the first time are forced to operate in an alien language. The absence of syllabuses or materials, the migration of families across language boundaries, and shortages of suitable teachers are a few typical examples. At secondary level, there is less room for manoeuvre, because the catchment area of many a secondary school crosses several linguistic boundaries; and I know from my Ugandan experience under Idi Amin that English was trusted as a non-partisan vehicle of communication, whereas such tribal languages as Luganda and Lusoga, and even the non-tribal Kiswahili, were not.

If we do as many Third World societies do—that is, sensibly accept the spilt milk of history and face the brass tacks of the present—we will find that English has been appropriated and is by and large being used to serve the ends of the peoples who need it. But the ends do not necessarily justify the means: the need to rely on English (or French or Urdu) for secondary and tertiary education does not justify the neglect of and even contempt for the pupil's own language that some societies are guilty of.

In many countries, the government could, if it only put its mind to it, decentralize education sufficiently for all or most of its primary school-children to start their schooling and become literate in their MT. Those who wonder why it matters so much that a child should be instructed in the MT should pause and imagine what it would have been like trying to become literate and operate at school in (say) Russian before, and perhaps even without ever, becoming literate in their own language; the intellectual difficulties and the emotional trauma can be tremendous. They ought then to consider the findings of such researchers as Toukomaa (1982), who regards MT instruction as 'the key to the entire development of the child'.

It is no excuse to complain that there is no standard script for a certain language; my experience of helping to create a 'typewritable' orthography for the Kayan/Kenyah languages of Borneo leads me to think that such problems are easier to overcome than some people would have us believe. Where there is no accepted orthography and next-to-nothing to read, even a makeshift spelling system will do for a start. Dialectal variations are unlikely to be any more problematic than they are in English. Nor is lack of teaching material a valid excuse: there is almost always a wealth of folk stories and traditional lore to use as a starting point. It seems to me self-evident that a willingness to read, and an ability to write with fluency will be achieved far more easily through the MT than through any foreign language, whether it is Standard British English being imposed on West Africans in Lagos and West Indians in London, or Parisian French being marketed in Mali, or Bahasa Malaysia being imposed on the gentle Bidayuh of Borneo.

I suspect that Rogers would wholeheartedly support me when I say that ELT practitioners are often superbly placed to lend their skills to the support of MT instruction. The principles and practices of TEFL have, after all, much in common with those of first-language teaching at primary level, and are even more similar to those needed for the teaching of a non-MT but local medium of education such as Kiswahili or Bahasa Malaysia. Without having to speak the local language, ELT staff can pass on their skills to anyone who speaks English. Again, when we find that we are dealing with illiterate secondary schoolchidren, our first thought should be how we can get them to read—not how we can get them to read English. Teaching them (or helping other teachers to teach them) to read their MT—or the local medium of instruction, if this is more appropriate—is almost certainly the best thing to do; and ELT staff should do this without feeling guilty because they are not doing the job they are paid to do. By getting children literate in a local language they facilitate the reading of English, and this *is* what they are paid to do, surely. Besides, in my own work overseas in Africa and Asia, I have proved to my own satisfaction that outsiders are far more likely to gain local cooperation in ELT matters if they show a willingness to help tackle the country's linguistic problem as a whole than if they confine themselves to 'pushing' English all the time.

It is this wider and very worthwhile extension of our profession which I would like to see pursued, both in this journal and in action: the application of our language teaching skills to the teaching of those indigenous (or, in the case of migrant populations, exotic) languages that are vital for the communication process that we call education. To continue Rogers' borrowed metaphor, perhaps what is needed is not the digging of new holes, but the widening of those we have already dug.

(*Originally published in Volume 38/2, 1984*)

Cem and Margaret Alptekin's paper looks at the role of teachers abroad who are native speakers of English. It stresses the dangers of allowing or encouraging expatriate teachers of English, and local teachers who follow their lead, to employ a methodology which combines language training and cultural awareness-raising, and may include considerable emphasis on the norms and attitudes of Anglo-Saxon countries. Unlike Rogers, the authors do not question the need for English language teaching around the world. What they stress is the necessity for this to be untrammelled by cultural and ideological propaganda. What most learners need is an additional means—English—of communicating freely about their own ideas and realities, and of gaining access to information and ideas from outside their own countries.

The question of culture: EFL teaching in non-English-speaking countries
Cem and Margaret Alptekin

Introduction

As the lingua franca of the twentieth century, English is one of the most important means for acquiring access of Anglo-American technology. As a result, there is a huge need to learn English in non-English-speaking countries—a need which creates a great demand for English instructors. Since this demand far outruns the available supply of qualified local teachers of English, many countries recruit teachers who are native speakers of English.

These teachers, most of whom come from Britain or the United States, bring with them the notion that a language and its culture are two inextricably related entities, and as such should be taught together. Resting on the empirically unverified theory of linguistic relativity, the implicit claim is that no real acquisition of the target language can take place without the learner's internalization of target language speakers' patterns and values. After all, so the belief goes, the new linguistic and cultural competence will enable the learner to develop new perceptions of reality and to behave differently in the light of such perceptions. What is implied here is that learners experience a series of cognitive and affective changes thanks to which they take on a new identity (Brown 1981)—an identity with both bilingual and bicultural features. Thus, foreign language teaching is seen as a pedagogical process aimed at changing the learner's behaviour by injecting new norms and values into it (Trivedi 1978). Since these norms and values involve learning to perceive the world as the speakers of the target language habitually see it, the foreign language teacher is often advised to persuade the learners that 'success in language learning depends upon the degree to which they integrate themselves with the "native environment" of the language, whether they are learning it in the country in which it is spoken or not' (Curtin 1979:281).

Attitudes to foreign language learning in English-speaking countries

In the chiefly monolingual and monocultural context of English-speaking countries, where there is little functional utility or social prestige to be gained from foreign language study, such preoccupations with the cultural aspects of foreign language acquisition appear to have been made its chief selling point in order to stem the general decline in enrolments in foreign language classes. Yet, due to the notorious lack of awareness about foreign languages and cultures in English-speaking countries (Fishman 1977, Moles 1979, Alatis 1979, Marchand 1979), it is quite apparent that foreign language study which is 'billed as a guarantor of international and intercultural communication and understanding ... does not even enable its graduates to sustain an ordinary conversation with a native speaker' (Wanner 1979:25). Under these circumstances, where foreign language study fails to realize the fundamental goal of enabling the learner to use the new language as a communicative tool, it is superfluous to speak of such justifications for target language acquisition as its potential for expanding the learners' range of cultural experience (Herron 1980:70) and developing cross-cultural awareness and appreciation (Elling 1980:92). In fact, the findings of attitude surveys conducted among foreign-language learners suggest that the acquisition of the new language causes neither an improvement in the subjects' overall attitudes toward the native speakers of the language (Teitelbaum *et al.* 1975, Oller *et al.* 1977, Ake 1982), nor a decline in their own ethnocentrism (Ake 1982).

The native English-speaking teachers of EFL who come to the host country naturally reflect the trends of their own culture in foreign language pedagogy, and believe that teaching the target culture is a *sine qua non* of teaching the target language. Otherwise, it is believed, students will be exposed to a hollow language devoid of cultural content and will be unable to identify with the English-speaking culture. The host country's educational policies which are related to social goals normally established by governmental priorities are thus ignored or marginalized.

Attitudes to EFL in non-English-speaking countries

In general, EFL instruction for the host culture is important because it affords a window on the world of advanced technology and industrial development. However, the cultural norms and values of the English-speaking world which come with the technical data and equipment are often considered to be 'alien and unacceptable features' of the target culture (Wilkins 1975:49), and not necessarily for chauvinistic reasons (Kehoe 1971, Berger *et al.* 1974, Schiller 1976, Olbert 1982, Alptekin 1982). Indeed, being at the receiving end of a virtually one-way flow of information from Anglo-American centers, the host country runs the risk of having its own culture totally submerged, and thus imposes restrictions in educational and cultural domains to protect its way of life (Rao 1976). For example, in Japan, English is generally taught not as a functional tool for cross-cultural communication in international settings, but as a codified system (Giesecke 1980) representing the linguistic characteristics of an idealized American or Briton (Nakayama 1982). Similarly, in China and Korea, the pedagogical focus seems to be on the grammatical features of English without regard for its communicative and/or cultural functions (Scovel and Scovel 1980, Evans 1980). Elsewhere in Asia, and also in parts of Africa and Latin America, there is a feeling on the part of the educated élite that English instruction in particular and modernization in general which has not been 'acculturated' and shaped to fit their country's needs constitute a threat to national identity. Thus, suggestions have been made to 'de-Anglo-Americanize' English, both in linguistic and in cultural respects, in order for the language to be in tune with the needs of the EFL learners in such countries as Japan (Nakayama 1982) and Venezuela (Thomas 1983). Moreover, there has been an increase in the production of local teaching materials that are culturally and experientially appropriate for learners in developing countries. In Kuwait, for instance, EFL texts are being prepared 'with the Kuwaiti situation in mind' (Hajjaj 1981). Likewise, China produces its own materials which are clearly modelled on British EFL texts of the 1960s, with one major variation—a thoroughly transformed cultural content that aims at reinforcing Chinese cultural norms and values (Scott 1980). Even in industrialized European countries, as Freudenstein *et al.* (1981) indicate, EFL learners want to acquire an international variety of English, independent of the cultural norms and values of native English speakers. In fact, many of these learners tend to reject the norms and values of the English-speaking cultures, but still acquire English satisfactorily, due to their wish to identify with international attitudes which have developed in such fields as pop culture, travel culture, and scientific culture where English happens to be the principal medium of communication (Ladousse 1982).

On a deeper level, the hosts' willingness to learn English in the context of national or international norms and values is indicative of their belief in the possibility of becoming bilingual without becoming bicultural—a phenomenon whose existence is pointed out by Paulston (1978:373). It is apparent that this concept of bilingualism without biculturalism, which seeks to dissociate the learning of the target language from its nationality-bound cultural context, soon clashes with the native English-speaking teachers' unwitting efforts to disseminate among their students the cultural norms and values of the English-speaking country as part of their foreign language teaching.

The failings of the 'guest' teacher

The conflict between the opposing pedagogical views of the 'hosts' and the 'guest' teachers of EFL is in many cases exacerbated by the latter's ignorance of the ways and minds of the local people and their language. In fact, it is quite ironic that, while espousing the idea that foreign language acquisition is a means to increase cross-cultural awareness and sensitivity, the guest teachers are often unable to understand the host culture or to speak the local vernacular. Another irony lies in their attempts to expose their students to the norms and values of the English-speaking culture in the students' own setting, while very often they themselves continue to remain monolingual and monocultural there.[1]

This monolingualism and monoculturalism eventually paves the way to mental and physical isolation from the host society. Given the linguistic and cultural difficulties involved in establishing meaningful relationships in the host culture, the guest teachers retreat into the comfort of an English-speaking enclave of compatriots, foreigners, and a few unorthodox local individuals. In addition to living in an enclave, there are other factors which reinforce the native English-speaking teachers' isolation and alienation. For one thing, they know that, at least officially, they are not expected to acquire the language of the hosts. For another, they are aware that the hosts' vernacular is unlikely to be useful once they are back in their home country, and they therefore fail to develop the necessary motivation to learn it. Furthermore, they are conscious of the temporary nature of their sojourn in the host country, and see little need to 'affiliate' with the hosts, either linguistically or culturally. Finally, as instructors in the host society, they feel they need to be treated as 'important', 'as bearing the cultural superiority that they suppose whoever asks for foreign teachers must concede' (Daniel 1975:63).

The consequences

Various pedagogical difficulties arise from this mismatch between the host country's and the guest teachers' patterns of thinking and behaving. First, the native English-speaking teacher's pedagogical attempts to modify the cognitive and affective behaviour of the students with a view to making them bilingual and bicultural are met with reluctance, if not resistance, by the students themselves. In fact, despite their desire to learn English, the students are often unwilling to receive the cultural load of the target language. Hence, it is not uncommon for many who do not want to be 'culturally assimilated' to give up on learning the target language. If, on the other hand, the native English-speaking teachers succeed in their pedagogical aims, it is not surprising, as Goke-Pariola (1982) indicates for the Nigerian context, to see students alienated from their own social setting as they become adjusted to the values of the Anglo-American world.

Secondly, teaching the target language along with the target culture is done on the somewhat unrealistic assumption that a language cannot be used if it is emptied of its cultural content. Advocates of this position claim that teaching English while, for example, referring to the culture of the student would be useless. They discount the psychologically sound and motivating effects of helping and encouraging students to use the new language to describe their own culture (Finocchiaro 1982:68), not to mention the facilitating effect that culturally indigenous materials can have on learners' fluency and grammaticality in target language use (Winfield and Barnes-Felfeli 1982). What they also ignore is the fact that, as the lingua franca of this century, English is used extensively by millions of people outside its original geographic boundaries to convey national and international perceptions of reality which may be quite different from those of English-speaking cultures. Brumfit (1980), for instance, points to the awkwardness of pedagogical practices which deny EFL learners the opportunities and occasions to express their own cultural needs and ideas in English:

> [No person] who is not intolerably alienated from his own environment is going to want to learn English in order to become an Englishman (or an American) to such an extent that he never uses it to express the ideology, the assumptions, the cultural basis of himself rather than of Englishmen. We have the strange paradox that in mother-tongue teaching we emphasize the clarity of the child's ability to express *himself*, while in the foreign language we demand that he express a culture of which he has scarcely any experience.... We need to devise a methodology which will enable the learner to *use* the language, not passively in relation to situations which are imposed by motivations and ideologies not his own, but actively as a product of his own needs.... The model of teaching which tells the foreigner to adopt our system is both untruthful... and unhelpful, because it implies that he cannot communicate without adopting our position unnegotiably (pp. 94–6, 105).

Third, using monolingual and monocultural native English-speaking teachers, who are incapable of escaping the powerful influences of their own culture, as pedagogical models for would-be bilinguals is paradoxical and counter-productive. Monolingual and bilingual norms and values are not alike. Not only do bilinguals store grammatical material differently from monolinguals, as Preston (1981) notes. They also have different attitudes toward native and non-native varieties of the language. Preston rejects the unrealistic goal of native-speaker-like performance in target language teaching and suggests that, both linguistically and psychologically, the most effective model for the learners is the successful bilingual. Similarly, Kachru (1977) and George (1981) criticize present-day EFL courses modelled on native-speaker competence for their lack of realism. According to Kachru, it is impossible to claim pedagogical and communicative universality for the concept of communicative competence in an international language like English, given the way functions of the language vary from one country to another. What might be acceptable, appropriate, and intelligible in the context of the United States, for example, might not necessarily be so in the English-speaking contexts of India, Nigeria, or the West Indies. Hence, he recommends that the criteria for a pedagogical model should change according to the educational, political, and linguistic characteristics of each country. George, on the other hand, indicates that EFL courses that aim to represent native-speaker communicative competence go beyond language into areas of social behaviour modelled on native-speaker norms and values. Although English is used around the world as a national and international language, such pedagogical practices, he claims, lead to the illusion that native-speaker presence is required whenever English is used. Smith and Rafiqzad (1979) provide empirical evidence which calls into question the practice of using native-speaker models in the instruction of English sounds. According to their findings, native-speaker phonology does not seem to be more intelligible to multinational audiences than non-native-speaker versions. If native-like pronunciation does not necessarily help in English for cross-cultural communication, why insist, they ask, on having native English-speaking teachers as performance targets in EFL classrooms?

Conclusion

If EFL instruction in non-English-speaking countries is to become effective and realistic, care must be taken by the ministry of education of each country not to let it either turn into a tool of Anglo-American sociocultural domination, or take on ethnocentric features in order to isolate itself from such domination. In practical terms, this means that less attention should be paid to teaching models based on native-speaker norms and values, and more to developing 'culturally neutral, non-élitist, and learner-oriented' EFL programs (George 1981:12). It also means that learners should be provided with opportunities to use English in relation to local situations and to international circumstances in which they are interested. Finally, along with teaching English in contexts which are culturally and cross-culturally relevant to students' lives, more effort should be made to recruit teachers among successful bilinguals—both from local sources and from English-speaking countries. Being less prone to mother-tongue and native-culture chauvinism, these people can serve as vivid and relevant pedagogical models in EFL. They can show the learners how it is possible to achieve cultural pluralism as a frame of mind, along with demonstrable competence in a given language. According to Bowen (1977), successful bilingual teachers in EFL programs have a psychological advantage over the monolingual native English-speaking teacher, since they can prove to their students that they, the teachers, have in fact acquired a foreign language, and that therefore the students can too.

Under these kinds of favourable and realistic learning conditions, EFL students in non-English-speaking countries can be expected to acquire a new identity as they become fluent in the target language. This will not, however, be a bilingual and bicultural identity subject to *anomie* and alienation. Rather, it will be an identity which is able to transcend the parochial confines of the native and target cultures by understanding and appreciating cultural diversity and pluralism thanks to the new language, while not losing sight of native norms and values in the process. In short, it is a bilingual and *intercultural* identity.

Note

1 It should be acknowledged, however, that there do exist native English-speaking teachers of EFL who are aware of the influences of their own culture on their thought and behaviour. As a result, they are more apt to learn the language of the hosts, and to develop empathy for them.

(*Originally published in Volume 38/1, 1984*)

Much more recently (after the period this collection covers), Luke Prodromou looked back at these three articles, and another by Cook (1983), in an interesting attempt to assess the implications of the thoughts behind them for ELT in Greece. His conclusion is that, while the lack of cultural relevance and the alien values of many of the ELT materials produced in Britain and the US may make them undesirable, there are ways of protecting the learner from these 'side-effects' of learning English. One is to try to ensure that the focus of lessons is within learners' potential range of experience. Many environments—and Greece provides a typical example—are rich in English language 'realia'. Signs and advertisements, as well as packaging, all provide useful instances of English. And there is no reason why learners who have no experience of the English-speaking world should not use English to talk about their own world.

English as cultural action

Luke Prodromou

A challenge

In his article *ELT Journal* 36/3, 'The world for sick proper', John Rogers challenged his readers to re-examine the role of English as a foreign language particularly in the context of Third World countries where English is often considered a passport to success by most people, but where most people are automatically excluded from realizing that success. This article takes its cue from Rogers in so far as it looks at the role of English in its broader social and political context, and it shares his concern for the way in which enormous resources are deployed in the teaching of English for what are, at the end of a very costly process, very meagre results.

A greater cause for concern is the ideological impact of English in developing countries, and here Rogers quotes Paulo Freire approvingly:

> There is no such thing as a neutral educational process. Education either functions as an instrument which is used to facilitate the integration of the younger generation into the logic of the present system and bring about conformity to it, or it becomes the practice of freedom.

Finally Rogers questions the validity of the accepted assumption that English is essential as an instrument in the struggle for growth and technological development, and refers to successful development programmes that 'do not rely on the importation of Western ideas and approaches'. Rogers concludes by suggesting that ELT experts should start digging other holes, such as the alternative approaches he himself puts forward in response to the mismatch between a country's real needs (cultural, political, economic) and the role of English in such countries.

A dilemma

Although Rogers' alternative approaches are tentatively put forward and based on experience of a wide range of developed and developing nations, his main point is clear: cut the teaching of English where it is not only an expensive luxury but where it also distorts a country's needs and raises false hopes in large sections of the population. English often encourages and reinforces the existence of bureaucratic élites in these countries. But he suggests what seems to be, ironically, an élitist solution to the problem: he considers L. A. Hill's proposal (1978) to teach English only 'to those students who (are) going to use it' as a 'very sensible proposal'. It is indeed 'sensible' seen from the perspective of those students who jump the social and educational hoops and reach tertiary education.

Thus, although one is in sympathy with the questions raised by Rogers, his answers 'select out' the weakest (*sic*) pupils as those who will have to do without English as a school subject. This seems on the face of it 'sensible'. But this is the old fallacy of 'selection of the best' resurrected: at what stage of the educational process is one ever in a position to say 'You will not benefit from X'? Besides, those who get to tertiary education are those who are in most cases more privileged socially in the first place: it is not English that creates the élites: the élites absorb and appropriate

English as they do so many other cultural benefits. Those who will miss out, were Rogers' solutions to be adopted, would be those who are not tertiary-level material, or who are not in a position to become tertiary-level material given the in-built obstacles in the societies under discussion.[1]

The 'uses' of English

Rogers also fails to consider English as an educational subject in its own right and assumes that its narrowly instrumental value is its only justification: 'Only a very small percentage will need English ... between 15 and 18 per cent of school leavers needed English for government or private company jobs ...' It is true that prevailing attitudes to English on the part of pupils and parents are predominantly utilitarian and materialistic. One may feel this is a good thing or a bad thing, but in proposing to limit the teaching of English to those who need it in the narrow sense of ESP, EAP, EST, etc., Rogers hopes to avoid courses becoming EFNPP courses (English for No Particular Purpose) and is implicitly accepting the utilitarian option. But by the same logic, many subjects in school curricula all over the world will not be 'needed' by most people: a very small percentage of pupils go on to university in any country, and very few of us make more than a very limited use of physics, algebra, and geometry in our daily lives on leaving school. If English is useless, I would like someone to tell me, twenty years after leaving school, why algebra is useful.[2]

Two options

It may be suggested that English is not like mathematics or algebra in that these subjects are, as it were, universal 'languages': they do not 'belong' (historically) to one particular culture and thus are not instruments of domination of one country by another. If one rejects the 'language of imperialism' argument then there is no need to confront the problem of cultural domination and alienation with which language teaching may in some contexts be inextricably tied up. But assuming one does recognize that language teaching has political implications, especially in developing societies which are culturally, politically, and economically 'peripheral', then there are, broadly, two options: first, to reject (or reduce, as Rogers suggests) the 'importation' of the language in question, thus limiting its function to one of technical usefulness, just as one would Western technology in general; or second, to treat the teaching of English in non-English environments as an educational issue in its broadest sense, i.e. (to use Rogers' own quotation from Paolo Freire's *Pedagogy of the Oppressed*), as a non-neutral process which recognizes the ideological nature of language teaching. By 'ideological' here I mean that what we teach and particularly the *way* we teach reflects our attitudes to society in general and the individual's place in society, and that our own educational practice is an implicit statement of power relationships, of how we see authority in the classroom and by extension in society outside the classroom.

Learning English for a change

To recognize this is the first step towards making the teaching of English more a process of developing self-awareness of the world outside the classroom: it begins to become 'the practice of freedom'. The teaching of English at primary and secondary school level for general purpose need not be, as Rogers fears, a waste of time and resources, and, worse, detrimental to the development of the individual and society. Just as the teaching of the mother tongue in Freire's *Pedagogy* becomes a process of increasing consciousness of one's society, so too may the teaching of a foreign language. Freire's *Pedagogy* aims to encourage the individual's capacity to act on his or her environment to change it for the better. The teaching of English may also, in a modest way, contribute to this process.

A plea for 'real' content

How? In 'What should language teaching be about?', V. J. Cook (*ELT Journal* 37/3) does not actually answer this question, but suggests that the content of most EFL textbooks is mostly 'imaginary' rather than 'real'. This distinction seems to be a useful one when considering the cultural factor in language teaching. Cook rightly stresses the need for more 'real' content as opposed to the entertaining (and not so entertaining) story-lines and 'situations' we find in most textbooks. Cook lists a wide range of sources of 'real' content which it is expected will motivate the learner instrumentally and/or integratively: other academic subjects may be taught through English; the students' own experiences may be the content of the lesson; language itself, literature, British and North American culture, and finally interesting facts are all valid sources of content in language teaching. Some of these content areas will be inappropriate in some contexts (for example, British and American culture in the 'world for sick proper' situations cited by John Rogers in his article), but what is valuable in Cook's approach is the stress on the variety of educational functions that foreign-language teaching is called upon to serve: the broadening of the learners' horizons, the 'development of the students' personalities and potentials' and the acquisition of 'more diverse ways of thinking'. All these reasons for learning English are additional to the strictly 'communicative skill' highlighted and highly valued by Rogers in 'The world for sick proper'. It seems to me that Cook's principle that 'different goals demand different content' may open the way to a more positive response to the questions raised by Rogers than the restriction of English to a select few.

The question of culture

Cook, however, is too general to be of much practical value, and his list of contents contains an omission to which I will return. First, I would like to look at a third article from *ELT Journal* which, it seems to me, confronts far more specifically and realistically than either Rogers or Cook the question 'What should language teaching be about?'. The article, 'The question of culture: EFL teaching in non-English-speaking countries' by Cem and Margaret Alptekin, does not doubt the need to teach English in response to the enormous demand for it, but, like Rogers, it identifies the problem of cultural domination: 'Indeed, being at the receiving end of a virtually one-way flow of information from Anglo-American centers, the host country runs the risk of having its own culture totally submerged' (Alptekin 1984). In response to this problem the authors put forward the following suggestions: (1) the acceptance of English as an international language with the variety of 'Englishes' to be found in different countries; (2) the production of local teaching materials 'that are culturally and experientially appropriate for learners in developing countries'; (3) the recruitment of teachers who are successful bilinguals who will be 'less prone to mother-tongue and native-culture chauvinism'.

If it's time, as Rogers says at the end of 'The world for sick proper', for ELT experts to start digging holes elsewhere, it seems to me that these suggestions by the Alptekins show us three locations where excavations could profitably begin. I have arrived at this feeling after ten years of trying to 'sell' communicative methodology and Anglo-American ELT textbooks to non-native-speaker teachers of English. Progress has been made, but after so much time, effort, and money, so much of the exhilarating clash of structural and functional syllabuses, more could reasonably have been expected. We have presented and perfected communicative techniques; but is technique enough? We have mobilized authentic materials: but whose authenticity was it in the first place? We have devised endless information gaps, but was the gap worth filling anyway? Globally designed textbooks have continued to be stubbornly Anglo-centric: appealing to a world market as they do, they cannot by definition draw on local varieties of English and have not gone very far in recognizing English as an international language either. What were they about? They were mostly about situations which were not only imaginary, as Cook says, but vacuous, empty of life. Even when the textbooks went technicolour, they were still marketing a black-and-white cardboard cut-out world. Native-speaker teachers have been the often reluctant or unwitting ambassadors of this world, but (whether knowingly or unknowingly) many native-speaker teachers have, because of their uncritical projection of Anglo-American culture, failed to take local sensitivities into account and have, as a result, made the learning process more difficult: 'The conflict between the opposing pedagogical views of the "hosts" and the "guest" teachers of EFL is in many cases exacerbated by the ignorance of the ways and minds of the local people and their language' (Alptekin 1984).

One may conclude from the three articles I have cited that one major problem we face in EFL situations is not how to deal with the cultural background (Anglo-American culture), but how to respond to the cultural foreground (local culture). English cannot be seen merely as technique or a vehicle for technology: it is both a set of communicative skills useful (if not essential) to plugging into Western technology and also an essentially educational process which happens to individuals in particular societies. As such a process English, like algebra, broadens the mind and makes it more receptive, critical and active: 'We have the strange paradox that in mother-tongue teaching we emphasize the clarity of the child's ability to express himself, while in the foreign language we demand that he express a culture of which he has scarcely any experience' (Brumfit 1980).

Taking my cue, then, from Brumfit and the other writers I have quoted, I would like to consider the role of English in Greece and the lessons to be learnt from this for the teaching of English in Greece and other comparable EFL contexts. I will look at some of the social functions of English in Greece which, taken all together, form the distinct variety of English most frequently encountered in the country: Greek English or 'Granglais'. Having defined and exemplified 'Granglais', I will then suggest some implications for the EFL classroom, and finally some techniques towards making the methodology we adopt more culture-sensitive. In broad terms, I will be describing the way the world outside interferes with what goes on in the classroom, and ways in which the teacher can intervene to reconcile the conflict between the real world on the one hand and the all too often 'imaginary' classroom world on the other.

The political background

The background against which the role of English in Greece should be seen includes certain crucial factors in Greek domestic politics and Greek perceptions of foreign involvement in Greece. English as a foreign language is perceived within the context of the role that Britain, the USA and recently the Common Market have played or play in Greece. Native-speaker teachers of English are often bemused and sometimes offended by what they consider to be their students' black-and-white or melodramatic view of foreigners. The British or North American teacher of English in turn finds s/he has offended a class of Greek students without understanding why. The 'guest' teacher would do well to be aware of the main political events in Greece since the struggle for independence in 1821. Indeed many regions of Greece became independent only in this century. Since independence Greece has had a succession of foreign 'protectors'. The main political events in modern Greek history should be seen in this context: the Civil War (1944–49), the Cypriot struggle against British rule (1955–58), the Colonels' dictatorship (1967–74), the Turkish invasion of Cyprus (1974), and the present tensions with Turkey over rights to the Aegean sea. In all of these landmarks of modern Greek history the role of 'foreigners' has been seen by most Greeks, whether rightly or not, as both prominent and hostile to Greek interests. The teacher of English should be aware that these are highly charged issues which have to a significant extent shaped the Greek view of foreigners and, of course, foreign languages (in this case, English).

But there are strong positive feelings towards Anglo-American symbols too, stemming from Britain's role in the resistance to the Nazi occupation; the impeccable reputation of British institutions such as the BBC; and universal, if sometimes reluctant, admiration for North American scientific and technological achievements.

The Greek motivation for learning English springs from this somewhat ambiguous orientation towards Anglo-American culture and more recently towards Europe and the Common Market. Since 1984 Greece has been a full member of the EEC, and her increased integration with Western industry and commerce, in addition to the increasingly sophisticated Greek tourist industry, has made English more prominent than ever before. Literally you see and hear English everywhere in Greece. 'Granglais' is the English one finds in Greece. It is found in many places, in the most unlikely places; it is heard on television in soap operas, documentaries, and, occasionally, commercials; it is heard on Greek radio in the idiosyncratic English used for reading the news to non-Greek speakers; it is heard on the BBC World Service, the Voice of America, and Radio Moscow (often invaluable alternative sources of information, given the partisan reporting of the Greek media). Our students listen to Granglais sung by British, North American, German, and even Greek rock groups: English is not only the language of international trade but also the language of international—and often national—rock music. Our students read the words of the songs on record sleeves, they sing the songs, they quote them at us. It is a brave or blinkered EFL teacher who ignores this rampant variety of English. The same students wear T-shirts with enigmatic and not so enigmatic slogans written on them: 'I love you', 'Peace', 'Jesus saves', 'No problem', 'Help yourself' or 'Get your hands off'. There are the stickers you find on the rear window of cars ('Nuclear power: no thanks', 'My other car's a Porsche'), and then there are the cars themselves, crowding the Greek roads in lexical sets: Senators, Consuls, Ambassadors; Escorts and Cavaliers. Computers in Greece, like everywhere else, are Apples, Acorns, and Apricots. The government has tried repeatedly to stamp out the christening of Greek shops with English names, but what can it possibly do about the products these shops sell? Whether Greek or imported products, they are wrapped and stamped with Granglais: Corn Flakes, Tasty Flakes, and Mars Bars. Go into a grocer's shop in the remotest mountain village and you are surrounded by English; look around you as you are making your way to that village through the beautiful Greek countryside and you suddenly find yourself in 'Marlboro' country. Even the graffiti on freshly painted walls, that most liberating of protest forms, is often written in an alienated Granglais.

Let us go back to the grocer's shop I mentioned earlier. In fact, we probably won't find it. There will be a supermarket in its place. The word 'supermarket' itself sums up more than any other what I mean by Granglais as a linguistic phenomenon—but as a cultural and political phenomenon, too. Here are the distinctive features of a Greek 'supermarket': (1) 'Supermarket' is an English word. (2) It is also a Greek word now (my mother-in-law, who doesn't speak English, does not use the available 'Greek' word, but 'supermarket' instead). (3) It is an imported concept and institution. (4) It sells lots of desirable goods, both Greek and imported. (5) It is a sign that Greece is a modern consumer society, buying and selling on a large scale. The fact that a large percentage of the goods sold in Greek supermarkets are foreign is, on the one hand, a sign that the country is culturally and economically developing in that it has money to spend on fulfilling a wide variety of material needs which it shares with the Western developed nations that export the goods. But this 'development' is ambiguous. The word 'supermarket' captures this ambiguity perfectly. The Greeks have a word for it, just as they do for 'computer', but the choice and use of such words is determined by the powerful hold that imported ideas, like imported goods, have on the Greek imagination. The prevalence of the English term 'supermarket' is a measure of the way Greek as a language and Greek culture are being shaped by external factors. Just as the supermarket is perceived both as a blessing and a curse, so too, attitudes to foreigners and their language are mixed. In our 'supermarkets', not even a tin of common-or-garden baked beans is as innocent as it looks in the rough and tumble of Balkan conflict. These beans, providing as they do (to quote the label) 'a nutritious, well-balanced meal', pose a serious threat, when multiplied a few million times, to the Greek farmer and the Greek economy, and if your economy is up the creek, then your culture may soon be without a paddle.

The problem is that the culture which has produced these beans and the language which advertises them has a secret charm. It is the charm of the exotic, the forbidden. While the government exhorts the Greek consumer to 'buy Greek', a well-known brand of cigarettes insists on playing on the selling power of all things foreign; the slogan on the huge advertising hoarding is one word: 'imported'. A distinguished Professor of Greek, F. Kakrides, expressed in a recent newspaper article what most Greeks feel about the political importance of foreign languages in Greece: 'every great power depends a lot on spreading its language, in furthering not only its narrow economic interests, but its prestige as a whole, its cultural reputation and political influence. Those who, for example, learn French do not only tend to prefer French products and visit France, but they also read French books, magazines and newspapers... in a word they act as "agents" not only for the economy but the culture of the country whose language and surely, to some extent, mentality they have acquired' (Kakrides 1986).

It seems, then, that the English language in Greece is a web of contradictions, pulling the Greek learner this way and that: it is perceived as the language of power, progress, and prestige, and at the same time the language of intervention into Greek cultural and political affairs. It is foreign and therefore good and therefore bad, at one and the same time.

Implications for the classroom

This paradox seems to me to be the starting point for understanding why a particular piece of 'authentic' material may fall flat in the classroom; why the functional syllabus does not always function, why communicative methodology does not produce much communication, why Council of Europe Needs Analysis has not met the Greek learners' needs. In the great Greek paperchase for qualifications, English is something you must acquire; as the language of foreign intervention it is something you distrust; in the snob value attached to things from abroad, it is an object of desire; at school it gets in the way of more prestigious lessons like Greek and Maths. As the language of Shakespeare, it is something one vaguely admires. In Greece, memories of deprivation in a village with no electricity make manual work a mark of poverty and failure: a foreign language may not open doors to a white-collar job, a permanent civil service post, but it certainly opens a window on to a better social position. Thus, the imminent introduction of English into the Greek primary school will be popular, yet in marked contrast to the contemporaneous attempt to ban English shop names.

In the classroom, these contradictions may make it very difficult to identify the needs of students. These tensions between positive and negative perceptions of English by the learner are compounded by the simple realization that perhaps as many as 90 per cent of Greek learners will never go on to make substantial use of the linguistic fragments we teach them for more than a few minutes during their entire life. Why does young Kostaki sit at the back of the English class reading his geography textbook? It is perhaps because we spend years teaching a subject which is, for most of the pupils, most of the time, a waste of their time and ours.

The classroom itself is often drab, with nothing on the walls—no sign that there is a world *outside* the classroom. The classroom is a small world, a community linked with the big world outside. It is an extension of that world. But we often behave as if our students, on entering our little EFL world, change: change utterly into little John Smiths or Janet Smiths; that, coming to learn English, they leave their three-dimensional humanity outside and enter the plastic world of EFL textbooks; textbooks where language is safe and innocent, and does not *say* or *do* anything. Our modern books are full of speech acts that don't *act*, don't mean anything to Kostaki. The problem is that Kostaki does not want or need to communicate with anybody in particular. Most textbooks project an Anglo-centric, male-dominated, middle-class utopia of one kind or another. The life has been taken out of this EFL textbook world; Janet and Brenda, Jim and Rod, are all dead, mere shadows strutting on the page, full of sound but no fury, signifying, literally, nothing.

When both the material we use and the way we use it are culturally alienating then, inevitably, the students switch off, retreat into their inner world, to defend their own integrity. In that sense, Kostaki's reading geography in the English lesson is a healthy sign. It is a sign that he is asserting himself over all that is trivial and dull. If Kostaki is not invited to speak as Kostaki but as a one-dimensional English schoolboy in a one-dimensional world, then he takes action: he channels his inventiveness into designing an aerodynamic paper aeroplane or does his geography homework.

The speech acts or functions in most textbooks are based on situations which most of our students will never have to function in: finding a flat in London, talking to landladies in Bristol, rowing on the river in Cambridge. The speech acts that accompany these contexts only *look* like speech acts; for the Greek EFL student, as opposed, let's say, to the migrant ESL student, they are unreal, impersonal, and inactive. They are pure fantasy. But this is what we spend most of our time doing, engaging the student and ourselves in a prolonged fantasy. The functional syllabus can be as alienating a fantasy as the grammatical system used to be.

For most of us involved in EFL in Greece, English is a game of let's pretend, and we have no choice but to play this game. Motivating the student will involve making this game intrinsically interesting; the material we are teaching may be rubbish, like most textbooks and like my examples of Granglais; but being good ecologists I'm sure we all believe in recycling rubbish and thus giving it new life. The language of our materialistic consumer society or of consumer products like most textbooks may, when processed and re-processed, become a game, an activity that makes the student think about language in Greek society; it may become, ever so slightly, the 'practice of freedom'.

I hope it is clear from what I have said about the role of English in Greece that teachers of English in Greece find themselves occupying a small corner of John Rogers' 'world for sick proper'. The familiar symptoms of uneven development are there: a demand for foreign languages on a grand scale, both in the community and by the state, in pursuit of personal fulfilment; and a demand for more technology and greater consumer affluence, even though there is not enough cake to make dreams a reality for all.[3] In the end one begins to wonder whether English and all it brings in its train is not getting the country more deeply involved in a rat-race in which it cannot compete, let alone win. And culture, if there is still time between one private lesson and another to think about it, becomes an alien, alienating product, imported like most other things found in the supermarket.

However, my response to the problem differs from that of Rogers. Rather than keep the product (ELT) as it is, but simply limit its consumption, I propose we recycle it and turn it to the students' advantage. Textbook material, whether locally or internationally produced, authentic English and local varieties of English, can all be sources of 'content', but they can at the same time be methodologically processed in such a way that they relate more closely to the culture and experience of the learners.

Besides, the trend in Greece is towards more, not less, language teaching. In 1981 there were an estimated 1,500 teachers of English in state secondary schools. By 1986 the Ministry of Education was planning for 4,270 graduate teachers of English in full-time posts in the state sector, and for 1,376 teachers of French. The introduction of English into the primary schools is imminent; there is an enormous and thriving private sector, and entries for the Cambridge exams were well over 20,000 in 1986 (and reportedly on the increase). This English language fever means Rogers' option of reducing the teaching of English is not realistic (or, in my view, desirable) in Greece, so we must come to terms with the problems I have outlined.

Proposals

I will, therefore, take one manifestation of this fever, Granglais, the English which Greeks see and hear all around them, and demonstrate how it can be incorporated into a methodology which sees the learning of English not just as the acquisition of a set of skills but as part of an educational process of personal development.

Cook (1983) suggested that the English language itself could be taken as the subject matter of the English lesson. If this means talking *about* the language, then there are obvious limits to how relevant this would be and for how long. Some of the ways in which I have used local examples of English do involve an element of talking about the language one finds in the environment, but at the same time I have also tried to make the process an active one, involving the students in a personal way in doing something with the language. My aim in using Granglais in class was twofold: to improve the learners' competence in English and to increase their awareness of what happens when cultures come into contact. As a bilingual myself, I was able to share with the learners my own insights into Anglo-American culture, and together we were making more conscious the way that culture influences the way we think and feel about Greek culture.

Here are some ways in which I have used local 'authentic' English in the classroom.

Graffiti

Text: Words written on walls by Greek football fans and others: *Black, plant, terror, love, thunder, wild, bull, evil, hawk, punk.*

Tasks:

1 Ask students to keep a record of such words in a special notebook.
2 Ask students to read out words/write on blackboard, and the rest of the class to identify where the words were found, who wrote the words,

and why they chose those particular words.
3 Students write their own graffiti (in their notebooks!) selecting appropriate words and explaining their choice.

Comments:

This task is appropriate for elementary level students, particularly boys who hate English but love football. Discussion includes why the graffiti is in English and whether it is right to deface public buildings and private property.

Shop names

Text: Names of shops/pubs/discos in Greece: e.g. *Woman's Club, Tunnel, His, Shaft, Record, Galaxy, For Ever, Smart, Family, Sweet Lady, Culture, Mayday, No Sense, Highway, Container, Corner, Volcano, Relax, Blow Up, Penny Lane, Fast.*

Tasks:

1 Ask students to write down on a piece of paper the (English) name of a shop/pub/disco they have been to recently. Papers are passed round the class and students try to identify what kind of place (pub, shop, disco) is being referred to.
2 Focus on one of the groups, e.g. shops: What kind of shop is it? (boutique, cafeteria, record shop, shoe shop . . .) Why was the name chosen? Are the goods sold Greek or imported? What kind of people shop there? (young, old . . .) Is it an expensive shop? Are the goods of high quality?
3 Classify names into nouns, verbs, adjectives, etc.
4 Ask students to suggest their own English names for pubs, boutiques, etc. Compare equivalent Greek words: why are English words often preferred?

Brand names

Text: Gillette, Weetabix, Pampers, Mickey Mouse, Kodak, Camel, Manex, Accumatic, Softex, Tasty.

Tasks:

1 Ask students to try and identify the kind of product that goes by the above brand names.
2 Read out (or expose gradually on the OHP) extracts from the 'blurb' on the packet, wrapping, box, or tube in which the products are sold, and ask students to match product with blurb, for example:

a healthy nutritional breakfast
Soft . . . Sanitary . . . Scented
American and Domestic Blend
Keep cool . . . Process promptly
Disposable Swivel Head
Published Weekly . . . Printed in Greece

Small ads in local English language newspaper

Texts:
Young lady wanted. Businessman plans to travel around Greece for business and vacations. English speaking, good-looking girl wanted to accompany him and especially to practise the English language. Preferably student. Contact his friend Mr. Jossif. Tel. 321–5320.

Experienced female hairdresser required for cruise ship. Tel. 418–0744.

Waitress wanted for a disco in Glyfada. Please call: 894–8545.

Tasks:

1 To identify the sources of texts, who wrote them, what they are about.
2 To prepare and practise a telephone call expressing interest, asking for further information and arranging an interview.
3 Role-play interview with various candidates for job; class votes on best candidate or funniest interview.

An English language newspaper will of course contain a wide range of texts such as the weather forecast, advertisements, what's on—cinema, theatre, museums—and the TV schedules in English. In EFL contexts these would be more relevant and motivating than similar texts taken from, say, *The Guardian*.

Conclusion

The use of local varieties of English is only one way in which we can as teachers, whether bilingual or not, be sensitive to the status of English as an international language on the one hand and the learners' cultural background on the other. It is also important to recognize the nature of language as carrying social, cultural, and ideological meanings and associations which are perceived differently by individuals, and particularly in EFL situations where cultures make contact and often collide. Both *what* we teach and *how* we teach will convey our beliefs and tacit assumptions not only about language learning but about education as a whole, of which foreign-language learning is, like it or not, a part.

As Abbott (1984) points out, it is not ELT experts or teachers who will, in the end, decide whether English is taught in EFL/ESL contexts, but governments in the countries concerned. It would be futile (and, as I have argued, unnecessary) to turn the tide back on English as an international language. Given that English will be the dominant international language for as long as western culture, science, and technology dominate world markets, then what we as teachers can do is to recognize the rich and varied uses of English on both a global and a local scale, and, wherever possible, to make pedagogic capital out of languages and cultures in contact. English is as useful a starting point for increasing learners' awareness of systems of communication as algebra or the label on a tin of (imported) baked beans.

Notes

1 Abbott (1984: 99) raises similar objections to Rogers' article in terms of equal educational opportunities. Abbott argues, as I do, for the broad educational value of a foreign language, but places his main emphasis on mother-tongue education in ESL contexts.
2 Abbott (op. cit.), again in response to Rogers' article, points out that the failure of pupils to learn arithmetic in primary schools does not lead to the removal of arithmetic from the curriculum.
3 Research into the foreign-language needs of Greek civil servants revealed that 100 per cent of those asked felt they needed a foreign language both in their professional and personal lives, and that reading was the skill most useful to them. The kinds of texts considered important were labels on commercial products (bottles, boxes, tins, etc.); advertisements, posters, brochures, etc.; and instructions (for assembling goods, how to make things), directions for use (medical) etc. The authors point out that there is a mismatch between the perceived need for reading and the emphasis on listening and speaking that is found in most coursebooks (Exarchou *et al.* 1983).

(*Originally published in Volume 42/2, 1988*)

The final paper in this section does not continue the examination of the whys and wherefores of ELT. It turns instead to the way in which the teaching of English to speakers of other languages is perceived by the outside world, in short with the 'image' of ELT. Harry Krasnick's concern is the way in which ELT, and in particular English as a second language in English-speaking countries, is seen by the community at large. The communities into which the ESL learner has moved temporarily or permanently, usually regard ELT as something inferior to mainstream education, and this may have a negative impact on prospective teachers, and through them on the learners themselves. As a countermeasure, Krasnick recommends that serving and prospective teachers of ELT should be made aware of the attitudes of the 'host community' to ELT and the situation in which ESL learners find themselves.

Images of ELT

Harry Krasnick

The role of images in instruction

It often seems to happen that when the need for a service or product is great and enthusiasm runs high, issues which are quite basic are overlooked. I believe this has happened in ELT, at least in some parts of North America. We have witnessed a series of attempts to improve curriculum and instruction in ELT, each one purporting to offer something which its predecessor had failed to deliver. Quite naturally, it has been these approaches, methods, and techniques which have attracted the most interest, as compared to the more mundane matter of teachers' intuitive views of what ELT is all about. In the result, the tendency has been to ignore, or at least take for granted, teachers' images of ELT. It is my belief, however, that these images have a significant effect upon ELT, notwithstanding their unofficial and unscientific nature, and that it would be wise to subject them to just a bit of scrutiny.

Images are a factor of considerable significance in ELT, as in any formal education, because *the ideal or intended curriculum is never implemented—it is the curriculum perceived by the classroom teacher which the students experience*. If there is a single conclusion common to nearly all studies of curriculum implementation, it is this one. In a field such as ELT, the gap between the curriculum intended and the curriculum delivered may be especially large. Variation in how teachers perceive and attempt to implement the curriculum may be attributed in part to pre-existing images of ELT which the teachers harbour. In order for the teacher's various opinions and views to warrant the term 'image', there must be something in the nature of a coherent pattern which can be recognized. Below I will attempt to describe three such patterns.

ELT as special education

One image of ELT presents it as a branch of special education. While there is no suggestion of physical handicap on the part of students, this image does portray the ELT student as having special (educational) needs. A limitation in terms of capacity for education is implied. The 'evidence' for this is immediate and striking: the student cannot communicate, or speaks strangely, haltingly. Trifonovitch (1981:214) reports having been told by several ELT instructors in Micronesia that 'they had no difficulty in teaching English in Micronesia, since they had already adequate training in special education and had had several years of experience in teaching the mentally handicapped'. One interpretation of these remarks is that they reflect a popular misconception that people who cannot speak English are not very intelligent, and that the experience of teaching mentally handicapped students had reinforced this belief in these particular teachers.

Two other ELT instructors' experiences on field trips seem to confirm the supposition that inability to speak English is believed to indicate intellectual deficit (in the world of everyday life). The writer took a class of adult ELT students to a museum in Vancouver, Canada. One of the museum volunteers, whose job it was to assist visitors to the museum in understanding and appreciating the museum exhibits, described to the class the long sea voyage from England to Canada undertaken by her ancestors. She then asked the students if they knew how many weeks there were in six months. A colleague had a very similar experience with a group of secondary students who were non-native speakers of English. On a visit to the main branch of the Vancouver public library, the students were asked by a member of the library staff if they knew the answer to what was an elementary problem in multiplication (ironically, among the students were a number who were rather well trained in mathematics—the type often seen with a calculator in hand). Other colleagues have reported similar occurrences, so experiences of this sort may be much more common than we realize.

The point in recounting these tales, and the quotation from Trifonovitch, is not to show that some ELT teachers in Micronesia and some public service personnel are thick-headed, but rather to raise the possibility that there exists in the 'stock of knowledge' shared by many members of a society (see Berger and Luckmann 1967) the idea that lack of fluency in the dominant language means low intelligence. To the extent that this is true generally, then the onus shifts somewhat, and the task becomes one of demonstrating the *absence* of the belief in ELT instructors. If the belief is held, it may well colour the teacher's image of ELT. It seems quite clear that this is the case for at least some ELT personnel. For example, an ELT supervisor in Vancouver told a number of his staff that teaching pronunciation to ELT students was something which required a speech therapist or perhaps a specialist in rehabilitative medicine. This individual had in fact hired two former nurses to teach English as a second language in his programme, and has never hired anyone with an advanced degree in ELT. In justifying his view that graduate training in ELT had little relation to teaching English, he posed this question: 'Who would you rather have take care of your young children, someone with a doctorate in child psychology, or someone who was a good baby-sitter?'[2]

ELT as non-education

A weaker form of the special education image also seems to exist. This is the view of ELT students as non-students, even when, as sometimes happens, the students are more intelligent and far better educated than the teacher. A group of highly intelligent, charming Libyan physicians studying English in Vancouver, for instance, were regarded by some of their teachers solely in terms of the 'problems' they caused in class on account of their superior communicative ability. Another example which comes to mind is that of a professor of philosophy from Czechoslovakia who was doing his own translation of works of philosophy at home but had to study Christmas carols in his ELT class at a local community college. These examples mean, not that general-purpose English classes ought to accommodate the intellectual needs of doctors and philosophy professors, but that the ELT students' *educational* needs may not be recognized. Since, as seems to be the case, they are not viewed as 'real' students, it follows logically that they do not have to learn anything of value beyond the language itself. One need never, therefore, confront what Herbert Spencer considered the basic curriculum question, 'What knowledge is of most worth?'

The image of ELT students as non-students may hold sway even with respect to students who have already been admitted to a secondary or post-secondary academic programme. What makes this image of ELT students possible is the view of ELT as a skill, rather than a subject. In British Columbia, Canada, for example, university students from overseas do not receive academic credit for learning English, while all anglophone students who study a foreign language—and it may be the language spoken natively by the overseas students—do receive credit. Sadly, even in some programmes in English for academic purposes, substantive learning is not pursued. The 'content' of the courses is not valued for its own sake. Instead, it is treated as practice for real learning, and hence there is very little sense of accomplishment or purpose on the students' part. This view of curriculum has its historical antecedents in the 'scientific curriculum' advocated earlier in the century, where education was seen as preparation for later life, rather than something intrinsically valuable or interesting (see Kliebard 1975).

There is in the grammar-based approach to ELT what may be a counterpart to the view of ELT students as non-students. In North America, where there has been widespread acceptance of communicative approaches, some teachers still display a devotion to grammar exercises which borders on worship. One explanation of why these teachers have not embraced the communicative approach is that they are among those who subscribe to the view of ELT students as non-students. For such teachers, even when ELT students have already had five to ten years of grammar-based instruction before entering the programme and still have not mastered English, the prescription is the same: more grammar. No 'real' education can be undertaken, in such teachers' view, until the students have proven themselves, have completed the rites of passage. This view, that subject-matter learning must be put off until the linguistic code has first been mastered, is difficult to maintain in the light of evidence available in North America which suggests that, on the contrary, language learning and subject-matter learning are quite compatible and can occur simultaneously (see Edwards *et al.* 1984). However, the image of ELT as non-education runs deep.

ELT as socialization

The role of ELT in socialization is clear in immigration policy, which requires independent (non-sponsored) immigrants to be able to speak and understand the national language and provides ELT for others; and it is implicit at the curricular level, in the specification of one or another variety of English as the target code (see Kachru 1982 and Smith 1981). As an image of ELT, however, socialization also involves the notion that

ELT students are in need of assistance. For instance, sociolinguistic or communicative competence may be seen in terms of avoiding giving offence to native speakers of English (see Paulston and Bruder 1976). Such views are often explicitly framed in terms of social etiquette, which of course underscores the socialization aspect. The image of ELT as special education is related too, in that training in basic social competence is a part of some special education programmes.

The socialization image calls upon the teacher to play the role of helper, which may in part explain the hiring of nurses as ELT instructors in preference to individuals with substantial formal education and experience in ELT: nurses are trained to aid those in need of assistance. The view of ELT students as deficient or needing socialization may well lead unaware ELT instructors to approach students in terms of their presumed dependency or need for aid in behaving properly; or it may lead them to interpret legitimate attempts on the students' part to protect their own individual interests as rude or disrespectful behaviour (that is, behaviour indicating independence may be misread as essentially unsocialized behaviour). In this sense, the students may come to be 'labelled' as incompetent and/or troublesome. Both views of the student—as untrained, and as unruly—are part of the image of ELT as socialization.

The problem of changing attitudes

The possibility that common misconceptions about ELT are imported into the classroom by the teachers is of more than theoretical interest, since it has been well established empirically that the teacher's *expectations* affect his or her own behaviour as well as the student's behaviour (see Cooper and Good 1983; Dusek and Joseph 1983). In ELT, the origin of the problem lies mainly in the fact that general curriculum and instruction issues are seldom included in ELT training courses, nor are relevant topics in the sociology of education or the sociology of knowledge.

One mitigating factor, however, is that many ELT teachers are not native speakers of English and most were themselves ELT students at one time or another. They may be counted on to be comparatively free of the notion that ELT is a form of 'special education' or remedial socialization.

On the other hand, all teachers, whatever their linguistic background, can do something to increase their awareness of their attitudes toward ELT students and ELT instruction. The easiest and most direct method consists simply of asking oneself what one's personal feelings and beliefs are regarding issues such as those raised in this article. However, the limitations of introspection as a method of changing attitudes should be borne in mind.

A more reliable, though more demanding, approach would involve the teacher in some type of *experiential* learning. This might be as simple as finding out directly from the students about their educational aptitudes and aspirations. A complementary approach would be that of getting an idea of the values and norms of their cultures which may lie behind some of the behaviour which leads to the view of students as being in need of re-socialization. Most teachers can locate one or more individuals in the local community who could provide a view of the world from the students' perspective (which, it should be noted, many students could not themselves provide at that point). What is most basic to all of this, of course, is that the teacher somehow be alerted to the fact that all of us, as members of our respective societies, are subject to being influenced by prejudiced views. Our students deserve careful consideration, and in our search for the latest, most modern methodologies, we ought not to take for granted anything concerning the essential nature of the enterprise.

Finally, it is possible to incorporate a suitable social science perspective into teacher training courses, if it is felt that this would represent a justifiable increase in the number of hours in the course. Relevant viewpoints could be drawn from several areas of education and sociology. However, the underlying issue here is whether those who are responsible for training ELT teachers themselves appreciate the relevance of the disciplines of sociology and education. I have suggested elsewhere (Krasnick, 1986) that the academic training undergone prior to entering the field of ELT has a considerable influence on one's view of ELT. Thus, in the present instance, ELT professionals from non-social science backgrounds may be slow to recognize the relevance of factors like those discussed in this article. If so, then we are dealing with still other 'images of ELT'.

Notes

1 This term is used in North American English to describe substantially altered educational programmes offered to students who have a variety of physical and mental conditions which make it difficult for them to benefit from ordinary programmes.
2 This individual was not one of the ELT teachers described by Trifonovitch (1981).

(*Originally published in Volume 40/3, 1986*)

Further reading

Readers may wish to follow up their reading of this section by referring to the following titles:

Ashworth, M. 1985. *Beyond Methodology*. Cambridge: Cambridge University Press (reviewed in *ELTJ*, 41/2, 1987).
Brumfit, C. J. (ed). 1983. 'Language Teaching Projects for the Third World.' *ELT Documents 116*. Oxford: The British Council/Pergamon.
Kachru, B. (ed.) 1983. *The Other Tongue*. Oxford: Pergamon (reviewed in *ELTJ*, 39/2, 1985).
Valdes, J. M. 1986. *Culture Bound*. Cambridge: Cambridge University Press.

SECTION 2

The communicative era: second decade

The papers gathered in this section were published in the *ELT Journal* between 1983 and 1986—at the beginning of communicative language teaching's second decade. Appropriately, the writers represent a whole spectrum of practitioners: classroom language teachers, materials writers, course designers, and applied linguists. They also include non-native speakers of English working in foreign language settings.

The papers explore in some detail the pros and cons, the whys and wherefores—one might say the pleasures and pains—implicit in the communicative movement. They are selected because none of them gives pat answers or simplistic advice to the hard-pressed language teacher who is trying to provide the best support feasible for his or her second language learners. Rather, the articles, some of which have of their own accord stimulated a lot of debate, collectively survey the landscape through which language teachers must find their paths.

The first paper in this section identifies what the writer considers to be the essential features of a communicative methodology, without intending to specify how they should interrelate. Jack Richards tries with some success to build bridges between the theories of communicative competence articulated by Hymes and others, and the task confronting the foreign language learner. He does this by re-expressing the theories as maxims not unlike Grice's in style and implication. These cover: the centrality of 'meaning'; the importance of native-speaker conventions and appropriacy constraints, and the essential role of discourse structure in determining the 'processes by which people communicate'. It is towards these that the balance in language materials and methodology has to be adjusted, he concludes.

Communicative needs in foreign language learning[1]

Jack C. Richards

The theme of language and the learner's communicative needs is a familiar one in language teaching. In recent years, applied linguistics has been revitalized by attempts to describe how language reflects its communicative uses, and by demonstrations of how syllabus design and methodology can respond to the need for communicative uses of language in classrooms and teaching materials. By considering some central aspects of communication, this paper attempts to contribute to our general understanding of how language use reflects underlying communicative needs. Five assumptions about the nature of verbal communication will be discussed, namely, that communication is meaning-based, conventional, appropriate, interactional, and structured. These will be discussed in relation to the communicative needs of second or foreign language learners.

Communication is meaning-based

Let us begin by examining basic 'survival' language needs, those for example of a learner who has an active vocabulary of perhaps two hundred words, a minimal knowledge of the syntax of English, but who is in a situation where English is required for simple and basic communicative purposes. The most immediate need is to be able to refer to a core of basic 'referents' or things in the real world, that is, to be able to name things, states, events, and attributes, using the words he or she knows. In addition, the learner must be able to link words together to make predications, i.e. to express propositions.

Propositions are the building blocks of communication, and the first task in learning to communicate in a language is to learn how to create propositions. Language is comprehensible to the degree that hearers are able to reconstruct propositions from the speaker's utterances (Wells 1981: 73–115). When the child says 'hungry' to its mother, the mother understands 'I am hungry'; from 'no hungry' the mother understands the child's message as being 'I don't want to eat'. From these examples we see that sentences do not have to be complete or grammatical for their propositional meaning to be understood. We often make good sense of a speaker who uses very broken syntax, just as we can understand a message written in telegraphese, e.g. *no money send draft*.

Sentences may contain more than one proposition. *The girl picked the red flower* contains the propositions *the girl picked the flower*, and *the flower is red*. Sentences may refer to the same proposition but differ in what they say about it. The following sentences all refer to the proposition *John married Mary*, but differ in what they say about it:

> When did John marry Mary?
> Why did John and Mary get married?
> Mary and John have been married for ages.

'Survival level' communication in a foreign language, however, implies more than the construction of propositions. Speakers use propositions in utterances in a variety of ways. They may wish to ask a question about a proposition, affirm a proposition, deny or negate a proposition, or express an attitude towards a proposition. They may use propositions to communicate meanings indirectly, as when the speaker says *I'm thirsty* but means *I'd like a glass of water*, the latter being the 'illocutionary effect' the speaker intends (see Austin 1962). Now, while the adult native speaker of English can use the resources of adult syntax to encode propositions in the appropriate grammatical form and to communicate a wide range of illocutionary meanings, the beginning foreign language learner finds that the demands of communication often exceed his or her knowledge of the grammar of English. The learner's immediate priority is to work out a way of performing such operations as stating, affirming, denying, or questioning propositions, as economically as possible, using only a partial knowledge of the vocabulary and syntax of the target language. Here the learner has similar needs to the child who is learning its mother tongue. Child language can be used to express complex meanings within the limits of a restricted grammatical system. 'Mother talk'—that variety of speech which mothers use when talking to young children—is simplified to make propositions and illocutionary intentions more readily identifiable (Goody 1978:24). Mothers' questions to children, for example, contain far more 'Yes-No' questions than 'Wh' questions, because propositions are more readily identifiable in 'Yes-No' questions.

How do foreign language learners communicate meaning when they lack the fully elaborated grammatical and discourse system of the target language? To answer this question, let us consider how a learner might try to express the meanings contained in the following sentences:

> John ought to have come on time.
> I regret I wasn't able to get to your class on time.
> I can't afford to buy that dress.

One strategy learners adopt in communicating complex meanings like this is to 'bring propositions to the surface' by expressing meanings and intentions *directly* rather than indirectly, and by expressing lexically aspects of meaning that in the target language are coded in the auxiliary system, in complex clauses, or by grammatical devices (Richards 1981; Dittmar 1981). The first sentence, for example, implies the proposition

John came late, and communicates the speaker's attitude towards this proposition. The meaning is roughly *Speaker disapprove that John came late*. This could be communicated by saying:

'Why John late?' (said with non-approving intonation), or,
'John late. That bad.'

(The distinction between propositions which are expressed, and those which are presupposed, is an important one, but will not be pursued further here.) The second sentence contains the proposition *I am late*, together with the speaker's expression of regret. It might be communicated by saying:

'I late. So sorry.'

I can't afford to buy that dress contains the propositions:

The dress is expensive. I don't have enough money to buy the dress.

It could be restated:

'The dress expensive. Cannot buy.' or
'Can't buy the dress. No money.'

This type of 'restructuring' is seen in the following examples, in which utterances in simplified learner syntax are compared with standard adult grammar.

Simplified utterances	Equivalent in standard adult syntax
Mary lazy. No work hard.	Mary can work hard if she wants to.
Tomorrow I give money.	You will have your money tomorrow, I promise.
You no money. I lend you.	I will lend you some money if you need any.
This way. See the map.	According to the map, this ought to be the way.
One day I go England.	I would like to go to England some day.

(De Silva: 1981)

Teachers too often resort to the type of language on the left in communicating with speakers of limited language proficiency. The following examples were produced by teachers who are native speakers of English:

1 A teacher is explaining the meaning of *wash*: 'In your house, you . . . a tub . . . you (gestures) wash.'
2 Here a teacher is explaining how to take telephone messages: 'I want to speak other person. He not here. What good thing for say now?'
3 A teacher explaining an interview procedure produced: 'Not other student listen. I no want. Necessary you speak. Maybe I say what is your name. The writing not important.'
4 And here is a teacher reminding her students to bring their books to class: 'The book . . . we have . . . (hold up book) . . . book is necessary for class. Right . . . necessary for school. You have book.'

(Examples from Evelyn Hatch, personal communication.) The examples above illustrate a linguistic system which can be used for communicating basic propositional meanings. Such a system is known as 'child language' when it is produced by infants learning their mother tongue, 'interlanguage' when it is produced by foreign-language learners, 'teacher talk' when it is used by teachers, and 'foreign talk' when it is produced by native speakers communicating with foreigners. The linguistic system behind this type of communication is one which uses a basic 'notional–functional' core of vocabulary items, a syntax which depends on simple word order rules (such as negating by placing the negative word in front of the proposition), and in which the communication of meaning is not dependent on grammatical systems of tense or aspect, auxiliaries, function words, or plural morphemes, etc.

The ability to use such a communicative system is crucial in the first stages of foreign language learning. We should consequently be tolerant of grammatical 'errors' from learners who are at this stage. They should not attempt active communication too soon, however. Before the learner is ready to begin speaking a foreign language, he or she should have a vocabulary of at least two hundred words and a feel for the basic word order rules of the target language. The learner needs to develop a feel for the system of basic word order (in English: subject predicate sentence order, adverb and adjectival positions, negation, question formation, etc.). When speaking is taught, the initial goal should be the production of comprehensible utterances through expressing basic prepositional meanings and illocutionary intentions.

Communication is conventional

While much of the learner's efforts in speaking a foreign language centre on developing the vocabulary and syntax needed to express propositional meanings, it is native-speaker syntax and usage that is ultimately the learner's goal. As language acquisition proceeds, the learner revises his or her ideas about how propositions are expressed in English. The learner's syntax becomes more complex as his or her knowledge of negation, the auxiliary system, questions, word order, embedding, conjoining, etc., expand. In short, the learner begins to develop grammatical competence.

Both linguists and applied linguists in recent years have emphasized the creative properties of grammatical systems. Language users were said to possess, as part of their grammatical competence, the ability to produce an infinite number of sentences, most of which are novel utterances. The learner's task was thought to be to 'internalize' the rules needed to generate 'any and all' of the possible grammatical sentences of English. The primary aim of language teaching was to create opportunities for these grammatical abilities to develop in language learners.

The fact is, however, that only a fraction of the sentences which could be generated by our grammatical competence are actually ever used in communication. Communication largely consists of the use of language in conventional ways. There are strict constraints imposed on the creative–constructive capacities of speakers, and these limit how speakers encode propositional meanings. In telling the time, for example, we can say, *It's two forty*, or *It's twenty to three*, but not *It's three minus twenty*, *It's ten after two thirty*, or *It's eight fives after twenty*. If I want you to post a letter for me I may say, *Please post this letter for me*, or *Would you mind posting this letter for me*, but I am unlikely to say, *I request you to post this letter*, or *It is my desire that this letter be posted by you*. Although these sentences have been constructed according to the rules of English grammar, they are not conventional ways of using English. While they are grammatically correct 'sentences', they have no status as potential 'utterances' within discourse, since they would never be used by native speakers of English.

This considerably complicates the task of foreign language learning. Once learners have progressed to the stage where they are beginning to generate novel utterances, they find that many of their utterances fail to conform to patterns of conventional usage, although they are undoubtedly English sentences. Constraints which require speakers to use only utterances which are *conventional* affect both the lexical and grammatical structure of discourse. The constraints on lexical usage manifest themselves in idiosyncracies and irregularities which particularly affect verb, noun, preposition, and article usage, and are usually rationalized as 'exceptions' or 'collocational restrictions' in teachers' explanations.

Thus teachers must explain that *a pair of trousers* refers to one item, but *a pair of shirts* to two; that we can speak of *a toothache* or *a headache*, but not *a fingerache*; that someone may be *in church*, but not *in library*. Conventionalized language is seen in many other features of discourse. For example:

a *Conversational openers*: *How are you?* may be used to open a conversation in English, but not *Are you well?* or *Are you in good health?*

b *Routine formulae*: Some conventional forms are expressions whose use is limited to particular settings, such as *Check, please*, said when a bill is requested in a restaurant.

c *Ceremonial formulae*: These are conventional phrases used in ritualized interactions, such as *After you*, said as a way of asking someone to go ahead of you when entering a room, and *How nice to see you*, said on encountering a friend after an absence of some time (Yorio 1980:437).

d *Memorized clauses* (Pawley and Syder 1984): The concept of conventionalized language usage may be applied to a broader class of utterances. These are clauses which do not appear to be 'uniquely generated' or created anew each time they are required in discourse, but which are produced and stored as complete units. Pawley and Syder cite the following examples:

>   Did you have a good trip?   Please sit down.
>   Is everything O.K.?   Call me later.
>   Pardon me?   I see what you mean.

They argue that speakers of a language regularly use thousands of utterances like these. Unlike 'novel' utterances (those which speakers put together from individual lexical items), these are 'pre-programmed' and run off almost automatically in speech production. Researchers in second language acquisition have observed that language learners also often use conventional formulae and memorized clauses as crutches in order to make communication easier. There is often a high frequency of them in their speech in the early stages of conversational competence (Schmidt 1981).

The fact that language is conventional has important implications for language teaching. Firstly, it suggests that there is reason to be sceptical of the suggestion that language cannot be taught, but only 'acquired'. Many of the conventionalized aspects of language usage are amenable to teaching. Secondly, applied linguistic effort is needed to gather fuller data on such forms (through discourse analysis and frequency counts, for example) with a view to obtaining useful information for teachers, textbook writers, and syllabus designers.

Communication is appropriate

Mastery of a foreign language requires more than the use of utterances which express propositional meanings and are conventional. The form of utterances must also take into account the relationship between speaker and hearer, and the constraints imposed by the setting and circumstances in which the act of communication is taking place. *What's your name?* is a conventional utterance, for example, but it is not an appropriate way of asking the identity of a telephone caller; in this case, *May I know who is calling?* is considered more appropriate.

Communicative competence (Hymes 1972) includes knowledge of different communicative strategies or communicative styles according to the situation, the task, and the roles of the participants. For example, if a speaker wanted to get a match from another person in order to light a cigarette, he or she might take one of the following courses of action, according to his or her judgement of its appropriateness:

1 Make a statement about his or her need: 'I need a match.'
2 Use an imperative: 'Give me a match.'
3 Use an embedded imperative: 'Could you give me a match?'
4 Use a permission directive: 'May I have a match?'
5 Use a question directive: 'Do you have a match?'
6 Give a hint: 'The matches are all gone, I see.' (Ervin-Tripp 1976:29)

Young children learning their mother tongue soon become skilled at using communicative strategies appropriately. Thus a child who wants something done may bargain, beg, name-call, or threaten violence in talking to other children; reason, beg, or make promises in talking to parents; or repeat the request several times, or beg, in talking to grandparents.

The choice of an appropriate strategy for performing a communicative task or speech act is dependent on such factors as the ages, sex, familiarity, and roles of speaker and hearer, which will determine whether a speaker adopts conversational strategies implying either *affiliation* or *dominance*. In the former case, 'Got a match?' may be considered an appropriate way of requesting a match, and in the latter, 'I wonder if I could bother you for a match?' (Brown and Levinson 1978). Foreign language learners typically have fewer alternatives available to them for performing speech acts appropriately. They may use what they consider a polite or formal style for all situations, in which case people may find them over-formal; or they may create novel ways of encoding particular speech acts, such as using *please* + *imperative* to make requests, regardless of whom they are talking to.[2]

Canadian researchers have investigated the problems which non-native speakers have when they are put in a situation where they feel they lack the means of speaking appropriately (such as when a person who has been taught to use a formal type of French needs a style of speaking suitable for communication in informal situations). It was predicted that speakers would show considerable discomfort in using a casual style, and that this discomfort would cause them to 'downgrade' the personality of the interlocutor and to judge that the interlocutor had formed a bad impression of them. It was argued that such speakers would have some awareness that they were not speaking in a suitably friendly and casual manner, and would conclude that they really did not like the person they were speaking to anyway. The results of the study supported this prediction. 'These findings have certain implications for second language learners who have only mastered basic vocabulary and syntax in their new language but have not developed skills in the domain of linguistic variability. Such people may find social interaction with native-speakers in their new language to be a relatively negative experience and may become discouraged from pursuing language practice with native speakers' (Segalowitz and Gatbonton 1977:86). Language learning texts have only recently begun to focus on the strategies learners need to perform various types of speech acts appropriately. In their texts the emphasis is not simply on teaching functions and their exponents, but on selecting appropriate exponents in different types of communicative situations. Textbooks thus need to give practice in performing particular speech acts with interlocutors of different ages, rank and social status, and practice in selecting language according to these variables.

Communication is interactional

The use of utterances which take appropriate account of the speaker's and the hearer's roles implies that conversation is often just as much a form of social encounter as it is a way of communicating meanings or ideas. This may be described as the 'interactional function' of conversation. It is the use of language to keep open the channels of communication between people and to establish a suitable rapport. Goffman has argued that 'in any action, each actor provides a field of action for the other actors, and the reciprocity thus established allows the participants to exercise their interpersonal skills in formulating the situation, presenting and enacting a self or identity, and using strategies to accomplish other interactional ends' (cited in Watson 1974:58). We see evidence of this at many levels within conversation. In the initial stages of conversation with a stranger, for example, speakers introduce uncontroversial topics into the conversation, such as the weather, the transport system, etc. These topics are carefully chosen so that there is a strong likelihood of mutual agreement. 'The raising of safe topics allows the speaker the right to stress his agreement with the hearer, and therefore to satisfy the hearer's desire to be right or to be corroborated in his opinions ... The weather is a safe topic for virtually everyone, as is the beauty of gardens, the incompetence of bureaucracies, etc' (Brown and Levinson 1978:117). These are examples of what has been called 'phatic communion'. 'Much of what passes for communication is rather the equivalent of a handclasp, or an embrace; its purpose is sociability' (Bolinger 1975:524).

The mechanisms of phatic communion include (a) the speaker's repertoire of verbal and visual gestures, which signal interest in what his or her conversational partner is saying (such as the use of *mmm*, *uh uh*, *yeah*, *really*, etc.); (b) the speaker's stock of 'canned topics' and formulaic utterances, which are produced at relevant points in discourse, such as the small talk which is required to make brief encounters with acquaintances comfortable and positive; and (c) awareness of when to talk and when not to talk, that is, appropriate use of turn-taking conventions.

Adequate management of these conversational resources is essential if we are to create a sense of naturalness in conversational encounters. Non-native speakers who lack the ability to use small talk and to exploit the interactional aspects of communication may find many encounters awkward and may avoid talk where talk would be appropriate.[3]

Communication as interaction is thus aimed largely at the need of speaker and hearer to feel valued and approved of. If our conversation-teaching materials primarily emphasize transactional skills, such as how to ask directions, how to order a meal, etc., learners may not have the chance to acquire the interactional skills which are also an important component of communicative competence.

Communication is structured

The last aspect of communication I wish to consider is its ongoing organization. This can be looked at from two perspectives: a 'macro' perspective which reveals the differences in rhetorical organization that reflect different discourse 'genres' or tasks; and a 'micro' perspective showing how some of the processes by which discourse is constructed out of individual utterances are reflected in speech.

Task structure

Communication consists of different genres of discourse, such as conversations, discussions, debates, descriptions, narratives, and instructions. These different rhetorical tasks require the speaker to organize utterances in ways which are appropriate to that task. When we tell a story, for example, we follow certain conventions. Stories consist of a setting, followed by episodes. The setting consists of statements in which time, place, and characters are identified. Episodes consist of chains of events and conclude with reactions to events. Most stories can be described as having a structure of this type, and it is this structure which gives them coherence. Just as a sentence is grammatical to the extent that it follows the norms of English word order and structure, so a story is coherent to the extent that it follows the norms of semantic organization which are used in English.

Other types of rhetorical acts derive coherence from norms of structural organization. When we describe something, for example, coherence in our description is determined by how appropriately we deal with such elements as the level of the description, the content, the order in which items are described, and the relations between items mentioned in the description (Clark and Clark 1977:232). In describing a landscape, for example, the writer must decide on the appropriate level of the description, and decide whether to focus on the general impressions of the scene or on every detail (as for example in a police report). The writer must also make decisions concerning content, which will determine which elements of the scene to include or exclude. Then the elements must be arranged in an appropriate order and the relations between the things mentioned must be decided. Some objects may be highlighted in the description, for example, and other items related to them. The result will be a coherent description, one which is organized according to appropriate norms for this type of discourse. Similar decisions must be made when we describe people, rooms, states, or events. If we adopt solutions that are conventional, we create rhetorical acts which are coherent.

Other types of rhetorical acts also develop in ways which are organized and structured. Conversations, for example, begin with greetings and progress through various ordered moves: the speaker's and hearer's roles are ascertained, topics are introduced, rights to talk are assumed, new topics are raised, and, at an appropriate time, the conversation is terminated in a suitable manner. The development of communicative competence in a foreign language is crucially dependent on the speaker's ability to create discourse that is coherent. Schmidt (1981), in his study of the development of communicative competence in a Japanese adult, studied how the subject's ability to perform coherent narratives and descriptions developed. At an early stage in his language development, the subject's attempts to narrate events suffered through the inclusion of excessive details presented in a random order, which made comprehension difficult.

Process structure

When we talk, much of our discourse is made up of words and phrases which indicate how what we are going to say relates to what has already been said. For example, our reaction to an idea or opinion may be to expand it, to add something to it, to disagree with it, to substantiate it, to give a reason for it, or to explain it. The following are examples of phrases or lexical items which may serve these or related functions:

When it comes to that	yes but
and another thing	well maybe
all the same	actually
consequently	anyway
in my case	as a matter of fact
all the same	to begin with
to give you an idea	

These have been termed 'conversational gambits' (Keller 1981), and they signal directions and relations within discourse. Evidence suggests that these contribute significantly to an impression of fluency in conversation. Course materials are now available which focus on these aspects of conversational competence. They are inappropriate, however, if they are used too often or in the wrong places, as in the following example:

To my mind I'll have another cup of coffee.

Conclusions

Theories about how we teach a foreign language reflect our view of the nature of language. While it is no innovation to define language as a system of communication, the way the dynamics of the communicative process influence the form of verbal communication is seldom fully appreciated. ESL/EFL materials too often focus only on the finished *products* of communication, rather than on the *processes* by which people communicate. A deeper understanding of the effects of communicative needs on non-native speaker discourse should make us more understanding of our students' difficulties in using English, and happier with their partial successes.

Notes

1 A plenary address given at the Japan Association of Language Teachers' Convention, Tokyo, November 21, 1981.
2 For example, 'Please, you carry this suitcase', said by a non-native speaker to a friend, where 'How about carrying this suitcase for me?' would be a more appropriate form; or 'Please. Bring more coffee', said to a waitress, where a more appropriate form would be 'Could I have another cup of coffee, please?' (Schmidt 1981).
3 For example, a foreign couple with a good command of English but lacking the ability to participate in ongoing small talk were judged as cold, stand-offish, and reserved by their American relatives (personal observation).

(*Originally published in Volume 37/2, 1983*)

The following paper comes at the question 'What does the communicative approach imply?' at an angle different from the one taken by Richards. The author's preoccupation is with the classroom consequences of the basic principles of the approach, and more particularly with the implications for Chinese classrooms (probably the most numerous in the world).

While much of Li Xiaoju's discussion refers to the key components implicit in the communicative approaches that were described in Richards' paper, she focuses her comments and questions on what are seen by many teachers in China—and almost anywhere else in the world—as 'difficulties' and 'problems' with this style of teaching. In particular, the author is concerned to break down the resistance to communicative approaches engendered by decades of working within the constraints of structural grading and the consequent emphasis on language form rather than use. She is also concerned to undermine the knowledge-orientated approach to language learning which measures progress in terms of items learnt (usually by heart) rather than by gains in competence.

This paper demonstrates poignantly the very real difficulties faced by those attempting to implement large-scale changes in classroom language teaching practice which involve ideological as well as practical shifts. The author provides vivid insights into the way entrenched teacher-centred procedures—in China, 'Intensive Reading' is an example—can act as effective barriers to changes requiring more independence and self-reliance on the part of learners. In addition, and at the same time, it highlights the essentially 'western' premises underlying the 'communicative approach', and begs the question: 'How can and should an approach such as this, conceived in an alien environment on the basis of alternative views of the world and the individual's place in it, best be applied in a totally different context?'

In defence of the communicative approach
Li Xiaoju

The CECL project

In 1979, with China newly emerged from its isolation from the outside world and EFL teachers in China just becoming aware of the need to update their teaching, two Canadian teachers and a Chinese teacher[1] were brought together at the Guangzhou (Canton) Foreign Languages Institute and given the task of developing a new set of EFL materials for students majoring in English in tertiary education in China. We named the project CECL[2] (Communicative English for Chinese Learners), because we intended to base the materials on the communicative approach, and because we wanted to make it clear that the materials are specifically for Chinese learners.

Three years' work on the project has involved us in all sorts of controversies. The approach we are trying to implement makes such a break with accepted EFL practice in China that we never expected our project to run a smooth course. The defence I offer may clarify things and may be of interest to colleagues in similar situations outside China.

Learning through use

That we consider it a primary principle in language teaching to have the students learn the language through using it will very likely go unchallenged anywhere in the world, including China. But here a problem arises: what do you mean by 'use'? To us, use means communication, and communication does not simply mean two people uttering sentences in turn. It takes for granted certain conditions. In a classroom context, there are, I think, three conditions that must be met before any activity can be called 'communicative'.

Real situations, real roles[3]

First, the situation must be real, and the role must be real. In our case, the English-using situations and roles must be 'real' to a Chinese foreign language graduate. For example, after graduation, some students will act as interpreters at meetings or negotiations, and others will read and summarize or translate news reports or technical literature. These are situations and roles that are real for our students, and therefore are what we try to simulate or reproduce for them when they are learning English.

Some teachers do not seem to realize there is any difference between a 'real' and a 'false' situation. So long as their students utter sentences in English, they think it is communication, good practice, and that through it they will acquire the competence to communicate in English. But is it likely that they will? Communicative competence does not mean the ability just to utter words or sentences. It involves the ability to react mentally as well as verbally in communication situations. The mental reaction is the root of the verbal reaction. Keeping the students out of real situations and requiring them merely to produce a verbal reaction is like keeping a plant away from the soil while trying to get it to grow and blossom. False situations do not produce mental reactions—even if they sometimes produce verbal reactions that sound appropriate.

However, far be it from me to disparage lively and colourful language activities such as role play, games, and drama, where the situations and roles are mostly not real in this sense. These activities serve many other purposes. For instance, they may serve to liven up the classroom, boost the students' motivation, develop their imagination, or cultivate their powers of reasoning or literary appreciation. But for the purposes of acquiring a working communicative competence, you still have to rely on down-to-earth communication practice—a great deal of it, too—in real situations and real roles.

Need, purpose, and substance for communication

When people ask questions, it is because they don't know the answer; when they speak or write, it is because they have something to say; and when they listen or read, they do it to get information or ideas. In other words, there is a need and a purpose for communication and something to be communicated. This need, purpose, and substance are what give rise to communication in real life. And therefore they are what we try to provide our students with when we want them to speak, write, listen, or read. We take care not to make students ask such questions as 'Is this a pen?' when everybody can see it is a pen, or to ask each other 'What is your name?' when they already know each other's names. For reading or listening, we wouldn't give our students the story of Lei Feng,[4] which every schoolchild in China knows by heart. Nor would we give them a set of pictures and make them say or write: 'This is Li Ming. He is going to school. Now he meets his friend Zhang Hua', and pretend that our students are 'doing very well' in spoken or written English. We don't think this *is* spoken or written English, because spoken or written English means communicating something through the spoken or written mode of English, and here the students are not communicating anything.

Many teachers constantly worry about their students forming bad language habits. But have they ever asked themselves whether this kind of empty talk might not lead the students to divorce language from communication? In fact this is a fairly common bad habit among Chinese foreign language students: the young interpreter may startle his or her foreign guest every now and then with lumps of memorized language that are completely out of place: the young Chinese postgraduate in a discussion with foreign colleagues may spin out a prefabricated speech, oblivious to what others are talking about.

Freedom and unpredictability

In real life, when you ask people a question, they always have the freedom to answer as they choose, so there is also always an element of unpredictability. In many language textbooks, however, when students are called upon to answer questions, they are often instructed to give only affirmative or negative answers, or 'full' or 'short' answers. In pattern drills, students are often required to give only one form of response, the only 'correct' one. Even in so-called 'conversation practice', students often simply recite a pre-written dialogue or utter sentences according to some prescribed pattern. There is no freedom, no choice, no unpredictability in this. In our opinion, it is not communication, since communication involves freedom and unpredictability.

This applies not merely to conversation or 'interactive' communication. In what is considered purely 'receptive' reading and listening there is also freedom and unpredictability. The reader or listener in a sense is free to negotiate and interpret meaning in his or her way, and at the same time is frequently unable to predict what he or she is going to read and hear. Language learners need to learn to handle this freedom and tackle this unpredictability. Yet 'traditional' teachers never give them a chance. They deprive learners of freedom by always giving them one 'correct' interpretation before they can do any interpreting themselves. They also remove any unpredictability from the text by filtering out whatever is unpredictable. If there are vocabulary or structural items that are not on the students' list of 'learnt items', these teachers will take them out. If there are ideas or concepts that the students are not familiar with, they will explain them beforehand. So the students are always in a protected position, where nothing is unpredictable or undecided. In real life, things are entirely different. Even after years of study and work, whenever you sit down to read or listen to something, say a newspaper article or a broadcast talk, can you ever be sure you won't come across any vocabulary items or structures that you haven't learnt before, or any ideas or concepts that are unfamiliar? In real life, there *is* no teacher to take such things out of the article or the talk or to explain them to you beforehand. And there is no teacher to give you the 'correct' interpretation; you have to manage by yourself.

So, if students are deprived of the chance ever to learn to cope with freedom and unpredictability at school, how can they manage when they are thrown into a real and unpredictable communication situation afterwards?

Form before use?

So far I have tried to establish one point—that learning a language by use (or communication), if taken seriously, involves some very specific requirements. In view of this, teachers might want to say that after all, language should be learnt first, and put to use afterwards, that students should be made to 'learn' bits of the target language by mimicry and memorization ('mim-mem'), and only after they have 'learnt' these things begin using them. With learning and using thus separated, people find a justification not to include the use of the language in the learning process. Learning a language comes to mean *only* the mastery of form. I would like to raise the following questions about this view:

1 In learning a language, is it possible to separate form from use? Even if it is possible, is it desirable?
2 Suppose we agree that language form has to be learnt before language use, can it be learnt by 'mim-mem'? And, again, even if it can, is 'mim-mem' the most desirable way even for learning form?
3 Let's suppose that bits of the form of a language can be learnt by 'mim-mem'. After you've learnt them, can you call them up for use when you are communicating? Some research shows that things learnt by 'mim-mem' are stored in a certain part of our brains and are retrievable when we are reciting, but very often not when we are actually communicating (cf. Lamendella 1979).
4 Let's furthermore suppose that forms learnt by 'mim-men' can be retrieved for communication. How do you know which is the appropriate form for a particular function in a particular situation and context?

Although learning the form of a language is necessary, it is not to be equated with learning its use. It is at best only a step towards learning use. After all is said and done, learning the use of language has to be achieved through use itself, that is, by communication.

Real language

Making the students learn through use naturally implies that the target language they come into contact with should be real, that is, authentic, appropriate, and 'global'. Quite a number of teachers seem to take the term 'authentic language' to mean standard native speaker language. In fact, it means language that is actually used in real communication situations, as opposed to language that is artificially made up for purposes other than communication. Specifically to us it means language that is used in communication situations that are *relevant* to our students. If after graduation our students have to read encyclopaedias, then the language of encyclopaedias is authentic for them. We can give them samples of it to read. If in actual work our students will have opportunities to listen to Africans speaking English, then African English is authentic for them. We will try to give them some samples of it to listen to. Of course, we also give them standard native-speaker English, because standard native-speaker English happens to be in actual use in communication situations that are relevant to our students.

Authentic language naturally entails appropriacy. Appropriacy is part of the authenticity not only of the language used, but also of the situation and the role. What is appropriate for our students is what is appropriate in the situations and roles that are relevant to them. Putting the students in false roles is likely to cause confusion about what is appropriate and inappropriate for them. Teaching the language as mere form, separated from use, situation, and role, is another practice that certainly does not help to sensitize students to appropriacy. It is only through use that appropriacy can be learnt and taught. On the other hand, if language is taught through use and for use, appropriacy is something you cannot ignore.

Another essential feature of authentic language is 'globalness'. By 'global language' I mean language that is whole and multi-dimensional, in which all sorts of forms may occur naturally as occasion requires. We believe that distorting language to fit it into a grading framework is not only unnecessary: it actually hinders the development of communicative competence in the learners. In a sense it is almost like a parent who is trying to help his or her children to learn about the world, and who is afraid to show them the world in full colour all at once, and decides to present it in monochrome first, adding other colours one by one at proper intervals. No one would claim that children seeing the world in full colour the first time they open their eyes are capable of comprehending everything there and then, but surely delaying revelation of the world's true colours would not help them to learn about it any faster.

Our own experience with the CECL project shows that not only are adult students able to cope with semi-authentic[5] and authentic language right from the beginning; in a very short time they even develop a palate for things authentic, so that if you give them any reading or listening text that seems phoney, they take one look at it and snort. My advice to teachers who have doubts about their students' ability to cope with authenticity is this: if you give your students a chance, you will find surprising potential in them.

The problem experienced by 'structuralists' over this is created by themselves. Since they have set up a rigid system of grading by structures, they have to keep to this system by sacrificing the authenticity, appropriacy, and globalness of the language they teach. From whatever angle you look at the matter, the sacrifice can in no way be justified. On the one hand, grading by structures is purely artificial and unnecessary; on the other hand, it is authenticity, appropriacy, and globalness all combined that constitute the communicative value of a language, without which the language becomes just a hollow carcass.

Grading

Another related argument has been raised against our approach. People say that because we insist on authentic, global, and appropriate language from the very beginning, there is no way we can grade our materials, and as a result we have simply thrown to the winds the time-honoured pedagogic principle of grading from easy to difficult.

We haven't thrown away the principle, and we naturally also grade our material. It is just that our concept of what constitutes difficulty and easiness does not seem to be quite the same as theirs. People are so used to textbooks concentrating on lexical and structural items that they take it for granted that difficulty or easiness can only mean difficulty or easiness of the *vocabulary* and *grammar* of the text. In fact, however, there are many other factors that contribute to the difficulty or easiness of a lesson, for instance, the task you require the students to do. That is how the CECL course is graded: by control of the tasks. Simple tasks are given to the students in the early stages, and more challenging ones in the later stages. Of course, how challenging a task is depends not solely on the task, but also on other factors, including performance requirements and the difficulty of the material. This, in turn, depends on conceptual, cultural, and linguistic difficulty. So, in this sense, we also take into consideration the linguistic level of the material.

Sufficient input

The learners must be provided with sufficient exposure to the target language. This again is a principle which nobody will object to theoretically. Yet when you put it into practice, you are sure to meet with resistance. Here I will try to answer two questions which reflect the prevailing attitude in China as regards this principle.

1 *Is the principle of 'learning sparingly but well' applicable to language learning?* The very nature of language and language acquisition contradicts this theory, which arises from a conceptual fallacy. One must remember that language is not knowledge, it is competence. In some ways, learning a language is like boiling a kettle of water. In normal circumstances a certain amount of water has to absorb a certain amount of heat in order to boil. This is a scientific fact and you never ask whether you can make a better job of boiling the water by reducing the heat. The only way to do a better job is to apply more heat, so that it will boil faster. Similarly, in language learning a person has to 'take in' a certain amount of language data in order to be able to internalize the system of the language and to acquire communicative competence in it. You cannot get around it by 'economizing' on the intake. The only way of doing a better job is to offer more language data and to help the learner deal with it.

There is a counter-argument to this which I would like to mention here. Some say that giving students such a lot of exposure to language is like throwing water over a duck's back. The water runs off and never penetrates. Well, our answer is: if the purpose is to get the duck wet to the skin and a pail of water has failed to achieve it, a sensible person would just add more water or, better still, keep the duck submerged in a pond. Reducing the amount of water to a cupful is just silly.

The crux of the matter lies in different interpretations of the term 'learning', as applied to language. In China when people say you have 'learnt' an English lesson, they generally mean you have looked up and memorized every single word, and translated and analysed grammatically every sentence in it. If you can't show them your notebook of new words and grammar items, they say you have learnt nothing. However, our materials are not meant to be 'learnt' in that way. Or, more precisely, language itself is not learnt that way. The very fact that our students have done the tasks required in the lesson means that they have learnt something: they have learnt some of the skills which go to make up overall communicative competence. At the same time, they also learn vocabulary and grammar, not by rote, but by assimilation and internalization. And that goes to make up communicative competence, too. Communicative competence, in fact, and not just how many words and how much grammar, is what we should be thinking of when we talk about learning 'sparingly' or 'extensively', 'well' or 'badly'.

2 *Can students digest such a great amount of language data?* That depends on what you mean by 'digest'. If it means memorization of every word and analysis of every sentence, of course they can't. We admit that our students did at first feel a little panicky when they saw a 'lesson' fifty or sixty pages long. Coming from schools where 'digestion' of a lesson *does* mean memorization of every word and analysis of every sentence, the students naturally have difficulty adjusting to a new way of learning. But as soon as they realize what is required of them, they no longer find quantity a problem.

Concern about students' 'indigestion' is, in fact, unwarranted. Let's suppose our students were not in China, but were learning English in an English-speaking country. Would we ever worry about whether they were able to 'digest' the enormous amount of language data they come into contact with? Would we forbid them to go out into the street or to talk to native speakers or watch TV? Actually, what teachers of English in China ought to be worrying about is not giving the students too much, but giving them too little.

Tasks and skills

Traditionally, a language lesson in China consists of a focus text and a list of language points drawn from the text. The language points are about grammar or vocabulary: they concern only the *form* of the language, since the sole objective of the course is to teach language form. Our objective is communicative competence, which, for pedagogical reasons, is broken down into communicative skills. To acquire these skills, the students are set tasks. We haven't thrown away grammar and vocabulary. They are just not the major content or objective of our lessons; they are dealt with only as and when the tasks require them.

Thus, what constitutes a lesson in our course is a series of tasks to be performed by the students. For instance, they may be required to read or listen to a report on, say, smoking, for a general impression, specified information, the main message, or the author's/speaker's attitude. They may at the same time be required to take notes, write a summary, transfer the information, or make some evaluation. They may be required to carry on a conversation, a debate, or correspondence with a foreign friend on such topics as the religion problem in China. These tasks, in their turn, involve different skills, such as the ability to skim or scan with the eyes or the ears, to read or listen between the lines, to get round some unfamiliar vocabulary or structural items so as to comprehend or express meaning by relying on the context, to recognize and to make use of various discourse signals, to employ one's own knowledge of the world, or one's reasoning, etc.

What has been the reaction of 'traditional' teachers to lessons which depart so dramatically from the familiar pattern? They miss the focus text—their nice, compact text of just the right length and level, in which they can find language points they want to elaborate on, and on which hours can be spent explaining, analysing, paraphrasing, asking questions, practising patterns, reading aloud, retelling, etc., until the students very nearly, if not literally, learn every word by heart. They say the CECL materials are all right for extensive reading, but not for intensive reading;[6] intensive reading is where students really learn things: extensive reading serves only to help consolidate or supplement what has been learnt in intensive reading.

Our answer to this is, first of all, we did not design a reading course, but an *integrated* course, in which students are supposed not only to use and develop all four major skills—listening, speaking, reading, writing—but also constantly to combine and integrate them in use, and therefore to develop not four separate skills, but rather composite skills involving sometimes one, sometimes two or more of the conventional four skills.

Also, even if we were discussing only reading and nothing else, I would say there are not just two kinds of reading—intensive and extensive—but many kinds. For example, the way you read a newspaper at breakfast is definitely not the same as the way you read a science thesis for research. And the ways you read a novel for pleasure or an almanac for reference are entirely different again. When you go into a library, you can spend just a few minutes going over a dozen books, then you may spend a whole month reading just one of them. Capable readers are always able to shift and vary their speed and mode of reading as the purpose and other circumstances demand. They have at their disposal several different reading skills from which they can at any time select and which can be combined. Therefore in training our students to read, we should help them to acquire this ability to shift, adjust, and combine, rather than turn them into some kind of robot fitted with only two reading programs— one for 'intensive' and another for 'extensive' reading.

There are teachers who cherish the illusion that, when the students have been taught intensive reading skills, extensive reading skills will take care of themselves. The fact is, extensive reading skills have to be taught too, and they are no easier than intensive reading skills. The way so-called 'intensive reading' is commonly taught in China not only does not help to promote extensive reading skills: it may actually fossilize the reading style of students so that they are hindered from ever reading efficiently. To us, intensive reading does not mean a focus on the individual words and sentences. It means getting at the interrelation between the parts of the discourse and between the discourse and its context, and eventually also getting at a fuller meaning of the discourse as a whole.

So far we have been discussing reading only to illustrate a point, which is by analogy also true of listening, and, in a converse way, of writing and speaking. To sum up, the traditional way of teaching the four skills and especially 'intensive reading' in fact reflects a superficial, segregative, and formalistic view of language skills and language. We need to find ways to treat language skills *integratively* within their sociolinguistic and psycholinguistic context. We believe dealing with them in terms of tasks is one such way.

Student-centredness

A communicative approach presupposes that students take the central role in learning. This idea of student-centredness is first of all embodied in the design of the syllabus. We claim that our communicative syllabus is student-oriented because it gears its objectives to what students actually need after graduation, and it is so designed that the students are given a chance to do the learning themselves, instead of having everything done for them by the teacher.

The traditional text-analysis syllabus cannot be considered a student-oriented syllabus, not simply because the teacher takes up almost all the time in class, but also because the content and design of the course are determined not by the students' needs, but by the 'texts' which have been selected solely for their 'literary value'. As to the structural syllabus, it is a syllabus designed and based on the analysis of the structure of the target language. We do not deny that the students need structure. The problem with the structural syllabus is that it deals with the structure of the target language as form existing independent of use and therefore as something that has to be taught according to its own internal system, regardless of the needs of the learners. In view of that, we don't think a structural syllabus can be called student-oriented, even if students 'speak' and 'practise' one hundred per cent of class time. We cannot evaluate the success of a lesson simply by counting how many utterances are made per students in one class hour. A student-oriented lesson may possibly be one where the students do not utter a single sound from beginning to end (for example in a speed-reading or listen-and-write lesson). The important thing is that full rein is given to their initiative and they are actively involved in communicative activities requiring speaking, listening, writing, or reading—and thinking. I have visited very impressive classes where the teacher and students perform a very 'lively' show. But there is an essential difference between a show and a communicative class. In a show, the actors/students do and say everything thinking, 'This is what the director/teacher wants me to do and say now', while in a communicative class there is no director: the students (sometimes with the teacher as just another participant) do what they need to do to carry out the given communication task.

So the teacher's role in a communicative class is completely different from that in any other type of class. In China, the tradition of the teacher occupying the centre in the classroom is still very much alive, and teachers on our project naturally feel a bit uprooted when they are removed from that position. Some of them are taking it pretty easy though, because now they don't have to prepare a 'lecture' for every class, or supply the 'correct' answer to every exercise the students do. Other, more conscientious teachers feel somewhat guilty because they 'have nothing to do in class' and don't think they are doing their duty. Of course, the communicative teacher's role is neither to give lectures nor to supply correct answers. And if teachers think it is their duty to take over everything from the students, then it would be much better for them to do nothing at all. To learn the language, the students themselves must go through the process of learning. The teacher's job is only to provide the *conditions* for this process, set it going, observe it, try to understand it, give guidance, help it along, analyse and evaluate it. It is also the teacher's job to help the students themselves understand this process, to turn it from an unconscious, irrational, patternless process to a conscious, rational and patterned process—patterned in an individual way for each student. That is what makes the communicative teacher's task so demanding. On the other hand, it is also a most rewarding job—a job full of interest, life, creativity, versatility, and possibilities, because the students are released from a passive role, and are now interested, alive, and creative.

Language learning—an active development process

The traditional text-analysis school looks upon language teaching as a 'knowledge-imparting' process, and language learning as a 'knowledge-receiving' process. The structuralist pattern-drill school, unlike the traditional school, lays down language skills as the objective. But language skills are conceived of as a set of habits, and language learning as a 'habit-forming' process. The communicative school, whose objective is communicative competence, regards language learning as an *active development* process.

Both the traditional and the structuralist schools treat language learners as passive recipients. They don't have to take any initiative. They just wait there to be filled with knowledge or to be trained in habits. The habit-forming process is rather like programming done on a robot: any initiative on the part of the robot is not only superfluous, it may actually get in the way. On the other hand, the communicative approach demands a high degree of initiative from learners. They are active agents throughout the process. Mechanically formed habits are only skin deep, whereas communicative competence is something that involves the creative functioning of the mind. And only one's own active efforts can ensure the development of such a competence.

In addition, neither the traditional nor the structuralist school gives sufficient credit to the learner's intelligence. All that 'traditional' teachers require of students is the ability to receive and store up in their heads the knowledge handed out to them. That presumably involves understanding what the teacher says. Yet it is a very passive kind of understanding. The structuralist teacher doesn't even require that much. His or her students are supposed to know only the surface meaning of the words they repeat, and even that understanding is not always necessary in order to do a pattern drill. The lessons and the drills seldom include anything that may require learners to stand on their own feet intellectually, let alone make any intellectual leaps. Everything is deliberately designed to require the minimum possible intellectual effort, and therefore also to involve the minimum risk of the learner making mistakes and forming bad habits.

I am not claiming that students going through traditional or structuralist courses do not use their intellect. Most of them do, in spite of the fact that it is not required of them. This is because they can't help using it if they are seriously trying to learn the language. My argument against both these schools is this: since it is a fact that our students are educated intelligent adults, and since they will try to employ their intellect anyhow, why not make full use of it to the advantage of the learning process, instead of ignoring or even suppressing it?

Moreover, we believe that the teacher's duty is not just to exploit the students' intellect but, even more important, to help develop it. This idea of development again distinguishes the communicative school from the other two schools. Neither of the latter includes in their concept of the language-learning process the idea of development.

The traditional school sees the language-learning process as one of quantitative increase—quantitative increase of knowledge of the target language. This is a view often held, even by teachers who wouldn't admit that they belong to the traditional school. Witness the fact that in English teaching programmes in China, no matter what level they are or what approach they profess to follow, a definite number of words and a definite list of grammar items are invariably laid down as final objectives. In our view, learning a language is a *developmental* process which must necessarily go beyond quantitative increase to qualitative change. Not that we do not consider quantitative increase necessary, but setting up such increases as final objectives will tend only to make the learners stop at them and never go beyond, and therefore never really learn the language.

The structuralists will also find this idea of development alien. Starting from the assumption that teaching a language means nothing more than training the learner in a set of habits, they naturally set about blocking off any possible diversions that may lead the learner into so-called 'bad habits'. Language learners are more or less looked upon as white mice in a maze who have an innate propensity to take the wrong turn when the opportunity arises. For instance, they have tendencies to let their first language 'interfere' with the second, to draw analogies between L1 and L2 learning experiences, to rationalize, to ask why, etc., etc. All these have to be kept in check, so that students may keep to the one and only correct route. In a word, for the structuralists the whole process of language learning is a disciplining process.

This is quite at odds with the rationale of the communicative approach. Those of us who have adopted this approach believe that learning a language should not mean restricting or thwarting learners. On the contrary, it should help them to grow and to mature. We believe that in every learner there is potential to be developed, and we have our eyes on this, rather than on any 'undesirable' tendencies. Learning a language will help learners to develop this potential, and, in turn, only by developing it can they learn a language. In a narrow sense, communicative competence is developed, and in a broad sense the learner also develops as an intelligent being. We consider that a foreign language course has failed if a learner coming through it has gained nothing beyond the language, or, in other words, hasn't become a fuller person who can play a really useful role in international communication between cultures, which of course goes far beyond mere linguistic exchange.

Those are the differences between the communicative view and the traditional and structuralist views of the language-learning process. These differences actually go deeper: they have their roots in differences in philosophy of education. The view that language learning is acquiring knowledge comes from the idea that to educate is to impart knowledge; the view that language learning is habit formation is based on the idea that to educate is to discipline; while the view that it is competence development has its origin in the idea that education is development. Since in China the knowledge-imparting plus disciplining theory is still fairly universally accepted, and not only in language teaching, it really is not surprising that a communicative approach to EFL should meet with stubborn and protracted resistance.

A criterion for judging performance

Since the goal for our programme is communicative competence, naturally the criterion for the assessment of the students' performance is *effective communication*. This may not be so obvious as it sounds. It implies that the performance being assessed must not be recitation, mimicry, copying, or reproducing formulae. If what you require of language students is the ability to use the language in communication, it stands to reason that you should test and judge them as they use the language in communication. You would think a driving test crazy if after a series of lessons it tested candidates, not in driving a car, but in drawing a picture of a car. Yet when students are given a test in English in China, it is often their ability to memorize words, formulae, and texts—not their ability to communicate—that is tested.

Another argument which sounds almost as obvious is that the communication we judge our students by ought to be relevant. For instance, we shouldn't judge our students' performance in such communication situations as ordering groceries or applying for a job. The reason is simply that it is highly unlikely that they would ever need to do these things in English in real life.

Relevance is also something we have to bear in mind when we measure effectiveness. We cannot talk of a performance being 'effective' or 'ineffective' without reference to the situation, the role, and the task. The crudest kind of survival English, which may be fairly effective for an immigrant applying for a dish-washing job in a New York Chinatown restaurant, cannot be considered an effective means of communication for a member of a Chinese official delegation visiting the New York State University, for example. In our understanding, effective communication entails two things: linguistic accuracy and sociolinguistic appropriacy. Inappropriate performance, even if it is perfectly accurate linguistically, can never be really effective as communication, not only because it doesn't produce the desired effect, but also because it sometimes produces the opposite effect. On the other hand, linguistic inaccuracy also prevents communication being carried on effectively. It follows logically that the requirement we set for accuracy is higher: we demand accuracy in actual communication, while the structuralists ask for accuracy only when form is isolated from use.

Some people say that students who are taught with our communicative materials make more errors in their English than those taught according to a structuralist approach. Even if there is some truth in this, it does not discredit the approach. Suppose you give students only one page of materials every week, and all they have to do is to memorize and recite things from this single page: certainly they won't make many mistakes. But if you give students fifty pages of materials per week and ask them to use what they get from them creatively, you are giving them many more chances to use the language, and also many more opportunities to make mistakes. Consequently it is natural that they make more mistakes, at least in the earlier stages. We certainly wouldn't try to cut down the students' errors by cutting down their chances of using the language. On the contrary, we know that it is only through use—plenty of use—that accuracy and appropriacy will come and communicative effectiveness increase. It is communicative competence that we aim at, and therefore it is communicative competence that we should test. It is a deplorable fact that in China, English tests and examinations have not yet gone beyond linguistic form, and learners' performance is still assessed only in terms of *linguistic* competence. As the saying goes, the examination is the piper that calls the tune. Perhaps the tide will turn only when language testing has changed its focus.

Notes

1 Wendy Allen, Nina Spada, and the author. Among others who worked on the project are: Tim Lockwood, Carol Pomeroy, Caz Philcox, Susan Maingay, and Gail Langley.
2 The project was originally named ECP (English for Communicative Purposes), which was later changed to CECL.
3 'Real' is used here as opposed to 'false', in the sense of 'relevant to reality'.
4 Lei Feng was an ordinary soldier of the Chinese People's Liberation Army. He did a lot of good deeds and became well known throughout China.
5 This refers to those parts of the materials written or rewritten by the materials writers, where no materials of appropriate length, topic, difficulty, etc., are available. What distinguishes 'semi-authentic' language from 'simplified' language is that the latter is fabricated to serve the purpose of teaching language forms, while the purpose of the former remains communication, and it therefore preserves the essential features of authentic language.
6 In China, 'intensive reading' is actually not a reading course, but the core course in EFL in which everything the teacher wants to teach (grammar, vocabulary, reading aloud, etc.) is taught through a written text.

(*Originally published in Volume 38/1, 1984*)

The following two papers really need to be read consecutively. In combination, they indicate just how much was—and is—felt to be at stake in the battle for the minds of language teachers, materials writers, and their managers.

Michael Swan's paper (originally published in two parts) raises in somewhat different terms many of the objections that Li Xiaoju was seeking to overcome. But the reasoning is different. The paper is written from the point of view of a materials writer who wants to stop what he sees as a bandwagon and to interrogate the drivers and musicians—and preferably to persuade passengers to get off!

Swan's entertaining dissection of what he views as shibboleths of communicative 'dogma' focuses on four leitmotivs of the literature on the approach, and consequently of this volume:

—sentence meaning vs. utterance meaning ('usage' vs. 'use', in Widdowson's terms)
—communication skills and strategies
—notional/functional syllabuses
—authenticity.

Swan may overstate his case, take other writers' words out of their full context, and be more reactionary than need be, but his paper provides a useful check (in more than one sense of the word) for those in danger of being tempted by new priorities and trendy terminology to believe that, magically, the new approach will solve all the foreign language teacher's problems—even though those in favour of the approach may expressly deny that it can.

The paper is overwhelmingly critical of the way in which the principles of the communicative approach have been articulated and promoted. Swan's aim, however, is not to say 'Forget all this—let's get back to the traditional values': he himself points out—and perhaps understates—some of the ways in which language teaching has progressed since the communicative era began.

In the second paper, H. G. Widdowson, one of the chief architects of the communicative approach, replies to Swan's lengthy critique. Widdowson's is an angry paper, and refreshingly free of the type of dissent wrapped up in polite circumlocution that characterizes much academic debate in print. Interestingly, he frames his counter-attack not as a point-by-point rebuttal but rather as a commentary on the nature of sound enquiry—and on Swan's failure, in Widdowson's opinion—to engage in it.

From the reader's point of view it is interesting to note the mismatch in levels of approach to the issues. While Swan attempts to remain at the level of classroom nuts and bolts—and in Widdowson's view is in danger of grasping mainly rusty and cross-threaded ones—Widdowson's interest is in 'enquiry' at a more theoretical level, and its essential role in providing guiding principles. He sees in Swan's attack an attempt to dismiss a majority of the insights gained and progress achieved through the debate and enquiry which surrounded the practical and pedagogic shifts which have taken place since the beginning of the Communicative Era.

A critical look at the communicative approach
Michael Swan

Introduction

There is nothing so creative as a good dogma. During the last few years, under the influence of the 'Communicative Approach', language teaching seems to have made great progress. Syllabus design has become a good deal more sophisticated, and we are able to give our students a better and more complete picture than before of how language is used. In methodology, the change has been dramatic. The boring and mechanical exercise types which were so common ten or fifteen years ago have virtually disappeared, to be replaced by a splendid variety of exciting and engaging practice activities. All this is very positive, and it is not difficult to believe that such progress in course design has resulted in a real improvement in the speed and quality of language learning.

And yet... A dogma remains a dogma, and in this respect the 'communicative revolution' is little different from its predecessors in the language teaching field. If one reads through the standard books and articles on the communicative teaching of English, one finds assertions about language use and language learning falling like leaves in autumn; facts, on the other hand, tend to be remarkably thin on the ground. Along with its many virtues, the Communicative Approach unfortunately has most of the typical vices of an intellectual revolution: it over-generalizes valid but limited insights until they become virtually meaningless; it makes exaggerated claims for the power and novelty of its doctrines; it misrepresents the currents of thought it has replaced; it is often characterized by serious intellectual confusion; it is choked with jargon.

In this article I propose to look critically at certain concepts which form part of the theoretical basis of the new orthodoxy, in an attempt to reduce the confusion which surrounds their use, and which unfortunately forms a serious obstacle to sensible communication in the field. I shall discuss in particular: (1) the idea of a 'double level of meaning' associated with such terms as 'rules of use' and 'rules of communication', and the related concept of 'appropriacy'; (2) some confusions regarding 'skills' and 'strategies'; (3) the idea of a semantic ('notional/functional') syllabus, and (4) the 'real life' fallacy in materials design and methodology.

I shall find it convenient to argue as if the Communicative Approach were a coherent and monolithic body of doctrine. This is, of course, far from being the case. Individual applied linguists and teacher trainers vary widely in their acceptance and interpretation of the different ideas which I shall discuss here. Some of the views quoted are becoming outmoded, and would not necessarily be defended today by their originators. But whatever their current status in academic circles, all of these ideas are familiar, widespread, and enormously influential among language teachers, and they merit serious scrutiny.

Meaning and use

A basic communicative doctrine is that earlier approaches to language teaching did not deal properly with meaning. According to the standard argument, it is not enough just to learn what is in the grammar and dictionary. There are (we are told) two levels of meaning in language: 'usage' and 'use', or 'signification' and 'value', or whatever. Traditional courses, it appears, taught one of these kinds of meaning but neglected the other.

> One of the major reasons for questioning the adequacy of grammatical syllabuses lies in the fact that even when we have described the grammatical (and lexical) meaning of a sentence, we have not accounted for the way it is used as an utterance... Since

> those things that are not conveyed by the grammar are also understood, they too must be governed by 'rules' which are known to both speaker and hearer. People who speak the same language share not so much a *grammatical* competence as a *communicative* competence. Looked at in foreign language teaching terms, this means that the learner has to be learn rules of communication as well as rules of grammar. (Wilkins 1976:10, 11)

This line of argument is often illustrated by instances of utterances which clearly have one kind of 'propositional' meaning and a different kind of 'function'. The coat example and the window example are popular. If you say 'Your coat's on the floor' to a child, you are probably telling him or her to pick it up; a person who says 'There's a window open' may really be asking for it to be closed. However, examples are not confined to requests masquerading as statements. All kinds of utterances, we are reminded, can express intentions which are not made explicit by the grammatical form in which the utterance is couched.

> ... this sentence (*The policeman is crossing the road*) might serve a number of communicative functions, depending on the contextual and/or situational circumstances in which it were used. Thus, it might take on the value of part of a commentary..., or it might serve as a warning or a threat, or some other act of communication. If it is the case that knowing a language means both knowing what *signification* sentences have as instances of language usage and what *value* they take on as instances of use, it seems clear that the teacher of language should be concerned with the teaching of both kinds of knowledge. (Widdowson 1978:19)

Put in general terms like this, the claim has a fine plausible ring to it—not least because of the impressive, if slightly confusing, terminology. There is of course nothing particularly novel about the two-level account of meaning given here. It has long been recognized that most language items are multi-purpose tokens which take on their precise value from the context they are used in. What *is* perhaps more novel is the suggestion that the value of any utterance in a given situation can be specified by rules ('rules of communication' or 'rules of use'), and that it is our business to teach these rules to our students. Neither Wilkins nor Widdowson makes it clear what form such rules might take, and so it is a little difficult to deal adequately with the argument. However, let us try to see what might be involved in a concrete instance.

Widdowson asserts, effectively, that a student cannot properly interpret the utterance *The policeman is crossing the road* (or any other utterance, for that matter) if he knows only its propositional (structural and lexical) meaning. In order to grasp its real value in a specific situation, he must have learnt an additional rule about how the utterance can be used. Very well. For the sake of argument, let us imagine that an international team of burglers (Wilberforce, Gomez, Schmidt, and Tanaka) are busy doing over a detached suburban house. Wilberforce is on watch. A policeman comes round the corner on the other side of the road. Wilberforce reports this to the others. Schmidt, who learnt his English from a communicatively-oriented multi-media course in a university applied linguistics department, interprets this as a warning and turns pale. Gomez and Tanaka, who followed a more traditional course, totally fail to grasp the illocutionary force of Wilberforce's remark. Believing him to be making a neutral comment on the external environment, they continue opening drawers. Suddenly Wilberforce blurts out, 'The policeman is crossing the road', and disappears through the back door, closely followed by Schmidt. Gomez and Tanaka move calmly to the wardrobe. They are caught and put away for five years. Two more victims of the structural syllabus.

Although the argument about rules of use leads to some very extraordinary conclusions when applied to particular cases, it occurs repeatedly in the literature of the Communicative Approach, and there is no doubt that we are intended to take it literally. Here is Widdowson again, this time talking about language production, rather than comprehension.

> It is possible for someone to have learned a large number of sentence patterns and a large number of words which can fit into them without knowing how they are put to communicative use. (Widdowson 1978:18, 19)

Well, no doubt this can happen. But is it necessarily or normally the case? One of the few things I retain from a term's study of a highly 'structural' Russian audio-lingual course is a pattern that goes something like this: *Vot moy nomer; vot moy dom; vot moya kniga*; and so on. I have done no Russian since, but I think I know when it is communicatively appropriate to say 'This is my room', 'This is my house', or 'This is my book' in that language, or most others. (And if I don't, it is not a communicative Russian course that I need; it is expert help of a rather different kind.)

Here is a final example of the 'usage/use' assertion; this time the term 'use potential' is introduced.

> Not until he (the learner) has had experience of the language he is learning as use will he be able to recognize use potential. (Widdowson 1978:118)

I have just looked up the Swedish for 'Something is wrong with the gearbox' in a motorist's phrase-book. It is (if my book is to be trusted) 'Någonting stämmer inte med växellåda'. I have no experience of Swedish 'as use'. However, I am prepared to hazard a guess that this expression's use potential is more likely to be realized in a garage than, for instance, in a doctor's surgery or a laundry (though of course one can never be certain about these things). I would also guess that this is true of the equivalent expression in Spanish, Tagalog, Melanesian pidgin, or any language whatever. And I know this, not because I am an exceptionally intuitive linguist, but because the fact in question is not just a fact about Swedish, or about language—it is a fact about the world, and the things we say about the world. A linguist may need, for his or her own purposes, to state explicitly that conversations about cars are likely to take place in garages, or that while 'The rain destroyed the crops' is a correct example of English usage, it is not an appropriate answer to the question, 'Where is the station?' But to suggest that this kind of information should form part of a foreign-language teaching syllabus is to misunderstand quite radically the distinction between thought and language.

Foreigners have mother tongues: they know as much as we do about how human beings communicate. The 'rules of use' that determine how we interpret utterances such as Widdowson's sentence about the policeman are mostly non-language-specific, and amount to little more than the operation of experience and common sense. The precise value of an utterance is given by the interaction of its structural and lexical meaning with the situation in which it is used. If you are burgling a house, a report of a policeman's approach naturally takes on the function of a threat or a warning—not because of any linguistic 'rule of communication' that can be applied to the utterance, but because policemen threaten the peace of mind of thieves. If you indicate that you are hungry, the words 'There's some stew in the fridge' are likely to constitute an offer, not because you have learnt a rule about the way these words can be used, but simply because the utterance most plausibly takes on that value in that situation.

Of course, cultures differ somewhat in their behaviour, and these differences are reflected in language. Although most utterances will retain their value across language boundaries (if correctly translated), problems will arise in specific and limited cases. For instance, there may be languages where all requests are marked as such (perhaps by a special particle or intonation pattern), so that a simple unmarked statement such as 'There's a window open' cannot in these languages function as a request. Speakers of such languages who study English (and English-speaking students of these languages) will need contrastive information about this particular point if they are to understand or speak correctly. Again, there are phrases and sentences in any language which conventionally carry intentional meanings that are not evident from their form. (English questions beginning 'Where's my . . .?' often function as demands; 'Look here!' is an expostulation; 'Why should I?' is not a simple request for information.) However, both the contrastive and the idiomatic aspects of language use have already received a good deal of attention in the past. Although the Communicative Approach may have some new information and insights to contribute (for instance about the language of social interaction), there is nothing here to justify the announcement that we need to adopt a whole new approach to the teaching of meaning. The argument about 'usage' and 'use', whatever value it may have for philosophers, has little relevance to foreign language teaching.

In a recent paper, Wilkins makes it clear that he has now come round to this kind of view.

> It seems reasonable to assume that the relation of linguistic and pragmatic features that we have referred to here is characteristic of all languages. If we consider second language learners, therefore, it appears that although there will be values, attitudes, norms, and even types of information that are culturally restricted and consequently not known to the learners, they will be aware that such a relation does exist in principle and that much of their previous experience will remain relevant in the second language. What the learners have to learn is less that there is a connection between language and context than the forms and meanings of the second language itself, together with whatever differences there are in the society that might affect the operation of the pragmatic element in communication. The learners will also know that if they can convey the meanings that they wish, even without making their intentions (i.e. illocutionary forces) explicit, the hearer has the capacity to make appropriate inferences ... Provided one understands the meaning of the sentences, in the nature of things one has every chance of recognizing the speaker's intention. (Wilkins 1983:31)

Appropriacy

The argument about a second level of meaning often surfaces in a slightly different form involving the concept of 'appropriacy'. This is the notion that our choice of language is crucially determined by the setting in which the language is used, the speaker's relationship with the listener, and similar matters. So important is this (we are often told) that appropriacy is the real goal of language teaching.

> What we want to do through language is effected by (the) relationship of (the) speakers, setting, etc. Grammar and lexis are only a small part of this. (Alexander 1977)

> Structural dialogues lack communicative intent and you cannot identify what *communicative operations* the learner can engage in as a result of practice. The result of purely structural practice is the ability to produce a range of usages, but not the ability to use forms appropriately. This is true even in cases where it looks as if communication is being taught. For example, the exclamation form 'What a lovely day' might be covered. But the interest is in the form, not on when and where to use it or what you achieve by using it. (Scott 1981:70, 71)

Nobody would deny that there are language items that are appropriate only in certain situations, or (conversely) that there are situations in which only certain ways of expressing oneself are appropriate. English notoriously has a wealth of colloquial, slang, and taboo expressions, for instance, whose use is regulated by complex restrictions. In French, it is not easy to learn exactly whom to address by the second person singular. Getting people to do things for you is a delicate business in most cultures, and this tends to be reflected in the complexity of the relevant linguistic rules. Although there is nothing particularly controversial or novel about this, it is an area where the Communicative Approach (with its interest in the language of interaction) has contributed a good deal to the coverage of our teaching.

We must understand, however, that 'appropriacy' is one aspect among many—an important corner of linguistic description, but not by any means a feature of the language as a whole. 'Appropriacy' is not a new dimension of meaning, to be added everywhere to lexical and structural meaning. It is a category that applies to certain items only: the same kind of thing as 'animate', 'countable', or 'transitive'. Items such as the imperative, *had better, bloody, I want, get* are marked for appropriacy in one way or the other; students have to be careful how they use them. But most items are not so marked. The past tense, for instance, or the words *table, design, blue, slowly, natural*, or the expression *to fill in a form*, or the sentence *She was born in 1940*—these items, and the vast majority of the other words, expressions, and sentences of the language, are unmarked for social or situational appropriacy of the kind under discussion. Consequently they cause the learner no special problems in this area.

What has happened here might be called the 'new toy' effect. A limited but valuable insight has been over-generalized, and is presented as if it applied to the whole of language and all of language teaching. Unfortunately, this is a common occurrence in the communication sciences.

Interestingly, the discussion of appropriacy often obscures a perfectly valid point about the need for increased attention to the teaching of lexis.

> We might begin our consideration of communicative language teaching . . . by looking at the discontent which teachers and applied linguists in the 1960s felt towards the kind of language teaching then predominant. This discontent is vividly expressed by Newmark . . ., who speaks of the 'structurally competent' student—the one, that is, who has developed the ability to produce grammatically correct sentences—yet who is unable to perform a simple communicative task. His example of such a task is 'asking for a light from a stranger'. Our structurally competent student might perform this task in a perfectly grammatical way by saying 'have you fire?' or 'do you have illumination' or 'are you a match's

owner?' (Newmark's examples). Yet none of these ways—however grammatical they may be—would be used by the native speaker.

Most of us are familiar with this phenomenon of the structurally competent but communicatively incompetent student, and he bears striking witness to the truth of the one insight which, perhaps more than any other, has shaped recent trends in language teaching. This is the insight that the ability to manipulate the structures of the language correctly is only a part of what is involved in learning a language. There is a 'something else' that needs to be learned, and this 'something else' involves the ability to be appropriate, to know the right thing to say at the right time. 'There are', in Hymes's . . . words, 'rules of use without which the rules of grammar would be useless'. (Johnson 1981:1, 2)

Now the 'structurally competent but communicatively incompetent student' pictured here certainly has a problem, but it is quite unnecessary to invoke nebulous abstractions such as 'appropriacy' or 'rules of use' to account for it. Newmark's student doesn't know enough vocabulary. He may be structurally competent, but he has not been taught enough lexis. He is unaware of the exact range of meaning of the word *fire* (and perhaps thinks it can be used in all cases as an equivalent of *feu* or *feuer*); he does not know the expression *a light*; he is (implausibly) confused about the meaning of *illumination*; he has not learnt the conventional phrase used for requesting a light. These are all lexical matters, and all the information the student lacks can be found in a respectable dictionary. It is perfectly true that 'the ability to manipulate the structures of the language correctly is only a part of what is involved in learning a language', and that there is a 'something else' that needs to be learned. This something else, however, is primarily vocabulary, and the Communicative Approach can hardly take credit for the 'insight' that language contains words and phrases as well as structures.

The teaching of lexis has certainly been greatly improved by the recent concern with communicative competence. Teachers and course designers are more aware than before of the vast range of conventional and idiomatic expressions that have to be learnt if a student is to be able to perform ordinary communicative tasks (such as saying she has been cut off on the phone, asking a petrol pump attendant to check his tyre pressures, or indeed asking a stranger for a light). If we are now adopting a more informed and systematic approach to vocabulary teaching, that is all to the good. But we should understand clearly that this is what we are doing. Inappropriate references to appropriacy merely confuse the issue.

Skills and strategies

Discussion of language skills is no longer limited to a consideration of the four basic activities of reading, writing, understanding speech, and speaking. We are more inclined nowadays to think in terms of the various specific types of behaviour that occur when people are producing or understanding language for a particular purpose in a particular situation, and there has been something of a proliferation of sub-skills and strategies in recent teaching materials. As we have seen, it is often taken for granted that language learners cannot transfer communication skills from their mother tongues, and that these must be taught anew if the learners are to solve the 'problem of code and context correlation which lies at the heart of the communicative ability' (Widdowson 1978:87–8). If, for instance, there is a special 'comprehension skill' involved in interpreting messages, then surely (it is claimed) we had better teach this skill to our students. Otherwise they will 'comprehend' the words they 'hear' as examples of 'usage', but will fail to 'listen' and 'interpret' messages as instances of 'use'; they will respond to 'cohesion' but not to 'coherence', and so on (Widdowson 1978 *passim*). (One of the most bizarre features of current terminology is the deliberate use of pairs of virtually indistinguishable words to illustrate allegedly vital distinctions. Faced with terms like 'use' and 'usage' or 'cohesion' and 'coherence', one really finds it extraordinarily difficult to remember which is which.)

One of the comprehension skills which we now teach foreigners is that of predicting. It has been observed that native listeners/readers make all sorts of predictions about the nature of what they are about to hear or read, based on their knowledge of the subject, their familiarity with the speaker or writer, and other relevant features. Armed with this linguistic insight (and reluctant to believe that foreigners, too, can predict), we 'train' students in 'predictive strategies'. (For instance, we ask them to guess what is coming next and then let them see if they were right or wrong). But I would suggest that if a foreigner knows something about the subject matter, and something about the speaker or writer, and if he knows enough of the language, then the foreigner is just as likely as the native speaker to predict what will be said. And if he predicts badly in a real-life comprehension task (classroom tasks are different), it can only be for one of two reasons. Either he lacks essential background knowledge (of the subject matter or the interactional context), or his command of the language is not good enough. In the one case he needs information, in the other he needs language lessons. In neither case does it make sense to talk about having to teach some kind of 'strategy'.

Another strategy which we are encouraged to teach is that of 'negotiating meaning'.

> ... speakers and writers perform an unconscious guessing game, because they have to establish what the agreed goals are (and this is not always clear, especially at the beginning of the conversation), as well as how much knowledge, or past experience, or understanding is shared. Thus if you ask me where I live, I may answer 'Britain' or 'London' or 'Surrey', or the name of the exact road, depending on why I think you asked me and how well I think you

> know south-east England. If I answer 'London' and you answer 'Whereabouts in London?' you are telling me that you want more specific information: we are negotiating about the purpose of the conversation, for you are showing that you really want to know, rather than just making a general social enquiry. . . . It needs to be emphasized that everyone, in any language, needs to develop the skills of adjustment and negotiation. (Brumfit 1981:6, 7)

The point is not always made with such unpretentious clarity.

> The shift towards a balance between form and function has had important methodological effects. If we see language as one part of wider social interaction and behaviour, deriving its communicative value from it, then we are compelled to introduce the *process* of interaction into the classroom. Learners now need to be trained and refined in the interpretive and expressive strategies of making sense amid a negotiable reality where the ground rules for understanding what partners mean are not pre-set entirely, nor unequivocal. In fact, learners have to come to cope with the essential problem of communication—to acquire the mutually negotiated and dynamic conventions which give value to formal signs. They have to learn how to agree conventions and procedures, for the interpretation of non-verbal and verbal language, with which they temporarily abide. (Candlin 1981:25)

Now this is very impressive, but it is simply not true. Language learners already know, in general, how to negotiate meaning. They have been doing it all their lives. What they do not know is what words are used to do it in a foreign language. They need lexical items, not skills: expressions like 'What do you mean by . . .?', 'Look at it this way', 'Whereabouts do you mean?', 'I beg your pardon', or 'No, that's not what I'm trying to say'. Of course, there will be cases where the mother-tongue and the foreign language differ in the detailed approach used for negotiation. Where this happens, we need to know specifics—at what point, and for what purpose, does language X operate a different convention from language Y? (Perhaps in language X it is rude to ask somebody what she means, for instance.) Such specifics can be incorporated in teaching programmes for speakers or learners of language X, and this can be very valuable. But in general there is not the least need to teach our students 'the interpretive and expressive strategies of making sense amid a negotiable reality', even assuming that we were able to define what this involves. And to talk in these terms contributes nothing whatever to our understanding of how to teach foreign languages.

Guessing, too, is something which learners are apparently unable to do outside their mother tongue.

> Clearly training in making intelligent guesses will play an important part in learning to understand the spoken form of a foreign language. (Brown 1977:162)

Assertions like this regularly pass unchallenged at conferences. As one reads the quotation, one is inclined to nod in automatic assent from force of habit: the sentiment is so familiar, so much part of the accepted orthodoxy. And yet, *why should* language students need training in making intelligent guesses? Are they less intelligent people, less good at guessing, than other groups in the population? Than language teachers, for instance? Is there any reason at all to suppose that they do not already possess this skill? And if they possess it, do we have any real evidence that they cannot in general apply it to learning a foreign language? And if we do not have such evidence, what are we doing setting out to teach people something they can do already? Most of the readers of this journal can probably understand the spoken form of a foreign language to some extent at least. How many of them have received systematic training in making intelligent guesses in the language in question?

It can happen, of course, that a learner has difficulty in transferring a skill from his or her mother tongue to the foreign language, especially in the early days of language learning. When this happens (as it can with comprehension skills), it *may* be worth giving specific practice in the 'blocked' skill in question. However, we need to know why the skill is blocked. If a learner seems to be understanding most of the words he or she hears but not really grasping the message (not seeing the wood for the trees), this may simply be due to anxiety. More often, perhaps, it is a matter of overload—the learner's command of the language is just fluent enough for him to decode the words, but this occupies all his faculties and he has no processing capacity to spare for 'interpreting' what he hears. The problem will go away with increased fluency; practice in 'global' comprehension may appear to go well and may increase the student's confidence, but I doubt whether a great deal can really be done to accelerate the natural progression of this aspect of learning. At higher levels, students may perform badly at classroom comprehension tasks (failing to make sense of texts that are well within their grasp) simply because of lack of interest; or because they have been trained to read classroom texts in such a different way from 'real life' texts that they are unable to regard them as pieces of communication. Here the problem is caused by poor methodology, and the solution involves changing what happens in the classroom, not what happens in the student. We cannot assume without further evidence that students lack comprehension strategies, simply because they have trouble jumping through the hoops that we set up for them.

This *'tabula rasa'* attitude—the belief that students do not possess, or cannot transfer from their mother tongue, normal communication skills—is one of two complementary fallacies that characterize the Communicative Approach. The other is the 'whole-system' fallacy. This arises when the linguist, over-excited about his or her analysis of a piece of language or behaviour, sets out to teach everything that has been observed (often including the metalanguage used to describe the phenomena), without stopping to ask how much of the teaching is (a) new to the students and (b) relevant to their needs. Both fallacies are well illustrated in the following exercise (Figure 1). It will be observed: (a) that the purpose of the exercise, as stated, is to develop 'conversational strategies' (a therapeutic procedure which might seem more relevant to the teaching of psycho-social disorders than to language instruction); (b) that students are taught a piece of discourse analysis and its metalanguage; and (c) that the actual English language input seems to be the least important part of the exercise—it is in fact by no means clear what

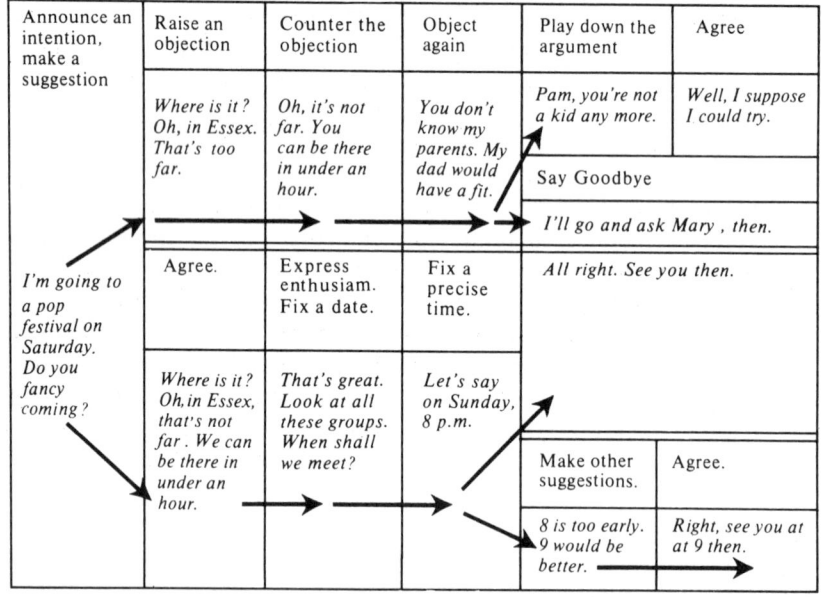

Announce an intention, make a suggestion	Raise an objection	Counter the objection	Object again	Play down the argument	Agree
	Where is it? Oh, in Essex. That's too far.	Oh, it's not far. You can be there in under an hour.	You don't know my parents. My dad would have a fit.	Pam, you're not a kid any more.	Well, I suppose I could try.
				Say Goodbye	
				I'll go and ask Mary, then.	
I'm going to a pop festival on Saturday. Do you fancy coming?	Agree.	Express enthusiasm. Fix a date.	Fix a precise time.	All right. See you then.	
	Where is it? Oh, in Essex, that's not far. We can be there in under an hour.	That's great. Look at all these groups. When shall we meet?	Let's say on Sunday, 8 p.m.		
				Make other suggestions.	Agree.
				8 is too early. 9 would be better.	Right, see you at at 9 then.

Figure 1: A 'discourse chain' from an experimental teaching unit 'I wanna have fun' by Ulrich Grewer and Terry Moston, first published in the Protokoll of the 7th Meeting of the Bundesarbeitsgemeinschaft Englisch an Gesamtschulen: 'Teaching Kits, Discourse Structure and Exercise Typologies', Hessen State Institute for Teacher In-Service Training, Kassel-Fuldatal (1975); reprinted in Candlin (1981) and reproduced here by permission of the publisher.

language teaching is going on here, if any at all. Exercises like this treat the learner as a sort of linguistically gifted idiot—somebody who knows enough language to express the (quite complex) ideas involved, but who somehow cannot put the ideas together without help. Normal students, of course, have the opposite problem: they know what they want to say more often than they know how to say it.

I have argued that the 'communicative' theory of meaning and use, in so far as it makes sense, is largely irrelevant to foreign language teaching. These considerations may seem somewhat over-theoretical. 'After all,' it might be objected, 'what does it matter if the theory doesn't really stand up? Theories about language teaching never do. The important thing is that students should be exposed to appropriate samples of language and given relevant and motivating activities to help them learn. This is what the Communicative Approach does.' I think there is something in this, and I should certainly not wish to condemn the Communicative Approach out of hand because its philosophy is confused. No doubt its heart *is* in the right place, and in some ways it has done us a lot of good. But theoretical confusion can lead to practical inefficiency, and this can do a lot of harm, with time and effort being wasted on unprofitable activities while important priorities are ignored.

Syllabus design

The incompetent school-leaver

> 'An English boy who has been through a good middle-class school in England can talk to a Frenchman, slowly and with difficulty, about female gardeners and aunts; conversation which, to a man possessed of neither, is liable to pall. Possibly, if he be a bright exception, he may be able to tell the time, or make a few guarded observations concerning the weather. No doubt he could repeat a goodly number of irregular verbs by heart; only, as a matter of fact, few foreigners care to listen to their own irregular verbs, recited by young Englishmen . . . And then, when the proud parent takes his son and heir to Dieppe merely to discover that the lad does not know enough to call a cab, he abuses not the system but the innocent victim.' (Jerome 1900).

Jerome K. Jerome was neither the first nor the last to observe that the language courses of his day were inefficient, or to propose ways of improving them. The learner who has studied the language for seven years, but who cannot ask for a glass of water, a cab, or a light for a cigarette, is regularly brought on to the stage to justify demands for a radical change in our approach to language teaching. Jerome's recommendations for reform were: more time, better qualified teachers, better coursebooks, a more serious attitude to language learning, and the application of common sense to education. These are modest, practical suggestions, but of course Jerome had no knowledge of linguistics. He would scarcely have expressed himself in such down-market terms if he had been writing today, with the benefit of an M.A. course in one of our better applied linguistics departments. Jerome would more probably have complained that his school-leaver knew grammar and words, but could not use them appropriately; could not express everyday notions, or perform basic communicative functions; lacked productive and receptive skills and strategies; was unable to negotiate meaning successfully; had learnt language on the level of usage rather than use; created text that was cohesive but not coherent; was not successful in relating code to context; and in general lacked communicative competence, which he could best acquire by following a good communicative course based on a scientific needs analysis. On the whole, I think I prefer the original formulation.

Defective language learning is often attributed to defective syllabus design: the student does not learn the language properly because we do not teach the right things, or because we organize what we teach in the wrong way. Recently the attention of linguists has been focused on meaning, and it has come to be widely believed that the secret of successful language teaching lies in incorporating meaning properly into our syllabuses. We can perhaps distinguish four common versions of this belief.

a. 'Older language courses taught forms, but did not teach what the forms meant or how to use them. We now do this.'

b. 'Older language courses taught one kind of meaning (that found in the grammar and dictionary), but did not teach another kind (the communicative value that utterances actually have in real-life exchanges). It is this second kind that we really need to teach.'

c. 'Older language courses failed to teach students how to express or do certain things with language. We must incorporate these things (notions, functions, strategies) into our syllabuses.'

d. 'Even if older structure-based language courses taught meanings as well as forms, they did so very untidily and inefficiently. A communicative syllabus approaches the teaching of meaning systematically.'

The first version (a) is no longer as common as it used to be, and it is not really worth wasting time on. I have discussed version (b) at length in a previous article (Swan 1985), in which I argue that the kind of meaning referred to ('rules of use') does not need to be taught, and cannot in any case be codified. Here I should like to deal principally with the issues raised by versions (c) and (d).

Meaning in older courses

Traditional structure-based courses have had a bad press. Current mythology notwithstanding, they did not systematically neglect the teaching of functions, notions, and skills. Older courses may indeed have failed to teach people to do some important things with language, and more modern materials, whose authors have access to checklists of communicative functions, have plugged a number of gaps. It is also true that many traditional courses adopted a very mechanical approach to drilling what was taught—that is to say, meaning was often neglected during the *practice* phase of a lesson. Nonetheless, it is quite false to represent older courses as concentrating throughout on form at the expense of meaning, or as failing to teach people to 'do things with language'. I have in front of me a copy of a typical structure-based beginners' course of the 1960s (Candlin 1968). The course has many of the typical defects of books of its generation (though these may seem greater to us, with our sharpened hindsight and different priorities, than they did to its users). However, by the end of Lesson 8, students have been shown perfectly adequate ways of performing the following language functions: greeting, enquiring about health, leave-taking, thanking, expressing regret, eliciting and giving information, offering, requesting goods and services, proffering, self-identification, asking for more precise information, confirming what has been said, exhortation, identifying and naming, describing, narrating, giving informal instructions, agreeing to carry out instructions, and enquiring about plans. 'Semantico-grammatical categories' are not neglected: students learn to talk about place and direction, to refer to states and processes, to describe past, present, and further events, to express concepts related to quantification, and so on. (In other words, they learn prepositions, verb tenses, singular and plural forms, etc. Structures have meanings, and traditional courses usually made a reasonable job of teaching them.) And of course the book provides a year's work on lexis—words and expressions are taught, and the notions associated with them are on the whole clearly demonstrated. Finally, the course (like many of its kind) uses the meaning category of *situation* as an organizing principle. Even if each lesson is designed to teach a specific structural point, it sets out at the same time to teach the language that is appropriate to a common situation. *Present-Day English* (like any book of its generation) does in fact have a quite clear and carefully worked out semantic syllabus. There are perhaps reasons why one might not wish to teach from this book, but it should not be accused of failing to deal properly with meaning.

Putting meaning first

For many people, the central idea in 'communicative' teaching is probably that of a 'semantic syllabus'. In a course based on a semantic syllabus, it is meanings rather than structures which are given priority, and which form the organizing principle or 'skeleton' of the textbook. Lessons deal with such matters as 'greeting', 'agreeing and disagreeing', 'comparison', 'warning', 'point of time', and so on. So we do not (for example) give a lesson on the comparative forms of adjectives, but on a notion such as that of relative size or degree, which may be expressed not only by using comparative adjectives but also in many other ways. In the bad old courses, where grammar was tidy and meanings untidy, students might learn comparative adjectives in June and the *as . . . as* structure the following February; they were never able to put together the various items they needed to express fully the notion in question. With a semantic syllabus, items which belong together semantically are taught together, even if they are structurally quite diverse.

The problem with this approach is obvious to anybody who has recently taught a beginners' class. Unfortunately, grammar has not become any easier to learn since the communicative revolution. If we set out to give a lesson to elementary students on the notion of relative degree, we are likely to run into difficulty straight away, for two reasons. First of all, the main syntactic patterns involved are complex (*as tall as*, *taller than, less tall than, not so/as tall as*, etc.), and if they are presented all together the students will probably mix them up, confusing *as* and *than* and so on. And secondly, it is not at all obvious to a learner how to form the comparatives of English adjectives: the rules are complicated, and can hardly be picked up in passing in the course of a notion-based lesson which introduces several other structural points at the same time. Experienced teachers often like to isolate and practise difficult structures (such as comparative adjectives) before combining them with others in realistic communicative work. They have excellent reasons for doing so.

Language is not *only* a set of formal systems, but it *is* a set of systems, and it is perverse not to focus on questions of form when this is desirable. Some points of grammar are difficult to learn, and need to be studied in isolation before students can do interesting things with them. It is no use making meaning tidy if grammar then becomes so untidy that it cannot be learnt properly. As Brumfit points out in his review of Wilkins's *Notional Syllabuses*, the teaching of functions and notions cannot replace the teaching of grammar. 'The point about the grammatical system is that a limited and describable number of rules enable the learner to generate an enormous range of utterances which are usable, in combination with paralinguistic and semiotic systems, to express any function. To ask learners to learn a list instead of a system goes against everything we know about learning theory' (Brumfit 1978).

Structural versus functional: a false dichotomy

We really need to question the whole idea that one syllabus, whether structural or functional, should be 'privileged', acting as the framework on which a whole course is built. Language courses involve far too many components, and the relationships between the components are far too complex, for us to be able to subordinate everything to a tidy progression of structures, functions, notions, or anything else. When deciding what to teach to a particular group of learners, we need to take into consideration several different meaning categories and several different formal categories. We must make sure that our students are taught to operate key *functions* such as, for instance, greeting, agreeing, or warning; to talk about basic *notions* such as size, definiteness, texture or ways of moving; to communicate appropriately in specific *situations* (for instance in shops, on the telephone, at meetings); to discuss the *topics* which correspond to their main interests and needs (for example tourism, merchant banking, football, physics). At the same time, we shall need to draw up lists of *phonological* problems which will need attention; of high-priority *structures*, and of the *vocabulary* which our students will need to learn. In addition, we must think about performance as well as competence: we will need a syllabus of *skills*, to make sure that our students are trained to become fluent in whatever aspects of speaking, understanding, reading, and writing relate to their purposes.

Rather than taking either meanings or forms as our starting point, therefore, we really need to look at the language from two directions at once, asking both 'What words and structures are needed to express meaning X?' (semantic syllabuses) and 'What meanings do we need to teach for word Y or structure Z?' (formal syllabuses). At first sight, it might seem as if semantic syllabuses and formal syllabuses ought ultimately to cover the same ground (so that if we have one we can do without the other). After all, if we have listed the meanings we want our students to express, and worked out what structures, words, and expressions are used to convey these meanings, this should surely provide us with a list of all the forms we need to teach, and it ought therefore to be unnecessary to list the forms separately. It is important to realize that this is not the case.

First of all, semantic syllabuses tend to list only items that are specifically related to the functions or notions included in the syllabus. More 'general-purpose' items slip through the net. If we make a list of high-priority functions and notions and write down all the words and expressions that are needed to handle them, there is no guarantee that we will include, for instance, the words *umbrella, control, move* or *rough*. These words are, however, common and important, and will need to be included in most intermediate courses. To be sure of plugging gaps of this kind, we shall need to refer to a traditional lexical syllabus based on word-frequency. The same is true of structures. Grammar items that do not have an easily identifiable 'meaning' (such as points of word order) tend to get left out of notional syllabuses, though they may be of great importance for the correct learning of the language.

Secondly, and conversely, traditional structural/lexical syllabuses are not very good at catching sentence-length idioms and conventional expressions such as 'Can I just break in here?' or 'I'd like to make a reversed charge call'. They may also fail to pick up special uses of 'standard' structures which are important for the expression of certain functions: for instance, the English use of the co-ordinate structure in threats ('Do that again and I'm going home'). To be sure of getting such items into our teaching programme, we need to look at lists of functions and notions and their exponents.

It is, therefore, essential to consider both semantic and formal accounts of the language when deciding what to teach. Failure to do so will result in serious omissions on one side or the other. (There is a well-known and deservedly popular 'communicative' beginners' course which gets through a whole year's work without teaching the names of the colours or the basic use of the verb *have*.) The real issue is not which syllabus to put first: it is how to integrate eight or so syllabuses (functional, notional, situational, topic, phonological, lexical, structural, skills) into a sensible teaching programme.

Integrating semantic and formal syllabuses

In discussions of communicative teaching, a good deal of confusion is caused by invalid generalizations. For instance, people often talk as if language courses had much the same shape at all levels from beginners' to advanced. In fact, the relative importance of the various syllabuses, and especially of the grammar component, varies crucially with level. It is fashionable to criticize old-style courses for being excessively concerned with teaching structure, and there is certainly some truth in the criticism. But it really applies only to lower-level courses (where grammar must in any case get a good deal of attention, even if this can easily go too far). At more advanced levels language textbooks have rarely given very much space to grammar: more typical concerns have traditionally been vocabulary-building, the teaching of reading and writing skills, literature and other 'cultural' matters, and the encouragement of discussion.

Equally, the role of 'grammar' in language courses is often discussed as if 'grammar' were one homogeneous kind of thing. In fact, 'grammar' is an umbrella term for a large number of separate or loosely related language systems, which are so varied in nature that it is pointless to talk as if they should all be approached in the same way. How we integrate the teaching of structure and meaning will depend to a great extent on the particular language items involved. Some structural points present difficulties of form as well as meaning (for example, interrogative and negative structures; comparison of adjectives; word order in phrasal verbs). As I have already suggested, it may be best to deal with such problems of form *before* students do communicative work on notions or functions in which they will have to mix these structures with others. Other grammar points are less problematic, and can be taught simultaneously with work on a relevant notion or function. (For instance, students might learn to use *can* in the context of a lesson on offering, or requesting, or talking about ability, ease and difficulty). Some functions and notions may be expressible entirely through structures which are already known: if students have learnt imperatives and simple *if*-clauses, and if they can make basic co-ordinate sentences, then they are already in a position to give warnings. Yet other functions and notions are expressed mainly through lexis, with no special grammatical considerations of any importance (for instance, greeting, leave-taking, thanking, speed, size).

How we organize a given lesson will therefore depend very much on the specific point we want to teach. A good language course is likely to include lessons which concentrate on particular structures, lessons which deal with areas of vocabulary, lessons on functions, situation-based lessons, pronunciation lessons, lessons on productive and receptive skills, and several other kinds of component. Many lessons will deal with more than one of these things at the same time. Designing a language course involves reconciling a large number of different and often conflicting priorities, and it is of little use to take one aspect of the language (structures, notions/functions, or anything else) and to use this systematically as a framework for the whole of one's teaching.

The importance of vocabulary

There is a certain air of unreality about the whole 'structural/notional' debate. Assertions which look plausible and persuasive when they are presented in general terms ('We should teach units of communication, not structures') tend to dissolve and become meaningless when one tries to apply them to specific cases. Part of the trouble is perhaps that pragmatics (the study of what we do with language) is grossly over-valued at the moment, in the same way as grammar has been over-valued in the past. The 'new toy' effect is leading us to look at everything in functional terms: we see the whole of our job as being to teach students to convey and elicit information, to describe, to define, to exercise and elicit social control, to express approval, make requests, establish rapport, warn, apologize, and the rest of it. It is important to remember two things. First of all, these functional categories are not themselves the names of things that have to be taught (though they may help to define how we *organize* what we teach). Students can already convey information, define, apologize and so on—what they need to learn is how to do these things *in English*. And secondly, when we have taught students what they need to know in order to carry out the main communicative functions, we *still* have most of the language left to teach. Students not only have to learn how information is conveyed or elicited, or how requests are made: they also have to learn the words and expressions which are used to refer to the things in the world they want to talk about, ask about or request. However good a lesson on the function of warning may be, it will not in itself enable students to say 'Look out—the top half of the ladder isn't properly fixed on'. Functions without lexis are no better than structures without lexis. And referential lexis is a vast field—it certainly makes up the bulk of the learning load in any general-purpose language course.

Stereotyped and creative language

An earlier linguistic school saw language use as being largely a matter of convention, involving a set of predictable responses to recurrent situations. Although this view of language is discredited, it is not so much wrong as only partially correct. A great deal of language does involve knowing what is conventionally said in familiar situations—interrupting, asking for a light, complimenting, leave-taking, buying stamps, correcting oneself and so on. This stereotyped, idiomatic side of language accounts for a substantial proportion of the things we say, and this is the area with which the Communicative Approach is perhaps mainly concerned, investigating the meanings we most often express and tabulating (in semantic syllabuses) the ways in which we conventionally express them. (For all its attention to meaning, the Communicative Approach has a strong behaviourist streak.)

Not all language, of course, is stereotyped. Since Chomsky's ideas became widely known, we have become accustomed to seeing language as something that makes infinite (or at least indefinitely large) use of finite resources. As O'Neill points out in his article 'My guinea pig died with its legs crossed' (O'Neill 1977), most utterances are not conventional responses to familiar situations. Students need to learn to say new things as well as old things. A learner of English may need to be able to say 'Could you check the tyre pressures?'; but he or she may also find it necessary to say 'The car makes a funny noise every time I go round a left-hand bend', or 'I nearly ran over a policeman just by the place where we had that awful meal with your hairdresser's boyfriend'. Sentences like these are not predicted by any kind of semantic syllabus; they can be generated only by constructing sentences out of lexical and grammatical building blocks in accordance with the various rules of phrase and sentence construction.

Simplifying somewhat, one might say that there are two kinds of language: 'stereotyped' and 'creative'. Semantic syllabuses are needed to help us teach the first; only structural/lexical syllabuses will enable us to teach the second.

Methodology

The 'real-life' fallacy

Teachers usually feel guilty about something: translating, or explaining grammar, or standing up in front of the class and behaving like teachers, or engaging in some other activity that is temporarily out of favour. Currently teachers feel guilty about not being communicative. Mechanical structure practice is out: it would be a brave trainee teacher who used a substitution table in his or her RSA practical exam.[1] Language work, we are told, should involve genuine exchanges, and classroom discourse should correspond as closely as possible to real-life use of language. Old-style courses, it appears, failed to take this into account. (At this point in the lecture the speaker usually does his 'Is that your nose?' number, where he reads aloud some appalling piece of pseudo-dialogue from a bad structure-based course and waits for the laughs.)

Of course one can hardly quarrel with the suggestion that classroom language should be as lifelike as possible. All other things being equal, authentic or natural-sounding dialogues are better models than artificial dialogues; it is good to demonstrate structures by using them as they are typically used in the outside world; writing and speaking practice should, if possible, involve genuine exchanges of information. The more we can (in Widdowson's eloquent formulation) 'contrive to make the language we present less of a contrivance', the better. And this is an area where the Communicative Approach has without question made an important contribution to language teaching. Whatever the defects of the communicative theory of language and syllabus design, the last fifteen years or so have seen enormous improvements in our methodology.

None the less, the classroom is not the outside world, and learning language is not the same as using language. A certain amount of artificiality is inseparable from the process of isolating and focusing on language items for study, and it is a serious mistake to condemn types of discourse typically found in the classroom because they do not share all the communicative features of other kinds of language use.

A common target for criticism is the use of questions to elicit feedback or to cue practice responses. If you say 'Is this my book?' or 'What am I doing?', it is objected that you are asking a question to which you know the answer already; the response will not convey any information, and the conversation is therefore condemned as a piece of pseudo-communication which incidentally gives a misleading picture of how interrogatives are used in English. Now conversations of this kind may not be very interesting, and we may well be able to think of better ways of getting the responses we want, but it is not true that no communication is going on. The questions have the communicative value (common in classroom discourse) of eliciting feedback—of asking students to display knowledge of a piece of information; the answers show whether the student does in fact possess the knowledge in question. Students are always perfectly well aware of the illocutionary force of questions and answers in exchanges like these (they have been in classrooms before), and they are in no danger at all of going out of the classroom believing, for instance, that English-speaking people are always asking questions to which they already know the answers.

A great deal of learning takes place in settings which are remote from the situation where the skills or knowledge will ultimately be used. Kittens playing on a living-room carpet are learning aspects of hunting: stalking, hiding, pouncing, biting, reacting at speed. The fact that they are learning these things in the absence of any real-life prey does not seem to detract from the value of the practice that is going on. Again, in many kinds of learning there is an element of 'mechanical' repetition that makes the activity at times very different from the goal behaviour that is ultimately envisaged. A boy who takes up the violin may dream of one day playing the Beethoven violin concerto to a packed concert hall. But if he is to realize this aim, he is likely to spend much of his time in the intervening years working alone doing very 'uncommunicative' things: playing scales, practising studies, improving his bowing technique, gaining a mastery of positional playing, and so on. Somebody who wants to break the women's 1,500-metre record will train for a long time before her big race. But comparatively little of her training will involve running the full 1,500-metre distance at racing speed; and a lot of what she does (e.g. interval training, callisthenics) will seem artificial and remote from what she is training to do. Learning a language is not altogether the same thing as learning to play the violin, run races, or catch mice, and analogies can be dangerous. However, it should be clear that effective learning can involve various kinds of 'distancing' from the real-life behaviour that is its goal. We do not therefore need to feel that there is anything wrong if, among our battery of teaching activities, we include some (repetition, rote learning, translation, structural drilling) which seem to have no immediate 'communicative' value. If *all* our exercises are of this kind, of course, it is another matter.

Communicative practice and 'information gap'

I have suggested that methodology is perhaps the area where the Communicative Approach has done most to improve our teaching. It is surprising, however, how often 'communicative' courses achieve the appearance of communication without the reality. A basic concept in contemporary methodology is that of 'information gap'. When one student talks to another, we feel that it is important that new information should be transmitted across the 'gap' between them. To this end, ingenious exercises are devised in which half the class are provided with data to which the other half do not have access; those who lack the information then have to obtain it by using language in an appropriate way. I do not wish to belittle the value of such exercises; the technique is a powerful one, and (if used intelligently) can generate interesting, lively, and useful work. However, the information conveyed should ideally have some relevance and interest for the students. If (to take a familiar example) I give a student a paper containing the times of trains from Manchester to Liverpool, purely so that he can pass on the information to another student who is not in Manchester and does not wish to go to Liverpool, then we are perhaps still some distance from genuine communication.

Perhaps no classroom exercises can completely achieve the spontaneity and naturalness of real exchanges, but there are certainly more realistic and interesting ways of organizing information-gap work than by working with 'imposed' information of this kind. Each individual in a class already possesses a vast private store of knowledge, opinions, and experience; and each individual has an imagination which is capable of creating whole scenarios at a moment's notice. Student X is probably the only person in the class to know the number of people in his family, the places he has travelled to, what he thinks of a film he has just seen, whether he is shy, whether he believes in God, and what is going on in his head while the class is doing an information-gap exercise. If student X can be persuaded to communicate some of these things to student Y—and this is not very difficult to arrange—then we have a basis for genuinely rich and productive language practice. In many contemporary language courses, communication of this 'personal' kind seems to be seriously under-exploited. The tendency to get students to exchange unmotivating, imposed information can even go to the extreme where much of their 'communication' is about the behaviour of the fictional characters of their coursebooks ('You are George—ask Mary what she does at Radio Rhubarb'). Role play and simulation are all very well in their places, but there are times when the same language practice can take place more interestingly and more directly if the students are simply asked to talk about themselves.

Authentic materials

Like many of the other issues in this field, the question of using authentic materials has become polarized into an opposition between a 'good' new approach and a 'bad' old approach. Many teachers nowadays probably feel, in a vague kind of way, that there is something basically unsatisfactory, or even wrong, about using scripted dialogues or specially written teaching texts. These are (we have been told) 'unnatural', and contrived; they tend to lack the discourse features of genuine text; they are fundamentally non-communicative (since they were written essentially to present language data rather than to convey information). Often, of course, this is all too true, and the general quality of published EFL dialogues and prose texts is a powerful argument for the increased use of authentic materials, whatever problems this may entail. However, it is important not to lose sight of the principles involved. There is nothing wrong in itself with creating special texts for specific purposes, and illustrating language use is a purpose like any other. People use deliberately simplified language when writing for children; when adapting scientific articles for laymen; when creating advertising copy; when writing leading articles in the popular press. Why not, then, when writing for foreign learners? Of course, we must be careful about quality: the language found in older-style 'John and Mary' type dialogues, or in some elementary story-lines, in so far removed from natural English that it does nobody any good. But this is an argument against bad scripted material, not against the use of scripted material in general.

In fact, it is obviously desirable to use both scripted and authentic material at different points in a language course for different reasons. Scripted material is useful for presenting specific language items economically and effectively: the course designer has total control over the input, and can provide just the linguistic elements and contextual back-up he or she wishes, no more and no less. Authentic material, on the other hand, gives students a taste of 'real' language in use, and provides them with valid linguistic data for their unconscious acquisition processes to work on. If students are exposed only to scripted material, they will learn an impoverished version of the language, and will find it hard to come to terms with genuine discourse when they are exposed to it. If they are exposed only to authentic material, however, they are unlikely (in the time available for the average language course) to meet all the high-frequency items they need to learn. And elementary students, faced with authentic material that is not very carefully chosen, may find it so difficult that they get bogged down in a morass of unfamiliar lexis and idiom. Eddie Williams, in a recent article, draws attention to 'the paradox that the use of authentic text with learners often has an effect opposite to that intended; instead of helping the learner to read for the meaning of the message, an authentic text at too difficult a level of language forces the reader to focus upon the code' (Williams 1983).

The mother tongue in foreign language learning

As far as the British version of the Communicative Approach is concerned, students might as well not have mother tongues. Meanings, uses, and communication skills are treated as if they have to be learnt from scratch. Syllabus design takes no account of the fact that students might already possess some of the knowledge that is tabulated in a needs analysis. (Munby's *Communicative Syllabus Design*, for instance (Munby 1978) makes no significant reference to the mother tongue at all.) Communicative methodology stresses the English-only approach to presentation and practice that is such a prominent feature of the British EFL tradition. (Perhaps because this has made it possible for us to teach English all over the world without the disagreeable necessity of having to learn other languages?)

This is a peculiar state of affairs. It is a matter of common experience that the mother tongue plays an important part in learning a foreign language. Students are always translating into and out of their own languages—and teachers are always telling them not to. Interlanguages notoriously contain errors which are caused by interference from the mother tongue; it is not always realized that a large proportion of the *correct* features in an interlanguage also contain a mother tongue element. In fact, if we did not keep making correspondences between foreign language items and mother tongue items, we would never learn foreign languages at all. Imagine having to ask whether *each* new French car one saw was called 'voiture', instead of just deciding that the foreign word was used in much the same way as 'car' and acting accordingly. Imagine starting to learn German without being able to make any unconscious assumptions about the grammar—for instance, that there are verbs and pronouns with similar meanings to our verbs and pronouns. When we set out to learn a new language, we automatically assume (until we have evidence to the contrary) that meanings and structures are going to be broadly similar to those in our own language. The strategy does not always work, of course—that is why languages are difficult to learn—and it breaks down quite often with languages unrelated to our own. But on balance this kind of 'equivalence assumption' puts us ahead of the game; it makes it possible for us to learn a new language without at the same time returning to infancy and learning to categorize the world all over again.

If, then, the mother tongue is a central element in the process of learning a foreign language, why is it so conspicuously absent from the theory and methodology of the Communicative Approach? Why is so little attention paid, in this and other respects, to what learners already know? The Communicative Approach seems to have a two-stage approach to needs analysis:

1 find out what the learner needs to know;
2 teach it.

A more valid model, in my view, would have four stages:

1 find out what the learner needs to know;
2 find out what he or she knows already;
3 subtract the second from the first;
4 teach the remainder.

Conclusion

Teachers do not always appreciate how much new approaches owe to speculation and theory, and how little they are based on proven facts. We actually know hardly anything about how languages are learnt, and as a result we are driven to rely, in our teaching, on a pre-scientific mixture of speculation, common sense, and the insights derived from experience. Like eighteenth-century doctors, we work largely by hunch, concealing our ignorance under a screen of pseudo-science and jargon. Speculation, common sense, and experience do not necessarily provide a bad basis to operate on, in the absence of anything better, and somehow our students do manage to learn languages. However, the lack of a solid empirical 'anchor' of established knowledge about language learning makes us very vulnerable to shifts in intellectual fashion. A novel piece of speculation can have an effect out of all proportion to its value, especially since the purveyors of new doctrines are rarely as humble or as tentative as the situation merits.

As the theoretical pendulum swings from one extreme to the other, each exaggeration is followed by its opposite. We realize that we have been translating too much, so translation is banned completely. Grammar explanations are seen to have been over-valued, so grammar explanations are swept away. Generation A spends half its time doing structure drills; for generation B, structure drills are anathema. Contrastive studies promise the moon and the stars; when the moon and the stars are slow to arrive, contrastive studies disappear from syllabus design as if they had never been. One approach fails to give sufficient importance to phonetics, or modal verbs, or functions; the next approach does nothing but phonetics, teaches modal verbs for thirty minutes a day, or announces that functions are more important than grammar, vocabulary, and pronunciation put together. Arguments for the current view are invariably highly speculative, extremely plausible, and advanced with tenacious conviction; if one looks back fifteen years, one can see that the arguments for the previous approach (now totally discredited) were equally speculative, just as persuasive, and put forward with the same insistence that 'this time we've got it right'. Each time this happens, the poor language teacher is told to junk a large part of his or her repertoire of materials, activities, and methods (because these are no longer scientific) and to replace them by a gleaming new battery of up-to-date apparatus and techniques. The students, as a rule, learn about as much as before.

It is characteristic of the Communicative Approach to assess utterances not so much on the basis of their propositional meaning as in terms of their pragmatic value. We should perhaps apply this criterion to the Communicative Approach itself. As with a religion, it may be more sensible to ask, not 'Is it true?', but 'What good does it do?' This is not a difficult question to answer. The Communicative Approach has directed our attention to the importance of other aspects of language besides propositional meaning, and helped us to analyse and teach the language of interaction. At the same time, it has encouraged a methodology which relies less on mechanical teacher-centred practice and more on the simulation of real-life exchanges. All this is very valuable, and even if (as with religions) there is a good deal of confusion on the theoretical side, it is difficult not to feel that we are teaching better than we used to. By and large, we have probably gained more than we have lost from the Communicative Approach.

In the same way, we shall probably benefit from the next language teaching revolution, especially if we can keep our heads, recognize dogma for what it is, and try out the new techniques without giving up useful older methods simply because they have been 'proved wrong'. (The characteristic sound of a new breakthrough in language teaching theory is a scream, a splash, and a strangled cry, as once again the baby is thrown out with the bathwater.) Above all, we must try not to expect too much. New insights can certainly help us to teach more systematically and effectively, but it is probably an illusion to expect any really striking progress in language teaching until we know a great deal more about how foreign languages are learnt. For the moment, talk of 'revolution' simply does the profession a disservice, raising hopes that cannot be fulfilled, and soliciting an investment of time and money which is out of all proportion to the return which can realistically be expected from the new methods. (It is a shock to realize that, after more than ten very expensive years of 'communicative' teaching, we cannot prove that a single student has a more effective command of English than if he or she had learnt the language by different methods twenty years earlier. Our research depends to an uncomfortable degree on faith.) The Communicative Approach, whatever its virtues, is not really in any sense a revolution. In retrospect, it is likely to be seen as little more than an interesting ripple on the surface of twentieth-century language teaching.

Note

1 The examination leading to the Royal Society of Arts Diploma in TEFL.

(Originally published as two articles in Volumes 39/1 and 39/2, respectively, 1985)

Against dogma: a reply to Michael Swan
H. G. Widdowson

Michael Swan's paper is an admirably provocative piece, eloquently written and stimulating to read. This much should be acknowledged. It should be noted, however, that it is not to be read as dispassionate criticism of a careful analytic kind. It is, rather, an indictment, charged with feeling, almost as if Swan felt that the ideas he opposes were a personal affront. And the desire to have a dig at theorists and to pander to anti-intellectual prejudice at times reduces the discussion to farce. So with reference to its title, this paper is 'critical' only in the sense of being captious: it is not evaluative. Nevertheless, it does indicate areas of misunderstanding and misconception, and as such warrants a reply.

Dogma and enquiry

The first point I should like to make is a very general one about the purpose of intellectual enquiry. The ideas that have been put forward concerning a communicative approach to language teaching do not, as Swan himself acknowledges, constitute a 'coherent and monolithic body of doctrine', nor were they intended as a manifesto for revolutionary change. They cannot by definition therefore be a dogma. Swan represents them as such in order to make a better target for attack. This is, to say the least, regrettable, because these ideas were proposed (for the most part) in the spirit of positive enquiry and were intended to encourage teachers not to reject customary practices out of hand and embrace a new creed, but on the contrary to subject these practices and proposals to critical (i.e. evaluative, not captious) assessment. So the intention behind the enquiry was to act *against* the dogmatism of doctrine whether new or old, revolutionary or reactionary. Its purpose was to provoke, not to persuade; to liberate thought, not to confine it by the imposition of fixed ideas. Perhaps I might be permitted to give two quotations from my own work to correct the quite false impression of doctrinaire assertion that Swan, for some reason, wishes to convey:

> This book is not in any way intended as propaganda for a new 'communicative' orthodoxy in language teaching. It is, on the contrary, an appeal for critical investigation into the basis of a belief and its practical implications. I am not trying to present a conclusive case but to start an enquiry. (Widdowson 1978:x)

> Above all we must deny ourselves the comfort of dogma which deals in the delusion of simple answers. (Widdowson 1979:262)

My reason for drawing attention to this misrepresentation is not (principally) to express my resentment at unfair treatment, but to point to a consequence which nullifies much of Swan's own argument. For the effect of creating a dogma on which to practise his polemic is that he is led into contradiction by committing precisely the same error that he unjustly attributes to the approach he is criticizing. What he does is to dismiss one set of ideas as if they constituted a single dogmatic creed, but then replace them with a dogma of his own. Again, as Swan might himself put it, we hear a strangled cry as the communicative baby this time disappears down the plughole.

Questions arising

What the Swan dogma amounts to essentially, it would seem, is a reassertion of the traditional view that what learners need to be taught is grammar, lexis, and a collection of idiomatic phrases: their effective use for communicative purposes can be left for them to work out for themselves by reference to common sense and the experience they have of using their own language. Ideas about use and usage, the realization of appropriate meaning, communicative strategies, negotiation, and so on that all these theorists prattle about in their impenetrable jargon are so much moonshine and nothing more. One can almost see the groundlings rolling in the aisles with glee. This dogma is then itself directly contradicted by other remarks in the two articles. Swan talks approvingly, for example, about the teaching of notions and functions: 'We must make sure our students are taught to operate key functions such as, for instance, greeting, agreeing or warning'. But why should this be necessary if the function of an utterance (use) can always be inferred by a common-sense association of sentence meaning (usage) and situation, as has previously been claimed, and, in the case of warning, so amusingly (if tendentiously) demonstrated by the anecdote of Wilberforce and his accomplices? And if Swan accepts that functions need to be taught as aspects of language other than structure and lexis, how does he propose that this should be done in a principled way without invoking the ideas about use and usage he has so summarily dismissed? Again, Swan tells us that we need 'to make sure that our students are trained to become fluent in whatever aspects of speaking, understanding, reading and writing relate to their purposes'. But, according to the dogma, students already know how to do these things: all they need is a knowledge of English structures and lexis and these abilities will come of their own accord. So why do they need any training? Why indeed do we need to bother with teaching these abilities at all?

Again we are told that one of the reasons for poor performance at classroom comprehension tasks may be that 'the learner's command of the language is just fluent enough for him to decode the words, but this occupies all his faculties and he has no processing capacity to spare for "interpreting" what he hears'. But how is this possible if the ability to understand, that is to say to provide language items with appropriate communicative value in context, follows automatically from a knowledge of language combined with the skills the learner has already acquired from the experience of using his own mother tongue? According to the dogma which denies any relevance to the use/usage distinction, decoding and interpreting should not be different processes at all. Fluency (whatever Swan might mean by this) in the one ought not to be distinct from fluency in the other. This problem of poor performance may also, we are told, be caused by the fact that the learners 'have been trained to read classroom texts in such a different way from "real-life" texts that they are unable to regard them as pieces of communication'. But how can this be? If they know the language, why can't they automatically apply this knowledge?

And what, anyway, does it mean to say that learners treat texts in a 'different way'? How then is this distinct from regarding them as 'pieces of communication'? These questions can be clarified by reference to the concepts of cohesion and coherence and strategies of prediction and negotiation, but this kind of 'jargon' is inadmissible, so all we are left with is a befuddled vagueness which, to use Swan's own expression, 'contributes nothing to our understanding of how to teach foreign languages'. We are told that the inability of learners to regard texts as pieces of communication is the result of poor methodology and that 'the solution involves changing what happens in the classroom, not what happens in the student'. What exactly is it that might lead us to assess one methodology as poor, another good? What *sort* of change in the classroom is called for? And anyway what is the point, we might ask, of changing what happens in the classroom unless it brings about changes in the student?

Questions of this kind (in so far as they make sense) need careful and *theoretical* consideration. They cannot be resolved by bland statement.

Repeatedly we find in these articles assertions about teaching and learning which can be justified, or indeed understood, only by reference to the kind of idea that Swan ridicules with such relish. And not infrequently, as we have seen, such assertions actually presuppose the validity of these ideas even when they are intended to undermine them.

Approve with care

Elsewhere, what Swan conceives of as 'the communicative approach' is favoured with approving comment. It has, we are told, 'many virtues'. What are they then? It has 'new information and insights to contribute (for instance about the language of social interaction)'. What new information and what new insights? At times, Swan seems to suppose that the language of social interaction simply means the 'stereotyped, idiomatic side of language' to be learned as a collection of 'conventional and idiomatic expressions' of the kind provided by a notional/functional inventory. Even a cursory glance at the literature on the pragmatics of language use would disabuse him of such a simplistic notion. But then pragmatics, depending as it does on recognizing a distinction between usage and use, 'has little relevance to foreign language teaching' and is anyway 'grossly over-valued at the moment'. The communicative approach is, again, given credit for 'enormous improvements in our methodology'. 'Methodology is perhaps the area where the Communicative Approach has done most to improve our teaching'. What exactly are these improvements? On what principles are they based? And how have they come about, if they are based on ideas that are apparently so defective in theory and irrelevant in practice?

Unreasoned approval of the 'communicative approach' is no better than unreasoned condemnation. What we need is clear thinking and explicit, well-informed argument of the kind which Swan conspicuously fails to provide. He fails to provide it because he is more interested in attacking the 'communicative approach' than in seeking to understand and assess it, and so finds it convenient to invent a distorted version so as to present his own views more effectively. These views are represented as being in opposition to the ideas about communicative language teaching. But many of them, particularly those put forward in the second paper, have already been explored in relation to these ideas, although Swan, by ignorance or design, fails to acknowledge the fact. His discussion about the use of authentic data, for example, and the classroom replication of reality has long since been anticipated by others pursuing the implications of a communicative approach. Similarly there has long been a recognition of the importance of grammar and lexis and the need to teach them as an essential communicative resource. The difference is that these matters have been treated as issues to be thought out and not just pronounced upon. Most of those who have given any systematic consideration to the effective teaching of grammar, for example, would wish to question the proposal for a *separate* treatment of the formal and functional aspects of language which Swan (not very humbly or tentatively, I may say) puts forward with such apparent conviction:

> Simplifying somewhat, one might say that there are two kinds of language: 'stereotyped' and 'creative'. Semantic syllabuses are needed to help us teach the first; only structural/lexical syllabuses will enable us to teach the second.

This statement, we should note, presupposes both a theory of language and a theory of pedagogy. The least we might expect is that such theoretical presuppositions should be made as explicit as possible so that they can be brought out into the open and debated.

Of course it is more comfortable (and convenient) to deny the validity of theoretical enquiry and instead make easy appeals to prejudice in the name of experience and common sense. But if we claim that our activities have any professional status, then we have to accept the need for a careful appraisal of the principles upon which they are based. And this must require the exercise of intellectual analysis and critical evaluation not as specialist or élite activities, but ones which are intrinsic to the whole practical pedagogic enterprise. Naturally there are risks involved: ideas can be inconsistent or ill-conceived; they may be misunderstood or misapplied; they may induce doubt. Some of us believe that such risks are worth taking. For others the delusion of simple answers will always be available as an attractive alternative to thought.

(*Originally published in Volume 39/3, 1985*)

The Swan–Widdowson 'debate' was preceded by a fervent defence of the Communicative Approach by Li Xiaoju, a non-native speaker concerned with the teaching of English to Chinese learners. It is followed in the next paper by equally fervent remonstrations from a non-native speaker concerned with the teaching of English to Hungarian learners: Péter Medgyes' main point is that too little account is taken of the additional burdens which acceptance of the practical implications of the Communicative Approach thrust on the shoulders of non-native-speaking teachers. In particular, Medgyes' entertaining but none-the-less heartfelt essay challenges the assumptions made by 'theorists' that teachers will, after initial extra effort, easily be able to adapt to being omniscient, humanistic, and 'professionally sophisticated' enough to switch roles, and also be self-reliant for materials—as well as highly skilled users of the target language. 'We are in desperate need' he writes, 'of language-teaching experts who would work halfway between the zealots and the weary [the actual teachers]'. Certainly, the greatest danger of inappropriately mediated educational reform is teacher—and learner—alienation.

Queries from a communicative teacher

Péter Medgyes

Recently, I gave a lecture on the main principles of the Communicative Approach. The audience consisted of secondary-school teachers of English on an in-service training course in Budapest. After my talk, a colleague asked in a rather aggressive tone whether I would be willing to commit myself in practice to the Communicative Approach if I were to teach a group of, say, 15-year-olds. I quickly answered in the affirmative.

In retrospect, however, I am not so sure.

The communicative teacher

The communicative classroom requires a teacher of extraordinary abilities: a multi-dimensional, high-tech, Wizard-of-Oz-like superperson—yet of flesh and blood. He or she must be confident without being conceited, judicious without being judgemental, ingenious without being unbridled, technically skilled without being pedantic, far-sighted without being far-fetched, down-to-earth without being earth-bound, inquiring without being inquisitive—the list is endless. But above all he or she must be *learner-centred*. The term 'learner-centred' is the great gimmick of today; this slogan is tagged on to every single language-teaching approach, method, methodology, procedure, and technique, communicative and non-communicative alike. But the Communicative Approach, since it is far and away the most well-known approach, seems to be brandishing this magic compound with particular vehemence and dedication.

In what follows I shall try to elaborate on certain aspects of the Communicative Approach and the enormous difficulties it presents to the language teacher.

Needs analysis

The Communicative Approach claims that teachers should no longer be encouraged and trained to impose their own view of learners' needs and aspirations. Instead, they should gain a detailed knowledge of

—who the learners are;
—what they bring to class;
—why they have signed up for the course;
—what expectations they have from the course.

Having established this, teachers face a two-fold job. First they have to cater for the specific needs of the groups as a whole. This is a relatively easy task to perform, provided the group is homogeneous enough in terms of interests, occupation, age, cultural and educational background, linguistic level, intelligence, etc. But generally this is not the case. TENOR (Teaching English for No Obvious Reasons) is by far the most common category all over the world. As the future needs of most learners cannot be predicted with any degree of certainty, and because of lack of self-motivation, motivation has to be fostered by the teacher alone.

Besides considering the needs of the group, teachers also have to see to it that individual aspirations are given due attention. The group, which used to be regarded as a faceless, monolithic mass, is seen today as an organic unit comprising learners of the most diverse nature. Personal differences in age, motivation, intelligence, linguistic level, proclivity, etc., should not be disregarded. In brief, Communicative Teachers have to cope with problems arising from the dialectic relationship between group coherence and group divergence—a task of immense proportions.

Focus on content

Communicative Teachers must pay attention to meaning and form simultaneously. In past methods teachers were not expected to listen so closely to *what* the learners had to say as to *how* they said it, i.e. by what linguistic means the message manifested itself.

Audio-Lingual Teachers, for instance, were able to conduct a 45-minute period without bothering about the content of the discussion. If after an hour of practising the 'what make' construction in sentences like 'What make is your car?', a teacher were asked what makes of car the learners had, surely he or she would not remember anything—the questions had not been asked in order to elicit information, but to make sure that the class could adequately apply the structure. By analogy, good typists usually have only a faint idea of the general content of the message being typed, let alone the details. Their efficiency in both speed and correctness is said to increase in inverse proportion to understanding. Similarly, the more teachers focus on what the learners say, the less they are able to check learners' performance in terms of formal adequacy.

It follows from this that the Audio-Lingual Teachers' job was easier than their communicative colleagues'. The former had only the production of the correct structure to consider, whereas the latter attempt to reconcile in their work two opposing elements of linguistic practice: meaning and form.

Real interaction

Prior to the Communicative Approach, English teachers were subject teachers, like maths or history teachers. Their job was to impart knowledge *about* the English language, as well as to develop the knowledge *of* the English language as effectively as they could.

Communicative Teachers have a radically different task to face. It is one of the chief tenets of the Communicative Approach that the foreign language can be learnt only in *real* communicative situations where *real* messages are exchanged. Since there is no true communication without someone wanting to say or find out something, teachers have to create favourable conditions for such needs to arise and get expressed. They have to initiate and stimulate activities where the learners can participate not only with their 'learning' selves, but with their whole selves. Almost the same applies to the teachers. Abandoning the safe position of general language monitor in the class, teachers will supplement their 'teaching' self with the role of co-communicator.

Given that real-life conversations embrace, in theory, all human knowledge and experience, Communicative Teachers must be extremely erudite and versatile people. In contrast with the well-defined subject matter of traditional foreign-language teachers, Communicative Teachers' great encyclopaedic learning is accompanied by a desire to share their knowledge with others, while being open and modest enough to gain information from any source, including their own learners.

The humanistic attitude

Although the highly acclaimed Humanistic-Psychological Approach, as interpreted by Moskowitz and others, is in several respects clearly different from the Communicative Approach, 'only the most radical would see them as antagonistic and immutably uncombinable' (Roberts 1982:104). In both views learners are seen not so much as full-time linguistic objects at whom language teaching is aimed, but rather as human individuals whose personal dignity and integrity, and the complexity of whose ideas, thoughts, needs, and sentiments, should be respected. By specific means, foreign language teachers must contribute to the self-actualizing process of the individual, by striving to be 'humans among the humans' (Littlewood 1981:94), genuinely interested people. Involved on both an intellectual and an emotional plane, they do not *have to* open up, but *are* open to all the participants in classroom interactions. And what if they aren't? Communicative Teachers just won't get asked this question. They *are* open, that's all there is to it!

To be fair, all teachers have been psychologists over the centuries, whether or not they realized or accepted this fact. The difference between traditional foreign-language teachers and Communicative Teachers lies, among other things, in the degree of consciousness. The latter should be fully aware of the measures they should take as psychologist—pedagogues in general and as language teachers in particular. The scope and responsibility of Communicative Teachers is, therefore, greatly enhanced.

Communicative Teachers withdraw

Teachers' roles in relation to their students have definitely changed recently. Communicative Teachers are judicious enough to realize that they are not the sole repositories of truth, wisdom, and authority, but merely instruments to see that learning takes place. Therefore, they keep a low profile in all their functions: as controllers they relax their grip on the class; as assessors they resort to gentle correction; as organizers they set activities in motion and then stand aside; as prompters they perform with discretion; as participants, they play second fiddle; as resources, they offer help, but only when requested (Harmer 1983:200–5).

Communicative Teachers are well aware that the success of the learning process is largely dependent on their ability to withdraw. 'Withdraw' is a key word in their vocabulary. However painful it might be, they should no longer display their own cleverness as conversationalists, but should be ready to radically reduce teacher talking time. In return for their much-reduced role, they will allegedly find plenty of solace and reward in the rapid development of their students.

This retreat, however, should not mean relinquishing control over the class, since it would undermine the learner's most basic need, which is for security. Learner initiative and teacher control do not work in opposite directions, and the success of language teaching is not guaranteed by maintaining a balance between them. The idea Stevick suggests is that there must be a way 'which will allow the teacher to keep nearly 100 per cent of the "control", while at the same time the learner is exercising nearly 100 per cent of the "initiative"' (Stevick 1980:17).

The learner's place, then, is at the centre of a space which the teacher has structured (Stevick 1980:33). Communicative Teachers are like supporting actors in a play, who have hardly any words to say, yet are the most crucial figures, on whom the whole drama hinges. This withdrawn-and-yet-all-present attitude requires of Communicative Teachers an extremely high degree of personal subtlety and professional sophistication.

Away with the textbook!

For quite a long time the textbook was the bible and the teacher's manual the exegesis. Both reflected the decisions which had been made about what learners would learn, how they would learn it, and what sections of the work would receive most emphasis. All teachers were supposed to do was to plod on assiduously from one exercise to the next, from one unit to the next, from Book 1 to Book 2 to Book 3 and so on, until the whole series had been completed. The less devoted and more realistic were often brave enough, of course, to delete, add to, or modify anything in the script as they saw fit (Rivers 1968:368), but the indispensability of the textbook had never been seriously called into question.

But with the advent of the Communicative Approach, the textbook has become suspect. The arguments against it are numerous: it is too general, boring, stuffed with cliché characters; it usually restricts activity to language presentation and controlled practice instead of stimulating real interaction. In consequence, demands to do away with the textbook have become rife. What is advocated as a substitute is a wide stock of flexible and authentic 'supplementary' materials.

Lacking the perspective (and the time) to take sides in a theoretical issue of such magnitude, Communicative Teachers are faced with a dilemma: 'Shall I let go of the textbook for the well-known reasons or shall I retain it, as it still offers a wealth of information, discipline of structure, and easy access?' This dilemma presents itself with particular force to non-native teachers in non-English speaking countries, for whom the textbook ensures a great deal of linguistic safety.

The attitude of theory makers

Throughout this article, I have restrained myself from scrutinizing the theoretical basis of the Communicative Approach. My intention has been merely to shed light on certain difficulties which the concept of learner-centredness entails.

Oddly enough, theory makers play down these problems, making them appear as trifles in the light of the 'strengths' of the theory. Quite often, what requires an unusually high level of craftsmanship is declared to facilitate the teacher's work. 'You have to review your whole teaching attitude? A welcome expansion of your hitherto limited scope!' Or the ball is thrown back at teachers: 'You're asking why you should dump your familiar stock of techniques? But *you* yourself hated drilling, didn't you?' At other times the militancy of teachers is taken for granted: 'What can be more challenging than fighting in the vanguard against those outdated exam requirements? Or despairing teachers are comforted with the prospect of a rich harvest: 'I know you have to make a bit more effort at the moment. But it'll pay off in the long run, don't worry!' And if all these arguments should fail to soothe the teachers' agitated souls, they are openly flattered to their face; allusions are made to their human and professional virtues, to their persistence, dedication, and conscientiousness, to their inventiveness, flexibility, and resourcefulness, and above all to their excellent sense of humour. After all, on the morn of the battle, what could be more encouraging to the soldier than half a pint of rum?

Nevertheless, teachers' psyches teem with fears and anxieties, which are probably no less intense than those their students experience (Stevick 1976:85–6). The 'sickness to teach' is well described by Stevick: 'Will my students regard me as superior to them in knowledge, or will I come out looking ignorant? Will they accept me as superior to them in authority, or will I have a "discipline problem"? Will my students admire me, and will my colleagues regard me as competent? Will I continue to have enough students so that I can make a living for myself and my family?' (1980:108). These inherent worries are further aggravated by the incredibly high demands set by the Communicative Approach.

Apparently, communicative methodologists are deaf (or pretend to be deaf) to teachers' inaudible cries, in spite of the fact that they are no longer the ivory-tower scholars detached from everyday practicalities that their predecessors might have been. Some of them even try their hand at teaching. I have great respect for those methodologists who are willing to submit their hypotheses to the test with real learners, and for those materials writers who pilot their new-fangled activities on intensive crash courses.

However, it is impossible to be an active theory maker and an active practising teacher permanently. Teaching must be a full-time job and so must research work. One spends the best of one's time either theorizing, or thinking up the lesson plans for tomorrow. The theoretician's perspective must be totally different from the practising teacher's, whose daily stint averages 4–5 lessons day in, day out. It is precisely these treadmill language teachers whose real problems methodologists and materials writers seem to be oblivious and insensitive to. Sparkling ideas and glossy materials are tried out by a handful of teachers, and provided that they fare well with this *élite*, they are claimed to have passed the acid test.

The selected few

Who exactly these selected teachers are I can only guess. If not the most outstanding, surely they are the ones who, by sheer luck, have fewer lessons to teach, with brighter students, in smaller groups. Hence they are in a position to experiment with and give the green light to an approach as demanding in terms of time and energy as the Communicative Approach. Presumably it is also this *élite* that has the opportunity to exchange ideas at conferences, only to become inebriated and be carried away with their own well-informedness. On arriving home, they feel obliged to promulgate all the trendy thoughts they have picked up, never doubting that their message is true and will reach the general public.

As a matter of fact, it is not met with open rebuff. Teachers are clever enough to keep a low profile, shunning any overt conflict. This cautious attitude is due to several factors, such as lack of time, modesty, diminished self-confidence, exhaustion, and cynicism. But the main cause seems to be that the philosophy of the Communicative Approach, like that of all dogmas, is invulnerable. Only a fool would dare denounce the axiomatic truths it disseminates: humanism, care and share, equality, ingenuity, relaxation, empathy, self-actualizing, and the rest. Who would admit in public, or even to themselves, that these impeccable principles are mere slogans? How could one claim to be a true pedagogue, while declaring that the burden is far too heavy and that one would fain flush the whole lot down the nearest drain?

Conclusion

Nowadays we are in desperate need of language-teaching experts who would work halfway between the zealot and the weary. Endowed with a good deal of restraint, these mediators could act as filters, letting the moderate ideas through, while blocking the more far-fetched. This function should be performed primarily by *non-native teachers of English*. For all their goodwill, native speakers are basically unaware of the whole complexity of difficulties that non-native speakers have to tackle. Native-speaking teachers tend to ignore, among other things, the fact that a great proportion of the energy of their non-native colleagues is inevitably used up in the constant struggle with their own language deficiencies, leaving only a small fraction for attending to their students' problems. By putting an especially heavy linguistic strain on the teacher, the Communicative Approach further reduces the time non-native teachers have available for their students. Only non-native go-betweens would be capable of seeing these contradictions clearly.

For the moment, however, this halfway house is left unoccupied—in Hungary, at any rate. Hungarian teachers of English remain divided: the initiated few joyfully fiddle with the subtleties of the Communicative Approach, while the vast majority feel frustrated and helpless—but keep quiet about it.

(Originally published in Volume 40/2, 1986)

Professor Pit Corder, who had recently retired from his Chair at Edinburgh, agreed in 1985 to engage in a recorded discussion with Dick Allwright and the editor for eventual publication in the *ELT Journal*. The occasion provided a golden opportunity to pursue the question: 'What do recent advances in our understanding of the process of second language acquisition imply for formal language teaching?' It has to be remembered that those who initiated the communicative debate—Newmark, Widdowson, Wilkins, van Ek and others—did so on linguistic and sociolinguistic grounds. The nature of language and its role in communication meant for them that the tradition of language teaching established in the 1950s and 1960s was inappropriate and had to be changed. Coincidentally, the findings of (mostly small-scale) research into the processes of second language acquisition that burgeoned in the 1970s, particularly in the USA, also implied that a re-examination of language teaching practice was long overdue. Significantly, the conclusions of researchers seemed to reinforce many of the proposals made by the methodologists.

Pit Corder's starting point in this discussion is the belief, supported by some of the research, that language learners are 'programmed' to learn by a pre-ordained route, and therefore that teachers can no longer work on the basis of the belief that what they teach is what will be learnt. Given this situation, Corder emphatically favours procedures that involve the learner in motivating language-using tasks. But, as emerges from the discussion, if tasks are the ultimate communicative prescription, this makes life harder—rather than easier—for the teacher. He or she can no longer rely on a prescribed sequence of materials dictated by a syllabus, but must select (or construct), resource, supervise and evaluate tasks that are relevant and motivating for given groups of learners. The prospect—however tentatively presented—is an exciting but challenging one.

Talking shop

Pit Corder on language teaching and applied linguistics

Pit Corder: ... The trouble typically is that we always talk about teaching: 'Teaching, teaching, teaching', and not about learning. Teaching and learning are a combined operation, and the focus has been far too much on teaching for far too long.

Richard Rossner: But if learning is in some senses independent of teaching, what is the point of 'teaching' as we know it?

Pit Corder: Learning can only take place in an appropriate environment, and it's commonplace that it is the teacher's job to create a favourable learning environment. Essentially, the idea was that teachers possessed something that they handed over in a package to learners. This notion is still widespread, and, although there have been what would be regarded by many people as considerable shifts of emphasis from the teacher to the learner, if we come to examine them, this underlying notion that the teacher is the source of information hasn't really been affected. There is much more concern for and tenderness towards the learner, but the underlying view of what goes on in a learning–teaching situation has not been affected.

Richard Rossner: You said in one of your papers[1] that, until we undertake longitudinal research into the ways in which second languages are learnt in a 'free learning' situation, we won't make much headway in our understanding of how people learn second languages. Are we any closer now to understanding how learners learn?

Pit Corder: Very significantly so, not only in a free learning situation, but also in a formal classroom situation. Second-language acquisition (SLA) research started as a result of interest in first-language acquisition (FLA) research and in whether SLA was a comparable process. I suppose most people would have thought it wasn't, as second-language teachers were (and are) under the impression generally that what they teach gets learnt, whereas in the FLA situation there isn't any obvious 'teaching' going on. The famous morpheme studies[2] were based on the techniques of FLA research. By and large the results that came out were rather surprising, because they indicated that the learning processes were after all rather similar. Then people looked at learners acquiring second languages in the classroom and found that they followed rather the same course as 'free learning' acquirers. This raised all sorts of problems because it suggests that teaching doesn't make very much difference to the acquisition process,[3] at least not to the order of acquisition. One of the other suppositions that was tested was that the nature of the mother tongue must have an effect on the order of acquisition of the foreign language, but this was shown not to be the case either. It certainly affected the speed, but not the order. It seemed more and more as research went on that external factors played no role in the order of acquisition, only in speed. Practically everything that the SLA researchers found out was extremely uncomfortable for teachers, who naturally assumed that their efforts were more or less effective. They believed if you teach a person something, he or she will learn it; if you teach it intensively he or she will learn it quicker. It seems to be true of almost anything else. It's just that language is the odd one out. I think the acquisition of language is fundamentally different from the acquisition of any other kind of knowledge... One of the things that Krashen has been saying, of course, is that the sort of 'knowledge' that we talk about in the case of language is not the same thing as when we're talking about history or science or what have you...[4]

Richard Rossner: Does that mean that you accept the Krashen distinction between acquisition on the one hand and learning on the other, with no 'cross-feeding'?

Pit Corder: Yes, I do, though the notion is not new, as Krashen himself points out. The distinction between the ability to *perform* in a language and the ability to *talk about* a language goes back to the slogan that my generation was brought up with: 'Teach the language, don't teach about the language'. One is still puzzled about the relationship between the two. Krashen takes the extreme point of view that there is no relation between the two. Teachers are of course unwilling to go along with this, because it would imply that much of what they do is a waste of time... But if indeed we are programmed to acquire a language—and no one has been able to prove we aren't—then you can't at the same time say that what the teacher teaches 'leaks' into the process. Either you're programmed, or you're not, so to speak, and all the evidence is that you are, so it doesn't really matter what the teacher does at any particular point. He or she can't interfere with the program. So there can't be any seepage from what the teacher consciously teaches into the learner's acquisition... The syllabus that a teacher uses is essentially a linear one, a list of linguistic forms in a certain order. From all the evidence we have about the way linguistic knowledge develops spontaneously in the learner, that is not the way things happen. The spontaneous development of a grammar in the learner is organic. Everything is happening simultaneously. The growth is organic in the way that a flower develops out of a bud. You can't write a linear program for the process of flowering, because everything is happening simultaneously. You can look at the development of tense, of negation, of question forms, or anything you like, and you find that all these things are developing simultaneously. Any language teaching programme is forced to define itself linearly, but it is *not* the way learning takes place. So there is no way—and it has been suggested on a number of occasions—that, once we know what the developmental picture is, we will be able to write a syllabus to fit it. You can't write a syllabus that fits that kind of organic growth.

Richard Rossner: Does the organic growth encompass vocabulary and phonology as well as grammar?

Pit Corder: No. Everything I've said so far applies only to grammar. The acquisition of phonology is well understood from the work done on it twenty years ago. The mother tongue obviously does play an important part, and little work has been done on it recently, so far as I know. As far as the acquisition of vocabulary and semantics is concerned, my own frequently expressed opinion is that we know virtually nothing! The acquisition of vocabulary (lexis) seems to be largely context-dependent, that is, we learn precisely that vocabulary which at any particular moment we need to know.

Dick Allwright: Learners in class seem to focus their energies on lexis and ask questions about it, and possibly get all sorts of grammatical help via the lexis.

Pit Corder: Yes, the learner in the classroom is quite rightly concerned with getting messages across, and since the overwhelming majority of meaning is carried lexically, it's quite right that he or she should be concerned with lexis. If I was going somewhere and was asked whether I would prefer to take a grammar book or a dictionary, I would say: 'Give me a dictionary—I can do without the grammar; I'll make it up as I go along.'

Dick Allwright: But if we study the processes by which lexis is acquired, we may get closer to the way grammar is acquired. When I watch learners in class, I see them working on words, but I can see them getting all sorts of help with grammar in so doing. In a sense they put their agenda on the lesson through the questions they ask about words. So one might end up by seeing a natural process of grammar acquisition through the natural process of enquiring about vocabulary.

Pit Corder: Yes, and I think from the teacher's point of view that to concentrate on problems of vocabulary is a good strategy, on the grounds that grammar will look after itself. And I think that talking about the meanings of words may prove to be an interesting and useful way of acquiring vocabulary (whereas talking about grammatical structures is not a good way of acquiring grammar) . . . But the ultimate conclusion one is irresistibly drawn towards by the studies that have been made of SLA is that the best language learning is likely to take place when the learner's attention is concentrated on other aspects of what is happening, rather than on language.

Dick Allwright: But surely the best circumstances for acquisition might be when the focus is on language but not on its *form*, so that you are actually thinking about what language is doing, not trying to avoid thinking about what language is doing. It's a paradox, surely, to say that you really want to get your brain as far removed as possible from the object of enquiry, if there are ways in which you can get a focus on language—like talking about lexical meaning—which will be a route into other syntactic issues.

Pit Corder: Well, I would agree up to a point. But if your focus is entirely on something non-linguistic, you will in the course of concerning yourself with it *necessarily* be involved in acquiring the language which enables you to do what you need to. You've got to have something to attach the words to. It doesn't seem to me profitable to have a lesson dealing with words related to gardens, for example, unless you are actually engaged in gardening-related activities where the words are necessary in order to perform the activity. The priority is the *activity*: the words are a by-product of the activity, rather than the central focus... The advantage of allowing vocabulary to grow out of some meaningful and interesting activity is precisely that you are making use of a knowledge of the world to learn the 'structure' of the language.

Dick Allwright: What is sad about that is that we are having to recommend to teachers that the language is the last thing they should talk about. It doesn't seem to me useless to talk about what can be done with language... There are all sorts of things to be said about social and pragmatic uses of language that can be useful to learners.

Pit Corder: Well, I've not heard of any evidence one way or another from research about whether talking about appropriate use (in Widdowson's sense)[5] is a good way of teaching use of language... I think a lot of nonsense has been talked about the problems of acquiring the 'use' of second languages; on the whole the ways in which different languages are used are far more similar than is believed. The emphasis ten or so years ago on the teaching of language use was really a sort of reaction against our failure to teach the structure of language.

Richard Rossner: But an implication of this view of language learning is that there will be great uncertainty in the teacher's mind about what he or she should do precisely. Even if one accepts that optimum conditions for language learning have to be provided by the teacher, involving 'comprehensible input'[6] and meaningful tasks, as well as language awareness-raising activities, some tremendous questions still remain. What *kind* of comprehensible input—does it matter? What kinds of task?—does it matter? In what order?—does that matter? What guidance, if any, can applied linguistics offer in these areas? It is still the teacher's responsibility to provide a programme of work for his or her learners. What is to go into that programme?

Pit Corder: Well, I am firmly in favour of some sort of task-orientated syllabus. Further research is needed into how tasks should be selected, but in the first instance they are selected because they interest the learners—I've said many times that people learn a language if they are exposed to it on the one hand, and if they have a reason for learning it on the other, but that doesn't get you very far. In class students learn because they enjoy working on the tasks, solving the problems. So the syllabus is a sequence of problem-solving activities.

Dick Allwright: Doesn't this mean that it is not possible to provide a syllabus of tasks, but only a bank of them? One has to rely on the teachers' perception of what is right for their learners at a given point in their development. One can't prejudge the suitability or relevance of a task to any particular group at any point.

Pit Corder: I think that's right. Teachers are going to have a much more responsible role, because they're going to have to make decisions about what is right for their group of learners at that time, instead of simply working through a book . . . the qualities in a group that are needed for this kind of task are not necessarily linguistic abilities first and foremost; they are general intelligence or something similar. Linguistic abilities play a part, but only a part. The trouble is that, in the language-teaching situation, we find great variability in the learners because we are teaching language. If we were doing something else, we might find a greater degree of similarity between learners' levels of linguistic ability . . . I think that if, as seems to be the case, there isn't much difference in the ability to acquire the mother tongue, one shouldn't expect to find much difference in the ability to acquire a second language, other things being equal . . . which of course they aren't.

Dick Allwright: Are you saying that the emphasis on turning language learning into an academic subject has actually created artificial differences of ability among learners?

Pit Corder: Yes, I think so. It's nothing to do with people's innate ability to learn a second language, but has to do with variations in motivation, attitude, and so on; that's where the variation is.

Dick Allwright: Previously teachers using a book or following a clear-cut syllabus weren't asked to make decisions about what to teach at a particular time. The problem in teacher training is now that, with a task-based approach, teachers are not going to be asked to teach any particular language item at any time, but must select tasks according to criteria that up to now have hardly been included in teacher training: 'conceptual readiness' and 'interest readiness'.

Pit Corder: Absolutely. Task-based approaches will require a total rethink of teacher training. What the teacher using a task-based approach isn't going to need is any linguistic 'knowledge' of a conscious, deliberate sort. But teachers will need to be trained in task development and task selection, and to recognize when a particular task is appropriate for a particular group. What they won't need is grammatical theory.

Richard Rossner: But it is still not clear to me how the teacher, working in the context of formal education, which is permeated with the notion of 'systematic progress', is to adjust to the apparent randomness of task-based approaches and what you are saying they imply. If what you are saying is that, so long as the tasks are motivating and involve comprehensible input, it doesn't matter what the tasks are, how does one reconcile the formality of classroom learning with such randomness?

Pit Corder: I agree that it is a problem, but teachers have already moved on a long way, and the tight control over the forms that a teacher was permitted to use in front of a class, which we associate with the audio-lingual and structural days, has gone. All one is suggesting is a further step. But equally there is a problem getting *learners*, especially adult learners, to accept a different type of approach.

Dick Allwright: Of course a possibility here, related to the teacher's difficulty in selecting the right task for his or her group at a given time, is to involve the learners actively in the selection of tasks with the teacher. And this would alter the relationship between learners and teachers.

Richard Rossner: Would this make the teacher redundant?

Pit Corder: On the contrary, the teachers become more, not less, important. Tasks may involve relatively little in the way of written or spoken materials. The talk which goes on in the classroom is the major source of input. You can't do without the teacher . . .

Notes

1 'Idiosyncratic dialects and error analysis' in S. P. Corder: *Error Analysis and Interlanguage* (Oxford University Press 1981) p. 20.
2 'Morpheme studies' involved analysing the development of a single morpheme (such as possessive *'s* at the end of nouns/names) in an

individual learner or in a group of learners in order to see how long the acquisition of the element took and what the developmental stages were (cf., for instance, R. Ellis 1985, for examples and outcomes).
3 Krashen (for example in his *Second Language Acquisition and Second Language Learning* (1981) makes much of the distinction between unconscious learning ('acquisition') of language and conscious learning ('learning') of, for example, rules of grammar through drilling, in developing his 'Monitor Theory'.
4 Cf. Krashen (1981) and reviews of his work in *ELT Journal* 36/3 and 37/3.
5 Cf. H. G. Widdowson: *Teaching Language as Communication* (OUP 1978), Chapter 1.
6 'Comprehensible input' is another term deriving from Krashen's work: he sees exposure to instances of language that are 'comprehensible' to the learner and which contain language at a level just above his or her current competence as one of the keys to successful acquisition (cf. Ellis 1985).

(*Originally published in Volume 40/3, 1986*)

Further reading

Readers may wish to follow up their reading of this section by referring to the following titles:

Blair, R. W. (ed.). 1982. *Innovative Approaches to Language Teaching*. Rowley, MA: Newbury House.
Brown, G. and **G. Yule**. 1983. *Teaching the Spoken Language*. Cambridge: Cambridge University Press (reviewed in *ELTJ*, 39/2, 1985).
Early, P. (ed.). 1981. 'Humanistic Approaches: An Empirical View'. *ELT Documents 113*. London: The British Council (reviewed in *ELTJ*, 37/4, 1983).
Ellis, R. 1985. *Understanding Second Language Acquisition*. Oxford: Oxford University Press (reviewed in *ELTJ*, 42/2, 1988).
Howatt, A. P. R. 1984. *A History of English Language Teaching*. Oxford: Oxford University Press (reviewed in *ELTJ*, 40/1, 1966).
Krashen, S. D. 1982. *Principles and Practice in Second Language Acquisition*. Oxford: Pergamon (reviewed in *ELTJ*, 37/3, 1983).
Krashen, S. D. 1985. *The Input Hypothesis*. London: Longman.
Stern, H. H. 1983. *Fundamental Concepts of Language Teaching*. Oxford: Oxford University Press (reviewed in *ELTJ*, 38/4, 1984).
Widdowson, H. G. 1983. *Learning Purpose and Language Use*. Oxford: Oxford University Press.

SECTION 3

Issues in methodology and teacher training

The papers in this section appeared in the *ELT Journal* between 1981 and 1987. Though most of them were contributed by British writers, and all of them by native speakers, it is interesting to note that the contexts referred to are world-wide, ranging from Poland, West Germany, and the U.K. to Mexico, Morocco, Thailand, and India. To this extent, they illustrate one of the continuing phenomena in the world of English Language Teaching: the encounter between the native-speaker 'expert' on the one hand and local teachers and lecturers on the other. The political and socio-cultural issues raised by this encounter are explored in some of the papers in **Section 1** of this volume. Many of them have more or less predictable methodological implications, and these are highlighted in some of the articles included in this section. Similarly, many of the questions posed at the level of *approach* in the papers and letters in **Section 2** are echoed in very pointed and practical terms in the articles which follow. It is, perhaps, in the nature of articles on *approach* in language teaching that there should be more questions than answers, and that the debate should take place at a certain level of abstraction. By the same token, many of these articles on the *methodology* of teaching and teacher-training are noticeably solution-oriented, and for the most part context-specific.

This tendency is understandable, given the expectations which, rightly or wrongly, learners have of teachers, and teachers and trainees have of trainers, native-speaker or otherwise. The extent to which solutions proposed in articles in teachers' journals are transferable to other contexts is a matter for much staff-room debate. One prerequisite for 'transferability' seems to be that the proposed solution should be firmly rooted in *principles* which are perceived to be generalizable. In other words they should transcend the level of techniques or 'recipes'. One reason why these papers were selected is that they fulfil this prerequisite.

As was hinted above, however, not all of these articles are solution-oriented or based on case studies. Methodology offers fertile ground for open-ended debate. Put another way, a thinking teacher's evaluative criteria should and do extend beyond the simple question: 'Will it work in my classroom?' Many teachers also have a critical and evolving concern with the psychological, linguistic, sociological, and philosophical issues which underlie all sound practice in education. The routes which teachers may take to a consideration of some or all of these issues are examined in some of the papers focusing on teacher training.

The effects of recent changes in English Language Teaching are critically examined in several of the papers in **Section 2**. These changes have inevitably led to a certain amount of division and even to a polarization of views among theorists as well as teachers. In the first article in this section, Alan Maley takes a look at some of the binary choices which have faced teachers, materials-writers, and syllabus-designers through the early years of the communicative era: for example, acquisition versus learning, errors versus mistakes, simplification versus authenticity, structures versus functions and, as the sub-title of his paper signals, realism versus surrealism. His purpose in surveying these pairs of terms and the trends associated with them is not purely historical, however. He argues persuasively that we should continue to explore new areas and new informing disciplines in language teaching whilst retaining our links with previous good practice.

New lamps for old: realism and surrealism in foreign language teaching

Alan Maley

In recent years we have become more aware that the theory and practice of language teaching (and learning) is subject to a process similar to that described by Thomas Kuhn in *The Structure of Scientific Revolutions* (1970). Kuhn postulates long periods of stability, when one theory or 'paradigm' is dominant, followed by periods of intense and heterodox experimentation, before the emergence of a new paradigm. Looking back at the past ten years or so in the field of foreign language teaching, it is clear that we have been living through just such a period of professional insecurity, which, if Kuhn is right, should herald the emergence of a new paradigm.

At the heart of our 'professional insecurity' is the failure to provide a satisfactory answer to Stevick's riddle: 'In the field of language teaching, Method A is the logical contradiction of Method B: if the assumptions from which A claims to be derived are correct, then B cannot work, and vice versa. Yet one colleague is getting excellent results with A, and another is getting comparable results with B. How is this possible?' (Stevick 1976).

In this article I will not attempt to answer the riddle, but I will try sympathetically to examine the various elements in the current debate.

Views of language learning

Acquisition and learning

One of the more interesting views to have emerged is the so-called 'Monitor' theory developed by Stephen Krashen (1978). Krashen posits two quite distinct processes whereby the adult learner achieves competence in a foreign language. These he calls 'acquisition' and 'learning'.

Briefly, *learning* is characterized by the need for conscious effort of concentration on what is being learned. It proceeds in a logical, analytical, step-by-step manner, and involves the learner in the pain of forgetting, regressing, and re-learning. It is subject to a *monitor* mechanism—that is, a kind of psychological censor, which vets all items before they are uttered, and corrects them if it detects error.

Acquisition, by contrast, is a largely subconscious process, in which the human organism abstracts, processes, and organizes relevant information from the linguistic environment and stores it in long-term memory ready for immediate retrieval. In this case the monitor mechanism is by-passed. This is, then, a system not subject to rational or voluntary control. Provided there is an environment sufficiently rich in data, it will take place.

When we apply this theory to the day-to-day business of classroom teaching, it is clear that most of our procedures favour learning. It is, relatively speaking, easy to set up learning situations (even if no-one learns). That is what classrooms are, traditionally, for. But how can one arrange for acquisition to take place if it is by definition involuntary?

This is one of the teasers which, if Krashen's theory has any validity, our methodology must come to terms with. How can we by-pass the inhibiting effect of conscious processing and create the right conditions for acquisition? It carries in its train a whole host of minor puzzles: how is it, for example, that certain items are instantly 'acquired' by some learners and not by others, and that some items are resistant even to 'learning', and that these also vary from learner to learner?

Errors and mistakes

Research is tending to show that not only the first language, but also second languages, are acquired in a predictable order (cf. Corder 1979). We are all familiar with children who progressively eliminate typical errors (e.g. aberrant past tense forms in English like 'he catched') as they grow older. A similar, in-built progressive elimination of error is often observable in foreign learners of a language. The process of learning a foreign language can be likened to a series of steps on a staircase: on any given step, learners will exhibit the errors characteristic of that step. These will disappear as the learners move up to the next one. And they will do this when they are ready. In other words, each learner passes through a sequence of developmental stages. This is often obscured in classroom teaching by the fact that learners progress through the stages at different rates. But the order is the same for all. This helps to explain the apparent imperviousness of many, if not most, learners to correction procedures. No amount of correction will move them to the next step until they are ready for it.

There would seem to be at least two important implications in this for the classroom. Firstly, 'mistakes' should not carry a feeling of guilt or failure with them, since, when regarded as 'errors', they are a natural part of the learning process. Contrary to what some of us were brought up to believe, errors are an indispensable part of learning. Without them no true learning can take place (cf. Dakin 1973). Secondly, we should perhaps re-examine the amount of time spent on error correction, or at the very least modify our procedures so as to develop more responsible self-correction by the learners themselves. After all, if we cannot significantly affect the rate of error elimination, why spend one-third (cf. Flanders 1970) to one-half of classroom time on it?

Input and intake

There are two major and opposing theories of learning anything, not just languages. Let us characterize these as the 'pint pot' theory and the 'home-brewery kit' theory. The 'pint pot' theory sees the learning process as one of pure transfer of information/knowledge/skill from one receptacle to another: the teacher simply empties his or her barrel of knowledge into the students' pint pots. There is no organic interchange. It is the students' job to absorb as much of the elixir as they can and not to spill any! Intake—what learners take in—equals input—what the teacher puts in, according to this theory.

In Britain, it is common for people to make their own beer. They simply buy a kit with the ingredients; then, following the instructions, they brew it. The other view of learning is analogous to this: the teacher is seen as provider of raw materials and instructions on how to use them, and the learner then works on them at his or her individual pace and in his or her own style. Input is identical for all, but intake (and output) is different for everyone.

It is more convenient for teachers—and systems of education—to adopt a 'pint pot' approach. And it can be shown to work. It is possible for students to commit to memory large chunks of material from the foreign language and to reproduce it for examination or classroom purposes. But what is learned this way is all too often inaccessible for use in wider contexts. It is as if a psychological wall had been built around it, cutting it off from contexts of use. Language tends to become a body of knowledge, not a tool for communication.

Eureka!

Arthur Koestler's book *The Act of Creation* (1966) investigates in detail the processes of creative behaviour. Koestler draws attention to the work of Helmholtz, who postulated a three-stage process. He speaks of a stage of 'preparation', in which relevant data are gathered and subjected to examination and questioning. This is followed by a period of 'incubation', during which the mind works on the data at a subconscious or unconscious level. Finally, there is 'illumination' when, quite suddenly, things fall into place. The problem is solved, the invention is made, the poem is written. This final stage is often the result of what Koestler calls 'bisociative' thinking, when two apparently incompatible elements come together in an unusual arrangement which sheds new light on the problem.

Some innovative approaches to the teaching of languages such as The Silent Way, Suggestopoedia, Community Language Learning, and Total Physical Response, draw in some measure on the Helmholtz model. And there are surely lessons to be learned from it for day-to-day language teaching. In particular, it suggests a need to leave the learner time to process 'input' before expecting any 'output'; and the desirability of at least occasionally providing inputs to stimulate the 'bisociative mechanism'.

Views of language

The past ten years have seen a shift in the focus of attention from concern with the formal properties of language, to a view of language as primarily a vehicle of communication. This is reflected in the following areas.

Structures and functions

It was customary until relatively recently (indeed in many places it still is) to regard a language as being made up of a series of syntactic building blocks known as 'patterns'. These were isolated, ordered in a sequence from 'least' to 'most' difficult. Teaching materials were then devised to exemplify and give practice in them. The main criticisms levelled against such a procedure were that it focused on language as *form* rather that language as *use*; and that it rested on the unproven premise that, equipped with a set of structural building blocks, the student could proceed without difficulty towards constructing skyscrapers.

According to the notion/functional approach, on the other hand, the forms of language are subservient to the major use of language as a vehicle for meaning. Teaching syllabuses such as that proposed by Wilkins (1976) were to reflect this by concentrating on such major areas as time, and spatial relations, and communicative functions such as 'suggestion', 'obligation', and 'suasion', all of which can be expressed using many different language forms.

There is no doubt that this movement has caused a considerable change in the ways we view language, and in the content and procedures of teaching it. It is, however, not without problems: so far there is no universally agreed and adequate description of the 'functions' of language. It is also not clear how teaching a list of discrete *functions* is qualitatively different from teaching a list of discrete *structures*. The pendulum seems to be swinging back towards a mid-point of common sense, where structure/grammar is considered a necessary but not a sufficient component in a foreign language syllabus.

Sentence and discourse

Until relatively recently, the attention of linguists was limited to the sentence. Grammar included everything up to the end of the sentence, but nothing beyond it. Emphasis has now shifted towards an investigation of the devices used to link sentences together to form 'text' (written or spoken), as opposed to a haphazard collection of propositions. For example, it is clear that:

> 'Howard said he need go no farther. Do not use quotation marks. Where is my car?'

does not form coherent text. The three propositions are unrelated syntactically or semantically.

To date most work has been done on the written language (e.g. Widdowson 1978, Halliday and Hasan 1976). But the ways in which connected speech is structured have also formed the basis for some interesting work (e.g. Sinclair and Coulthard 1975). This has proved especially useful in the teaching of reading and listening skills, and has pointed the way towards the teaching of language in contexts of use, not simply as tokens illustrating the formal properties of language.

The negotiation of meaning: language as social interaction

Many people hold the view that meaning is somehow there, to be apprehended: that words are like trucks, each one carrying its load of meaning. However, a more complex view (cf. Widdowson 1978) holds that meanings are not externally given, but are dependent to a degree not hitherto suspected on other factors. Even so simple an utterance as 'What's the time?' can be variably construed according to such factors as setting (where it is spoken), topic (about what), participants (with whom), their respective roles and status, and the intention and mood of the speakers, etc. Such sociological and psychological factors deeply affect language and are in their turn affected by it. The meanings a writer conveys are similarly conditioned, and set off chain reactions of associative meanings in the reader, which necessarily vary from one reader to the next. The problem posed for teachers by such a view is considerable. To what extent can such things be taught? And if they can, how? (cf. Candlin 1981).

The renewed interest in the receptive skills, especially listening comprehension, and in more adventurous forms of production via role plays, simulation, and drama work has its origin in this question. On the one hand, we seek to expose learners to a broad range of language contexts to enable them gradually to form their own criteria for appropriacy of language use. On the other, we provide them with opportunities for trying out what they feel may be appropriate.

Programme design

Needs analysis

The idea of analysing the needs of language learners proceeds from the common sense notion that no-one is able to learn a language totally. Even native speakers use only a small part of the total resources of their language. Surely, the proponents of needs analysis argue, it is a waste of time to try to teach the whole of a foreign language? We should instead concentrate on what the learner will need to use the language for when he or she finishes the course. If we can develop a way of ascertaining in detail the needs of learners, then we can translate this into a syllabus, and from the syllabus derive appropriate teaching techniques and materials (Munby 1978).

There are, however, a number of practical and theoretical objections to such a view. In the first place, it is extremely difficult to predict the needs of a group (which is necessarily composed of a number of individuals, possibly with conflicting needs). Munby's model offers a procedure for defining an individual's needs, which are then extrapolated to a group, but the justification for doing this is tenuous. It has also been pointed out that, for a majority of learners, we simply do not know what uses they will find for the language at the end of their course. Moreover, any description of needs is static, not dynamic. There may well be, and there often is, a difference between the 'analysed' needs of learners (e.g. flight attendants) and their needs as perceived by themselves (i.e. their 'wants'), which evolve throughout the learning process.

At a more abstract level, it has been pointed out that needs analysis tends to reinforce a *product* view of learning, rather that a *process* view. If we know what the learner needs, we can pour it into his or her pint pot. The implication is that the syllabus designer always knows best. Clearly it is the syllabus designer's job to take decisions, but it has been argued that learners are not necessarily best prepared for a given set of terminal behaviours by giving them practice in these behaviours alone.

The analysis of needs, however, cannot be ignored. Used with a dose of common sense, it can eliminate much superfluous teaching and make way for what is truly useful.

Simplification and authenticity

There are two strongly held but opposing views on the matter of simplification. Some would argue that students cannot simply be left to deal with the awesome foreignness of the new language in all its manifestations, but must be helped by judicious simplification. They can then be exposed by small degrees to the full complexity of the language. Others claim that simplified materials are a poor preparation for the encounter with the real language outside the classroom. In their view, the course designer should be selecting appropriate authentic texts and devising exercises which facilitate learners' comprehension of these.

This discussion leaves to one side the question of the authenticity of learner *output*, considering only the authenticity of *input*. We should not, however, be concerned solely with input. How can we devise techniques which will allow learners scope to express themselves in the foreign language? It is conceivable that even simplified inputs can be made to produce a personalized response. (One heterodox suggestion is to encourage learners to formulate criticisms of the very material they are obliged to learn from!) It is also true, of course, that highly original techniques in the hands of an unimaginative teacher can stultify learning just as much as unoriginal ones.

The decline of the textbook

There is a tendency for the 'monolithic' textbook to give way to less rigid forms of instructional materials. These range from various types of supplementary materials which now surround the central core of many courses, or exist independently, to inventories of ideas for teachers, and to so-called 'modular' materials.

The module idea is a fascinating one; it attempts to reconcile the need for some kind of backbone to a course with the individual and changing needs of real learners. It also allows for the fact that learners in a single class may progress at different rates, have different interests, and be working on different materials at the same time. Taken to its extreme, it leads into the field of individualized learning, where the teacher provides the learners with guidance to a range of resources, but does not intervene unnecessarily in their learning.

It is interesting to note in passing that the increasing opportunities for choice in learning seem to be part of the wider pattern of enlarged choice about which Alvin Toffler speculates (Toffler 1981).

Is your syllabus really necessary?

It has always been customary, even before developments in systematic needs analysis, to base language teaching materials upon a previously decided list of items. These 'a priori' syllabuses assume a need on the part of the syllabus designer or textbook writer to select and order what is presented, usually according to its usefulness or frequency. That is, such syllabuses were, and are, linguistically graded.

An alternative (but one not often applied so far) is to devise a series of interesting activities, using more or less authentic texts, irrespective of linguistic grading except in the roughest sense. The activities are graded, not the texts. Only afterwards are the language items selected for attention and set out in the form of a checklist (cf. Maley *et al.* 1982).

The most compelling argument against 'a priori' syllabuses is the fact that they distort linguistic and situational reality by an over-concentration on certain language forms. Text functions as pretext. The strongest argument for 'a posteriori' checklists is this: if linguistic items are truly frequent and useful, then they can be presumed to occur naturally in representative samples of the language as normally used. There is, too, the logical incompatibility between the fact that all learners are different, and the imposition of a set programme which is identical for all. In purely practical terms, a syllabus is certainly of some use, especially for oral production and writing. One has to learn *something*, to start *somewhere*. But the argument for such a syllabus loses much of its force in a consideration of listening and reading comprehension, where the very essence of the skills is an ability to deal with the unknown and the unexpected, and to accommodate it in a framework of meaning.

Methodology

Accuracy and fluency

This distinction has been widely discussed in recent years (e.g. in Brumfit 1980). Accuracy activities typically focus on the *form* of the language and try to ensure that it is correct. The concern is with getting forms right. Fluency work, by contrast, is marked by a concern with developing the learners' ability to handle language interactions appropriately. This ability is built up through activities favouring relatively uncontrolled interchange in which errors are tolerated (provided that communication is effective), and through exposure to varied samples of the spoken and written language.

It is easier for teachers to organize accuracy work than fluency activities. No-one should be surprised, therefore, to note a predominance of accuracy work in classrooms. But if the foreign language is to become a living means for communication, then the balance between accuracy and fluency work needs to be redressed in favour of fluency.

Language-centred and task-centred approaches

Much classroom activity even nowadays is typically focused on the language as the prime target. There is, however, a danger that we may lose sight of the fact that language is essentially a means for getting things done. Some recent approaches have tried, as an alternative, to develop activities which are meaningful and interesting, and in which the learners can invest something of themselves. Absorption in the activity takes over from obsessive concern with the language. Such activities may take the form of problem-solving (in the broadest sense), drama work, simulations, or self-discovery. The claim is that, by losing themselves in the task, learners lose inhibitions when using the language. In order to complete the task, of course, it is necessary to engage in language activity (reading, writing, speaking, listening, and usually a combination of two or more of them). However, this is no longer an end in itself, but a necessary step on the way to a non-linguistic outcome.

The politics of the classroom

Methodology is often a reflection of the power relationships obtained in a given classroom. A host of studies (e.g. Flanders 1970; Barnes 1976; Stubbs 1976) testify to the way typical classroom interactions are teacher-dominated, leaving little psychological space for student initiative. Much teaching, for example, is still of the 'lockstep' variety. That is, everyone in the class is put through the same hoops at the same time, irrespective of individual ability or inclination.

While it is true that it is the teacher's responsibility to provide a framework of overall control within which learning can take place, an over-emphasis on control will stultify the learning process. Too often teachers lose sight of the fact that only the learners can learn: teachers cannot learn for them.

How then, can teachers change the power structure in positive ways? Even quite minor physical changes, such as the way desks are arranged, whether the teacher sits or stands, and where he or she is, can make a great difference. The procedures adopted can likewise modify relationships significantly. For example, having students ask each other questions, or working in groups, will shift the emphasis away from domination by the teacher. The form of activity may also be significant. For example, a problem-solving activity involving the exchange of information between groups is learner-centred rather than teacher-centred. But the overriding factor will be the attitude of the teacher. It is a sad observation that many teachers who exercise rigid control do so because of insecurity. They are worried about their inability to operate in a situation where not everything is under their control. This is a natural enough fear, but one which experience of a more relaxed approach usually proves unjustified. It is fear of the unknown more that anything else.

Psychological factors

Learning styles

It is now commonplace that no two learners are alike in their mode and rate of learning, and we are beginning to know a little more about just how they may differ. There are those who prefer a linear approach, in which every step is exhaustively explained before passing to the next, and who are uneasy when faced with the unexpected or the unexplained. Others seem at home in situations where they are invited to come to conclusions for themselves, often on the basis of insufficient data. These are the 'holistic' learners, who see the wood and do not trouble themselves unnecessarily about the trees. Similarly, there are the convergent thinkers, who tend to seek reassurance in the right answer (and every question must have one!). Whereas divergent thinkers are rarely satisfied with the most obvious answer. They go on looking for others, and will even accept the fact that there may be no answer (Hudson 1966). There are, too, 'visualizers' and 'verbalizers', and manipulative and intellectual approaches (Boekaerts 1979).

The implications of all this for the classroom seem to be three-fold. Firstly, we should not adopt a normative attitude to these differences. There is nothing inherently inferior or superior in any learning style. It is simply a fact to be taken account of. Secondly, we need to offer a variety in teaching which will give equal opportunities to people with differing styles. A purely rational explanation of a rule of grammar would usually be absorbed by only a part of the class; a visual representation would account for a further proportion; a visual plus a manipulative presentation—for example via the 'Silent Way'—would reach still others (cf. Vester 1978). Finally, such varied alternatives may help individuals to develop their latent abilities. Rational types may find release in intuition, verbalizers in visualizing, and so on.

The threat of learning and the zest of risk

From the point of view of the learner, there seem to be two alternative, and fluctuating, views of learning. One of them highlights the feeling of threat to self-esteem which accompanies the act of learning (cf. Rogers 1969). It is claimed that adults in particular develop negative feelings in a learning situation, because they feel that their whole personality is put at risk and that they are in danger of losing their self-respect if they admit to not knowing. Thus, learning turns into a protective affair, where people learn things simply to shield themselves from the accusations of stupidity emanating from the teacher, their peers, or their conscience. Lozanov (1978) has also pointed out the way in which most classroom situations give off the negative suggestion that what is to be learned is difficult and unlikely to be learned successfully, so that learners are immediately faced with an impossibly high wall to scale. 'Suggestopoedia' (Lozanov's approach) and approaches based on Counselling Learning seek to reduce threat-induced resistance by creating an atmosphere of non-judgemental acceptance and supportiveness.

The other view, however, regards all learning as a risk-taking business. Without exposing oneself to risk and the possibility of error, no learning takes place. And risk entails danger. The best kind of teaching, according to this view, prepares learners for the encounter with the unknown, and does not give them feelings of false security.

Conclusion

Realism tends to be associated with the solidly based, the well founded, and the serious; surrealism is associated with the zany, the 'lunatic fringe', and the irresponsible. Yet, if we wish to take account of even some of the factors discussed above, I believe that our teaching procedures have to look more surreal than real. If we wish to favour 'acquisition', for example, or revise our view of error, allow for the difference between 'input' and 'intake', and allow space for the Eureka principle, and if we are to take account of individual learning styles in a less rigidly controlled framework where authentic tasks make up much of the programme, there will be changes in methods, materials, and techniques.

Such changes have already begun to happen. There is now an almost bewildering variety of published materials. Ideas flow and are exchanged in a plethora of conferences and articles. To return to the theory of scientific revolutions, one begins to wonder whether it can be applied to language teaching. We do not for the present seem to have rejected one paradigm in order to accept another—unless the absence of a paradigm is itself paradigmatic! We seem, rather, to find it exhilarating to ride the surf-wave of change—and to try to keep our sense of balance.

(Originally published in Volume 37/4, 1983)

In one section of his paper, Maley refers to 'the decline of the textbook', and this theme is the primary concern of the articles by Dick Allwright and Robert O'Neill which now follow. Allwright queries the value of *teaching* materials which leave the learner little room for manoeuvre, and argues the case for more *learning* materials on the grounds that teachers often work too hard in classrooms while learners are frequently understretched. Hand-in-hand with the call for learning materials goes the realization that the shake-up in the teacher/learner/materials relationship posited in the article will result in a need for more *learner-training*. Allwright's mention of this in 1981 presages an increasing interest in the topic in the following years. It is a theme which is also taken up in later articles in this section.

What do we want teaching materials for?

R. L. Allwright

The question

In this paper I will focus on the sorts of publications we might want publishers to promote, in terms of the sorts of jobs we might want teaching materials to do.

To ask 'What do we want teaching materials for?' is unfortunately a premature question. To say 'What do we want materials to *do*?' may clarify the problem, because it may remind us that, if we are thinking about the role of teaching materials in the whole teaching/learning operation, then we ought first to ask 'What is there to be done?' This question deliberately avoids reference to teaching or to the teacher, because I wish, at this stage, to leave 'who should do what' in the management of language learning an open question.

'To be done' suggests action, but in fact there are three phases in management, rather than one. There are things to decide, actions to be taken on the basis of those decisions, and a process of review to feed into future decision-making.

Figure 1 should help reinforce this point, with its circularity and overlapping segments indicating the dynamic interrelationships involved. After a *decision* has been taken—say, to use a particular textbook for a particular course—some *organization* is necessary—namely the purchase and delivery of an adequate quantity of the books to the classroom —before the decision can be fully *implemented*. The use of the textbook, for a sensible review to be possible, has then to be *monitored* to permit *evaluation* of its use and effectiveness, and the result can then go forward to inform subsequent decisions.

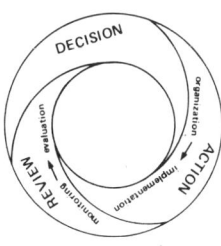

Fig. 1. Decision, Action, Review.

In addition it seems necessary to take a preliminary look at two different approaches to the question of the role of teaching materials. On the one hand there is the DEFICIENCY view. According to this view, we need teaching materials to save learners from our deficiencies as teachers, to make sure, as far as possible, that the syllabus is properly covered and that exercises are well thought out, for example. This way of thinking might lead, at one extreme, to the idea that the 'best' teachers would neither want nor need published teaching materials. At the other extreme we would have 'teacher-proof' materials that no teacher, however deficient, would be able to teach badly with.

On the other hand, there is the DIFFERENCE view, which holds that we need teaching materials as 'carriers' of decisions best made by someone other than the classroom teacher, not because the classroom teacher is *deficient*, as a classroom teacher, but because the expertise required of materials writers is importantly *different* from that required of classroom teachers—the people who have to have the interpersonal skills to make classrooms good places to learn in. For some this conception may seem to 'reduce' the teacher to the role of *mere* classroom manager. For others, it 'frees' the teacher to develop the expertise needed for dealing with practical and fundamental issues in the fostering of language learning in the classroom setting.

Both the DEFICIENCY and the DIFFERENCE views have enough truth in them to be worth holding in mind simultaneously as we move towards a management analysis. Both views are based on the assumption that decisions are best taken (and 'acted upon', and 'reviewed') by those with the relevant expertise. Although this must, at first sight at least, seem entirely reasonable, it does ignore the important possibility that, at least in some not very improbable circumstances, the question of *who* takes the decision, etc., might be more important than the question of *whether* or not the 'best' decision is always taken. We shall need to return to this issue later. Now it is time to introduce an analytical answer to the question 'What is to be done?'

The analysis

This analysis of the issues involved in the management of language learning is simplified for the sake of exposition. (See Appendix 1 for the same analysis elaborated into 27 separate points.) It is not intended to be especially radical or controversial in its division of language teaching and learning into four main areas. It may be surprising to see 'Guidance' given a section to itself, but otherwise the content should be familiar and, I hope, generally uncontroversial. The novelty, if there is any, consists mainly in presenting the analysis without reference, at this stage, to 'who should do what', or 'what should be covered by teaching materials'.

Goals

Four main points need to be made about goals:

1 Points of view

In considering goals, at least four different points of view need to be taken into account.

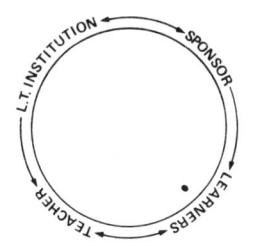

Fig. 2. Points of view.

Figure 2 attempts to show, by means of the one-way and two-way arrows, that language teaching institutions and sponsors may interact and negotiate goals for particular courses, but that language teaching institutions may impose goals on teachers, and sponsors may impose goals on learners. Teachers and learners then meet and may also get involved in negotiation of goals.

2 Types of goals

At least two types need to be distinguished here: goals for oneself and goals for others. All four 'points of view' represent people or institutions who must be expected to have personal goals. Teachers wish to develop their teaching careers, language teaching institutions want to survive financially and with enhanced prestige, sponsors want to further their own interests, and learners, we hope, want to learn the language. The first three, however, have goals for the learners as well as for themselves. They not only *have* goals, they may seek to *impose* those goals on the learners. Hence:

3 Probability of conflict

Given these complications, it is not surprising if a conflict of goals is found. Teaching materials, of course, are chosen at least partly because of the learning goals they embody, but these, we know, are not the only goals involved in the whole management of language learning. This brings us to:

4 Materials may *contribute* in some way, but they cannot *determine* GOALS.

The role of teaching materials must then be relatively limited. No matter how comprehensively the materials cover learning goals, they can never even 'look after' everything to do with goals, let alone actually determine them.

Content

There are three main points to be made about content, and then four categories of content to be described (but see Appendix 1 for a more detailed analysis).

1 Input

We have got used to the input/intake distinction (cf. Corder 1967) in recent years but only in terms of input from the teacher. Learners in classrooms, however, listen to each other as well as to the teacher, and are exposed, potentially, to much more language than is focused on in teaching. I wish to distinguish between 'what is taught' in the classroom, and 'what is available to be learned' there, as a result of the interactive nature of classroom events. If, for example, the teacher explains something in the target language, the language of that explanation is available to be learned. It constitutes potential 'intake'. Similarly, all the things that get said when errors are being corrected constitute potential intake, as do all the things said in the target language by other learners.

2 'Emergent' content

If we define 'content' as the sum total of 'what is taught' and 'what is available to be learned', then it becomes clear that 'content' (potential intake) is not predictable. It is, rather, something that emerges because of the interactive nature of classroom events.

3 Materials may *contribute* in some way, but cannot *determine* CONTENT.

Again we find that the role of teaching materials is necessarily limited. Even what learners learn is in an important way independent of the materials used.

This notion of content needs further analysis (see Appendix 1) but here I can simply indicate four main types of content:

a. The target language itself

b. Subject-matter content

This may include knowledge about language in general, about target language culture, literature, etc. In the ESP (English for specific purposes) context, subject-matter may be an important part of 'what is taught', or it may be simply the 'carrier' of all the language content.

c. Learning strategies

Part of the content of instruction (both that which is 'taught' and that 'available to be learned') may be learning strategies, that is, ways of dealing with language input to turn it into intake, or means of generating input (see Seliger 1980). Although the learning of learning strategies has not, traditionally, been an explicit goal of language instruction, it has become, recently, much more usual to give it emphasis, as in 'study skills' courses for foreign students, for example. But all courses, not just those labelled 'study skills', could well aim to help learners with learning strategies, as an obvious part of the management of learning. Learners themselves, of course, may well want to become better language learners. We shall return to this issue under the heading 'learner-training' later.

d. Attitudes

It is well accepted that one of the goals of school language instruction is to improve the attitudes of speakers of different languages to one another.

However seldom this may be achieved, the development of positive intercultural attitudes remains important, but it is not often discussed as part of the *content* of instruction. Even where attitudes are not being explicitly 'taught', however, they are almost certainly 'available to be learned' in *any* language classroom, from the teacher and from everyone present. They include attitudes to learning, of course, and not just language or intercultural attitudes. To summarize, anyone involved in the management of language learning has necessarily to deal with attitudes as part of what learners may learn.

This analysis of CONTENT has pointed to some of the many complexities involved: enough, I imagine, to reinforce my contention that not too much can be expected of teaching materials.

Method

Here there are three main issues that have to be attended to (decided, acted upon, reviewed) in the management of language learning.

1 Learning processes

The fundamental question is 'What learning processes should be fostered?' This is clearly central for all concerned, from curriculum developers to the learners themselves.

2 Activities

The next question is 'What activities, or what learning tasks, will best activate the chosen processes, for what elements of content?' A less deterministic version of this might be 'What activities or learning tasks will offer a wide choice of learning processes to the learner, in relation to a wide variety of content options?' This amendment suggests, I think correctly, that we can neither predict nor determine learning processes, and therefore perhaps should not try as hard to do so as we usually do in our teaching materials.

3 Activity management

The third basic question is 'How can we manage these activities (set up group work, run simulations, etc.) so that they are maximally profitable?' (i.e. minimizing the management risks discussed in Allwright 1978): for example, who will work best with whom, how long can be allowed for any particular activity. Such questions may be the subject of suggestions in teaching materials, but detailed local decisions are clearly beyond the scope of publications.

Again we come up against the fact that teaching materials are necessarily limited in scope. They can, and do, contribute to the management of language learning, but cannot possibly cope with many of the important decisions facing the 'managers' working in their various situations.

Guidance

I am using the term 'guidance' to refer to all those things that can be expected to help people understand what they are doing and how well they are doing it. The scope of the term thus ranges from the provision of a full-scale grammatical explanation, to the mere nod from a teacher to signify acceptance of a learner's pronunciation. It also covers, of course, guidance about method (e.g. instructions for simulation) as well as about content, and guidance about appropriate standards of attainment. These are major issues in the management of language learning, involving decisions, for example, about the most helpful type of explanation to offer for given aspects of the language, and about the type of error treatment that will help an individual learner.

Clearly, in the circumstances, there is again a limit to what teaching materials can be expected to do for us.

This analysis has quite deliberately been presented without raising the important question of 'who should do what'. That we can cover in the next section. Meanwhile, the analysis should have reinforced any doubts there might have been about the viability of 'teacher-proof' teaching materials! The whole business of the management of language learning is far too complex to be satisfactorily catered for by a pre-packaged set of decisions embodied in teaching materials. This is obvious if we recognize that, while teaching materials may *embody decisions*, they cannot themselves *undertake the action* and the review phases of the management process. Of course very few writers actually claim that their teaching materials can do everything, but a surprising number do state that their materials are entirely suitable for the learner working neither with a teacher nor with fellow learners, and this implies strong claims for what the materials can do. In turn it suggests a possible need for a 'learner's guide' to language learning, of which more later. Meanwhile, the main point is that the management of language learning is inevitably complex.

Implications

So far I have delayed answering the question in my title and have preferred instead to consider a more fundamental question: 'What is there to be done in the management of language learning?' In this section I shall deal with implications for teacher-training, then with those for what I will call 'learner-training', and finally with implications for materials themselves.

Implications for teacher-training

The main implication is clear: if we subscribe to the 'deficiency' view of the role of teaching materials, then we are forced to admit that teaching materials cannot possibly make up for all our possible deficiencies as teachers. Perhaps teacher-training, then, should be based on a 'management of language learning' analysis, and should concentrate on those areas of teacher expertise (like the action and review phases, for example, or the practical business of classroom interaction management) that cannot be safely left to materials. This is hardly a new idea for teacher-trainers, but it does seem worth emphasizing here.

If that was the only implication for teacher-training of the analysis presented above, little would have been gained. The analysis, by highlighting the complexity of the teacher's job, also sheds light on a common problem found almost every time that teachers are observed or observe themselves. It is the problem of teacher 'overload'. Teachers, it appears, seem to do 'all the work', and exhaust themselves in the process. As Telatnik noted in the diary she kept as a teacher (Telatnik 1980) 'I'm working harder than they are'. This might not matter, if teachers could keep up the pace without running into trouble, but the evidence (mostly informal, but see Allwright 1975, McTear 1975 for specific examples) suggests that teachers who do so much work in the classroom run foul of a number of management risks (see Allwright 1978 for a fuller analysis) and typically fail to present the language to be learned as clearly as they had intended (because they may offer off-the-cuff explanations that are faulty, or treat errors inconsistently, or leave the learners in doubt about what they are supposed to be doing, etc.).

The obvious answer would be to offer more training to produce more efficient classroom teachers who could cope with the inevitably large workload without falling foul of the risks. If, however, we entertain the possibility that teachers are not just doing 'too much' work, but doing work that the learners could more profitably be doing for themselves, the immediate implication for teacher-training must be that teachers need to be trained *not* to do so much work, and trained instead to get the learners to do more. Hence the concept of 'learner-training', since it is unlikely that learners will be able to share the burden without some preparation.

Implications for learner-training

Teacher 'overload' often entails learner 'underinvolvement' since teachers are doing work learners could more profitably do for themselves. Involvement does not just mean 'activity', however. It is not just that learners are not busy enough. 'Involvement' means something more akin to Curran's 'investment' (Curran 1972 and 1976), which suggests a deep sort of involvement, relating to the whole person. This sort of 'whole-person involvement' should be related not simply to 'participation in classroom activities' but to participation in decision-making, and in the whole business of the management of language learning. (It is, after all, their learning that is being managed.) But we should not expect the learners to be already expert at the sorts of decision-making (and action and review) involved in the management of language learning. We must therefore consider ways of conducting learner-training. Before doing that, however, there is a further point to be made about the possible benefits of greater learner-involvement. One of the 'management risks' is 'spoon-feeding', and this shows up most obviously in the treatment of error: teachers seem to prefer supplying the correct answer to asking the learner to think again (see Lucas 1975; Fanselow 1977; see Cathcart and Olsen 1976, for evidence that learners, as things are, prefer it too). If learners could be trained to take much more reponsibility for identifying and repairing their errors, for developing their own criteria of correctness and appropriateness, then we could expect a direct improvement in their language learning. At least in this area, then, and no doubt in others as well, the investment of time in training learners to assume a greater share of management responsibilities should bring dividends in the short term as well as in the long, both directly and indirectly.

But what ideas do we have for 'learner-training'? Of course, very many teachers practise 'learner-training' already, but I wish to give ideas for learner-training the prominence I believe they deserve. Thus, rather than attempting a comprehensive review of learner-training as currently practised, I shall instead report on personal experience with a course designed to foster learner-training and English-language training simultaneously.

In 1978 I was asked, through the British Council, to direct the Polish Academy of Science's annual three-week 'English seminar' for their research scientists (who work in the Academy of Science's various research institutes across Poland). From the outset it was agreed that the course (repeated in 1979) should be aimed at learner-training, at helping the participants become the sort of learners who could effectively go on with their language learning after the course was over, even if no further courses were available to them. At the same time it was of course agreed that we should directly help the learners with their English. We could not offer the 'future-orientation', as we called it, while neglecting the present need.

In planning the course, the first essential was to think of ways of getting the learners to accept the innovation—a preliminary, but fundamental, problem of learner-training. What has developed over the two years is firstly a 'warm-up system' whereby prospective course-members receive, a few weeks in advance, a letter describing the intended nature of the course and asking them to come to it having thought about their learning priorities and their preferred ways of learning English, and some introductory activities for the start of the course, consisting of 'workshops' at which participants are given the task of producing personal profiles of their learning needs, and of their preferred language learning strategies (see Appendices for copies of the profile sheets). These profiles then constitute the paper input to interviews of each learner by two of the tutors (one of whom, for the sake of the less confident learners, is a speaker of Polish). At these interviews the priorities emerging from the profiles are discussed, to make sure we know what the learner intended and to make preliminary decisions about the learner's learning. At this stage we tutors only have an outline structure for the course, in the form of a suggested daily timetable. The learners are asked if they can already see how this structure might facilitate or frustrate pursuance of their personal priorities, and we discuss what adaptations might be possible on either side. For example, a person who wished to get much more writing practice than was allowed for in the timetable was invited to use 'Private Consultation Time' (described below) for this purpose. From these workshops and interviews we hope learners emerge with a clearer idea of what they want from the course and how to get it (within our necessarily imposed 'future-oriented' scheme). On the other hand, we tutors emerge ready to meet and take decisions about grouping the learners, assigning tutors to groups and planning the first lessons. One of the course-members (the one chosen to be student-representative) is present at our meeting to help in the important decision-making.[1]

The second essential element in our course-planning was to find a course-structure that would offer us and the learners a framework which was clear enough to satisfy our need for order, and yet which would be flexible enough to take into account the fact that we would not know much about our learners' needs until the course-members actually assembled.

The structure we developed consisted of three main timetabled elements:
1. Class Time.
2. Self-Access Time.
3. Private Consultation Time.

(There was a fourth element, the writing workshop, which was important in its own right but less important structurally; see below.)

These three elements were given equal time (90 minutes each in a 6 × 45 minute timetable) in the order in which they are listed above. To meet the demand for writing work and simultaneously to reduce the demand at any one time on the self-access facilities, the 'Self-Access Time' alternated daily with a writing workshop, so that half the participants (25 to 30 people) worked on their writing while the remainder used the self-access facilities. These comprised four rooms: a listening centre, a 'communication room', a 'language workroom', and a 'reading/writing room'. (The self-access facilities were also available at untimetabled times in the early afternoons and throughout the evenings and weekends.) There were also social activities each evening, if only films to watch.

The three timetabled elements were allotted equal time to reflect their equal potential, and also to avoid the implications of the bias in favour of class time. The intention was that the three modes of learning should complement and feed into each other. 'Class Time' was therefore used not only for familiar language learning activities but also as a training ground for decision-making. (For example, learners were asked as part of their 'homework' to study in groups available textbooks and select appropriate exercises to propose for use in class.) In this way Class Time was used to help learners learn how to make best use of Self-Access Time. Individual or small-group problems that could not be appropriately dealt with in class could be dealt with by the learners in Self-Access Time, or in Private Consultation Time, when time could be booked for private discussions with the tutors. Our monitoring of what learners chose to do in Self-Access Time and of what sorts of problems they brought to us in the Private Consultation Time fed into our decisions about the best ways of spending Class Time. It was particularly interesting that often the learners brought *learning* problems rather than *language* problems to these Private Consultations. For example, they wanted advice on how to deal with a listening comprehension problem after they had exhausted listening comprehension materials in our listening centre.

Halfway through the course we interviewed the learners again to discover whether they felt that their learning priorities (in terms either of language or of learning stratagies) had changed, whether they found current course activities profitable, and whether they felt the course was helping or hindering in any way their pursuance of their priorities. Thus we continued to involve learners in the decision-making, the action based on those decisions (although we tutors accepted the greater share of responsibility for the organization and implementation with respect to class time and to the course as a whole) and in the reviewing of both decisions and action. We were asking the learners to monitor continuously and evaluate before taking more decisions. The mid-course review did all this in a relatively formal way, but the decision-action-review cycle was of course more often handled informally, whenever tutors and learners discussed the selection of materials during Self-Access Time, for example.[2]

The third essential task in our planning was to think ahead to possible follow-up activities. We could not hope to make our 'future-oriented' course credible if we gave the future no thought ourselves. In practice, however, there was little we, as visiting tutors, could directly plan. We could only hope to persuade the Polish Academy of Science and the British Council of the potential value of making provision for learners who might be ready to make much greater demands on their facilities and supporting services. No persuasion was in fact needed, and it is good to be able to report progress in the development of year-round self-access facilities and the creation of an English 'club' for Polish Academy scientists wishing to continue their learning of English in a non-class setting.[3] With more money more could be done, of course, particularly for learners away from the main centres. We have also evolved a follow-up questionnaire (distributed several months after the end of the course) to help us find out what learners themselves are doing to build on the three-week course, and to get their advice for future courses and follow-up activities.

This Polish Academy of Science course has been described at some length (though still very sketchily) to reinforce the point that learner-training is a concept with implications that go well beyond the classroom. Of particular importance, I believe, are the implications for course structure, since without such changes 'learner-training' may ultimately lack credibility.[4] Also of obvious importance, however, are the implications for teacher-training, to which I will now return.

Further implications for teacher-training

Learner-training is not going to be done well by teachers who believe that, since only they have the necessary expertise, only they can be allowed a responsible role in the management of language learning. Teachers need to be trained to help learners develop their expertise as learners. Apart from the practical problems this involves, there is also the problem of what the teacher is to do with whatever pegagogic expertise he or she already has. How can we put our expertise in the business of language learning 'at the diposal of' the learners, so that it is neither imposed upon the learners nor devalued by them (in their new-found independence)? We call teachers 'masters' rather than 'servants', and yet, in the best traditions of domestic service, it is servants who have the expertise, as cooks or valets, and so on, and their problem is identical to the teacher's problem as I have outlined it: how to make their expertise available without imposing it (because that would be presumptuous), and without having it devalued (because then they would not get the rewards their expertise merited). It may help, then, (and it may be salutory for other reasons) to see teachers as 'servants' rather than as 'masters'. Of course, it is not in the best interests of domestic servants to train their employers to do without them, but in education the situation is different: in education, since courses are necessarily finite, there is an obvious need for teachers (servants with expertise) to help their learners become independent of them (to develop their own expertise as learners) so that they can continue to learn efficiently after the course is over. In order to achieve this, without either imposing their expertise or having it devalued, I suggest that teachers, in addition to their role as 'activities managers' in the classroom, need to accept the roles of:
1. 'ideas' people, ready with practical advice about language learning strategies and techniques, both for classroom and for outside use; and
2. 'rationale' people, ready to discuss language learning and justify their opinions and advice.

These are certainly the qualities we needed as tutors in Poland, especially during Self-Access and Private Consultation sessions. Somehow, we need to encourage the development of such qualities in teacher-training. At the same time we should explore the possibility that there might be a role for materials writers in all this.

Implications for materials

In the type of language learning described above, we are not going to want, I suggest, materials that pre-empt many of the decisions learners might be trained to make for themselves. We are going to need *learning* materials rather than *teaching* materials.

The most obvious and radical form for 'learning materials' to take would be that of a learners' guide to language learning. It is difficult to find many examples in publishers' lists at the time of writing, although there is work in progress. The research so far is by no means conclusive, but any such guide could profit from the work of Rubin, and of Naiman and his colleagues (see Rubin 1975, and Naiman et al. 1977), on the characteristics of the 'good language learner'. One possibility would be a guide to 'independent' language learning, for learners without teachers. Such a guide could include advice on how to establish one's priorities, advice on the most productive ways of exploiting native speakers and other useful people (like off-duty teachers), and also advice on the sorts of exercises a learner might devise for personal use, or perhaps for use with friends. It is too early to know what problems there might be in writing such a guide (although we can predict some, of course) but that should not prevent us from exploring the concept.

An alternative learners' guide might be produced for classroom language learning. Such a guide could include much of the same material as for independent learners, but would focus on how to exploit the classroom as a language learning situation without making it more difficult for other learners to do the same, and without antagonizing the teacher; on how to make full use of the teacher's expertise without becoming dependent upon it, and how to develop your own expertise as a learner. At its simplest this may involve suggesting the sorts of things learners might do to obtain repetitions of clarifications of things said in the classroom.

The difficulties with such learning materials as commercial publications might be considerable, if we aimed them primarily at the 'captive' learner (who, by definition, has not *chosen* to study a language) in our state school systems. It would seem more sensible to aim them at the 'non-captive' learner, the sort of learner who, in Britain, might buy a 'teach-yourself' book and/or voluntarily enrol in evening classes. The captive learner is unlikely to have the strength of motivation required to purchase an extra book, and may well resent it if such a thing is imposed by the teacher. For such learners something much less ambitious, probably locally produced, would seem preferable, something that could be highly specific and therefore more directly useful to poorly motivated learners. One possibility, in such circumstances, would be to make the production of a local guide a task for one generation of learners for the sake of future generations, who would then have the task of updating the guide as and when necessary.

Apart from 'learners' guides to language learning' there are other possibilities for learning materials. If, as I have suggested, the teacher needs to be an 'ideas' person and a 'rationale' person, there is a potential need for 'ideas' books and 'rationale' books.

Under the heading of 'ideas books' I suggest we should first include books full of ideas for content. In circumstances where there is easy access to 'raw' data in the target language (e.g. newspapers, magazines, etc.) it may be quite unhelpful to suggest that teachers should look to specialist language teaching publications for content ideas. But in the many settings where 'raw' data in the target language is not at all easily available there is little reason to complain if teachers resort to specialist publications. There are examples on publishers' lists already but there could be room for many more perhaps, if teachers demonstrated a willingness to use such collections of ideas rather than fully predetermined courses.

Another need is for ideas for activities. Although language drills are 'activites' under any general definition, what I have in mind here is more restricted in scope and biased towards relatively extended activities, for which we could still use plenty of ideas. Under this heading we could ask for more published simulations, for example, more role-play ideas, and more ideas for communication games (but see the British Council work at ELTI for major contributions in these areas[5]). Another need is for more ideas for what I call 'filler' activities, that is, short, easily interrupted activities that the quicker groups can use during group work to supplement extended activities, while waiting for other groups to catch up. In my experience such 'activities ideas materials' (for example the Canadian 'Gambits' materials by Keller and Taba Warner 1976) can be passed to learners for them to make their own selections (perhaps leaving the teacher to look after the organizational problems that arise, once the learners have made their decisions). Again the important point is that such materials will flourish on publishers' lists only if teachers are willing to use them in preference to fully worked out course books.

When we talk about 'rationale books' we are at our furthest from 'normal' teaching materials, but teachers trying to share management responsibilities with their learners will need not only 'ideas books' but also books that help them understand the thinking that lies behind their teaching and thus may help them explain it to their learners. Of course there are plenty of books about the general background to language teaching[6] but relatively few deal with the most recent ideas in a manner that is accessible to the majority of teachers. Again I am not advocating something new: rather I am trying to draw attention to and reinforce a change of emphasis that is already perceptible. It is a change that could perhaps be productively accelerated if its relation to a general change in the conception of teacher and learner responsibilities for the management of language learning was more widely accepted.

Summary and conclusions

I started with a question: 'What do we want teaching materials for?' I attempted to answer it through an analysis of what there is to be done in the management of language learning. This analysis, with its obvious complexity, carried implications for teacher-training that themselves led to the concept of 'learner-training' as a necessary development if learners are to share management responsibilities properly.

'Learner-training', I argued, has important structural implications for language courses, and this point was illustrated from my experience in Poland. This led to further implications for teacher-training, because of the difficulties it creates with the teacher's expertise, specifically with how the teacher can sensibly put his or her expertise at the disposal of the learners. From this I moved on to consider the implications for materials. Most obvious here was the change from 'teaching' materials to 'learning' materials, leading to support for the notion of 'learners' guides' to language learning, and for 'ideas' and 'rationale' books for teachers. Throughout this latter section I was concerned to point out that I was describing a change already in progress, and attempting to reinforce it and perhaps accelerate it.

Finally, I should return to my title. I hope I have dealt with both the straight and the ironic interpretations of my original question. If I have not dealt with them satisfactorily, I hope at least I have raised questions that others will be prompted to pursue. The most important point for me is that materials should be related to the conception of the whole of language teaching and learning as the cooperative management of language learning.

Notes

1 See also related work at CRAPEL (Nancy, France) and at the School for International Training (Brattleboro, Vermont).
2 Anyone who knows anything about teaching will know that reality cannot possibly have been so neat. It was not so neat, but this brief account, for all its over-simplification of what was organizationally very complex, will perhaps indicate what we were trying to do, and what we to some extent succeeded in doing. There are numerous practical problems involved in the introduction of such a course structure. We think we sorted out a lot of them, but many remain unsolved.
3 See Ruth Hok's 'Some thoughts on study circles and their potential for language teaching' in *TESOL Quarterly*, March 1980.
4 At the same time, those who cannot make radical structural changes should not be discouraged from trying 'piecemeal reforms' and finding ways of making them credible to their learners.
5 Of special interest are:
   a. the issue of *ELT Documents* devoted to *Games, Simulations and Role-Playing* (1977/1);
   b. the film *Communication Games in a Language Programme;*
   c. the book *ELT Guides No. 1* (Byrne and Rixon, eds.): *Communication Games*, published by NFER.
6 See Corder's *Introducing Applied Linguistics*, for an excellent example.

Appendix one

The twenty-seven point management analysis

Language teaching analysis
The role of the teacher and the role of the teaching materials

A. Goals

Materials may or may not embody a fixed set of aims and objectives. Some materials serve highly specific aims and are difficult to use for other purposes. Other materials are much more flexible and consist of ideas that can be exploited for a variety of purposes. The teaching, whether helped by the materials or not, must reflect the relative weightings assigned to the aims, and also attend to the sequencing of objectives.
1 Long-term aims.
2 Short-term objectives.
3 Relative weightings.
4 Sequencing.

B. Content

What we teach is of course the 'language' but this needs a lot of further analysis, because we may also want to teach (and/or learners may want to learn) features of target language discourse, and features of the target culture. Also we may include subject-matter from other disciplines (as in ESP). Some of the subject-matter we use may be there just to carry the language practice, and not to be learned (e.g. conversation topics, or the content of drill items).
5 Target language content.
6 Target discourse content.
7 Target cultural content.
8 Target subject-matter content.
9 'Carrier' content.

What we teach may also include selected learning strategies and techniques, because we may want our learners to be *better learners* after whatever course we are giving them, so that they can carry on learning effectively, perhaps even without a teacher.
10 Target learning strategies to be developed.
11 Target learning techniques to be developed.

What we teach may also include attitudes, in the sense that we would hope our learners would develop positive attitudes towards both their current learning and their future use and learning of the target language, etc.
12 Target attitudes.

Lastly, after selection, matters of weighting, of timing, and of sequencing have to be attended to.
13 Assignment of weightings to all elements of content.
14 Assignment of time to all elements of content.
15 Sequencing.

C. Method

Determining how all the various elements of content are to be learned is obviously a complex matter and involves thinking about the learning processes to be employed, the activities or tasks that will draw upon those processes, and about how to relate content, in all its complexity, to the activities or tasks. Then the actual performance of the activities or tasks has itself to be thought about: the amount of time needed, the nature of the groupings, etc.

16 Selection of learning processes to be employed/exploited.
17 Selection of learning activities/tasks to be employed/exploited.
18 Allocation of time.
19 Allocation of people.
20 Allocation of space.
21 Sequencing.

D. Guidance

'Guidance' refers to information about the goals of the course, the target content, and about the learners' mastery of it all. It will also cover instructions about learning activities and tasks.

22 Explanations/descriptions of goals, all types of content, and of learning activities/tasks.
23 Cues/hints to draw attention to criterial features of target content.
24 Immediate yes/no feedback (knowledge of results).
25 Evaluations of learner progress (including tests).
26 The timing of 22–25 (exactly when to do what).
27 The setting of standards of performance for all aspects of target content, and for classroom behaviour in general.

Appendix two

```
++ very high    – low           Name ........................
 + high         – – very low
 0 medium                       Date ........................
```

Needs	Frequency	Importance	Proficiency required	Proficiency now	Confidence

Need— What do you use English for? What do you do with English?
Frequency— How often do you have this particular need?
Importance— How important is it to you (professionally and/or personally) to perform well in this situation?
Proficiency required— How good is it necessary to be *at English* to perform well in the situation?
Proficiency now— How good are you already?
Confidence— How sure are you about your judgement of your own proficiency?

For example:

You may need to be able to write scientific papers in English. Perhaps this does not happen very often (FREQUENCY − −), but it is very important when it does (IMPORTANCE + +). You may feel that it is necessary to be very good at English (PROFICIENCY REQUIRED + +) in order to write scientific papers, and you may feel that, at present, your own proficiency (for writing) is much lower (PROFICIENCY NOW −). You may be absolutely certain of this (CONFIDENCE + +) because you have just been trying to write a paper and have found it extremely difficult.

	++ very high − low				
	+ high − − very low		Name		
	0 medium		Date		
Learning Activity/strategy/technique		Frequency	Enjoyment	Usefulness	Efficiency
_____		_____			_____
_____					
_____		_____			

What do you actually *do* in order to learn?
Frequency— How often do you do it?
Enjoyment—How much do you enjoy/like doing it?
Usefulness— How much does it help you?
Efficiency— How good/efficient are you at doing it?
           Are you getting the most out of the activity?

(Originally published in Volume 36/1, 1981)

The underlying message of Allwright's article, as well as the challenge implicit in its title, must have caused a few moments of questioning around the publishing houses. ELT publishing has been a growth area for twenty years or more and the combination of calls like Allwright's for more learner-centredness, along with the move towards the selection and exploitation of authentic materials, supported by ever-more-sophisticated photocopiers, has been a legitimate cause for concern to publishers and authors alike. For better or worse, however, the textbook has been a part of educational tradition since the age of mass printing began, and teachers and learners throughout the world have come to rely on it. Better, argues Robert O'Neill, to fall in with the consequences of this tradition, and to choose a textbook which provides a useful starting point, than to flounder around inexpertly trying to produce poorly conceived materials of your own on pieces of paper which learners are only too likely to lose.

Why use textbooks?
Robert O'Neill

This article is not designed as a direct reply to Dick Allwright's paper 'What do we want teaching materials for?' There are two basic reasons why it is not. First, I think it perfectly possible to agree with many of his assumptions and still believe in the use of textbooks for a variety of purposes. For example, I agree that we should not attempt to predict the learning process of the learner in the way that some textbooks appear to do. But I shall argue that this is by no means typical of all textbooks. I can also agree that some textbooks promote over-involvement of the teacher and under-involvement of the learner. But this does not mean I think it is impossible for textbooks to be designed to promote loosely co-operative styles of learning in which the learner often takes the initiative in deciding what is the best step forward. Indeed, I believe that a number of contemporary textbooks *are* designed in this way. I can also agree that in some cases it may well be best to begin with a clean slate and rely only on materials designed after contact with a particular group and close analysis of their needs. However, I think the situations in which this is possible are far less common than Dick Allwright appears to believe. Certainly they are far less common than the particular circumstances he argues from. Relatively few groups are sponsored by organizations like the Polish Academy of Sciences, or have the favour of a British Council subsidy. Teachers and classes are often thrown together in schools or institutions in which there is relatively little time for careful analysis of each group's needs. In such cases it is often far more practical to choose from the considerable and growing variety of published textbooks. I shall argue in any case that often there is far more similarity between the needs of apparently different groups that we realize.

My second basic reason for not designing this article as a direct reply to Dick Allwright's question 'What do we want teaching materials for?' (and by teaching materials he means textbooks) is that I think it is far better to set out the positive advantages of using textbooks, as I see them, and to allow readers to judge for themselves between our two arguments.

About two years ago I happened to be teaching English in a German shipyard. It was an intensive course of about six hours a day, over six months, for a small group of German technicians who were expecting to train a contingent of Iranians how to maintain and repair six submarines undergoing construction in the yard. The Iranian government had stipulated that all this instruction between the Germans and the Iranians was to be done in English. (This was a few months before the downfall of the Shah.) I was only one of the teachers; each of us did an intensive three-week stint and then handed over to another teacher. When my turn to hand over came, I went over with my replacement what I had done. He was a young, intelligent teacher who had just finished a course in applied linguistics at a British university. 'My God, you haven't been using a textbook, have you?' he said when he saw my notes. It was as if one doctor trained in the latest medical techniques had discovered that a colleague had been bleeding one of his patients with leeches. Indeed, I had been using a textbook for one central part of the course. My replacement believed that this was inherently wrong. His objections boiled down to the fact that he didn't want the people he was teaching to know what he was going to do the next day. 'It takes away the element of suspense. Besides, I don't like using other people's material. It's so uncreative!' he exclaimed. His attitude, although extreme, was not untypical. There are many teachers who share his views almost as an article of faith. A great deal of their training reinforces this attitude. For example, it seems to be widely believed by candidates taking the RSA Certificate for Teachers of English as a Foreign Language that they dare not teach from a textbook in the practical lessons they are required to give before an examiner. If they do, they will almost automatically be failed. Textbooks are 'out', home-produced materials are 'in'.

I began to think about my own reasons for using textbooks on that course in Germany and on others. I was, in fact, using more than one. There was a technology-oriented textbook consisting mainly of short texts describing basic workshop procedures and practices. There was another 'general coursebook' at about intermediate level, which I used for teaching or re-teaching the basic grammar almost everyone in the group needed (even though some described themselves as 'advanced'). What were my reasons?

1 A great deal of the material, although not specifically designed for this group, was very suitable for their needs.
2 The two textbooks made it possible for the group to look ahead to what we were going to do or to look back at what we had done.
3 The textbooks provided materials which were well-presented, which could be replaced by me or by someone else only at great cost in terms both of money and of my own time.
4 The textbooks allowed me to adapt and improvise while I was teaching. Each reason, however banal, needs some additional clarification. Let me go through them again and enlarge upon them.

My replacement at the shipyard believed almost as an article of faith that any materials that were commercially available, as these were, could not possibly be suitable for this particular group since they had not been specifically designed for it. 'Only materials arising out of experience teaching the particular group can be valid for it,' he stated dogmatically. 'Whoever wrote these books has never seen this group or the inside of a shipyard. This group has its own needs and we must provide materials specifically designed for those needs.' But I and the teacher who had preceded me had not selected any old materials. We had spent several days scouring bookshops in London, looking for things we thought might be suitable. After all, there are a number of things almost any group studying technical English will have in common. Although one group's needs diverge at various points from another's, there is often a common core of needs shared by a variety of groups in different places studying under different conditions at different times. For example, the technical processes described in the textbook on workshop practices introduced a great deal of basic technical vocabulary describing many of the machines and tools shipyard technicians use. More importantly, we did not expect the book to provide us with the exact instructions our technicians would later give to their Iranian apprentices. It is a dangerous delusion to suppose that textbooks can do this and it is quite false to believe it is necessary for textbooks to do so in order to be useful. What this particular textbook could and did provide us with were examples of instructions which our learners could adapt and transfer to their particular uses. In other words, it provided us with a grammatical and functional framework within which we could work. It is nonsense to argue that this framework is never the same from one group to another even though the ultimate, specific uses two groups may make of the language may differ. The framework is as much a result of the language itself as it is of the learner's needs. Are there many learners, for example, who do not need to learn how to explain cause and effect, to make requests, to suggest things, to ask for other people's opinions about things and to give their own, or to make basic tense distinctions such as past and present? Is there any significant use of English which escapes the need to express modal distinctions such as 'You can do it', 'You should do it' and 'You must do it'? In other words, do not almost all learners at elementary, intermediate, and even many advanced levels have to learn the same basic grammatical and functional framework in order to make use of the language in their own particular ways? Of course there are many ways of illustrating and exemplifying this framework so that different learners will see its relevance to their purposes, but this hardly means that the same textbook cannot be used successfully for a wide range of different groups. Almost always a textbook can be found which will provide the core language which is necessary and useful for a group whose needs may at first sight seem unique. Groups vary enormously in their composition and level. They vary even more, perhaps, in what will interest them and sustain their motivation. But there is an immense variety of textbooks to draw upon.

The second basic reason for using the particular textbooks we had chosen was that the books made it possible for learners who, for various reasons, had missed lessons to catch up. They also made it possible for the class to prepare in advance for lessons. There is a curious, sometimes submerged, but still formidable school of thought in the language teaching profession that would if possible discourage learners from doing this. As my replacement said, he didn't want the group to know what he was going to do because it removed the element of surprise. I sympathize with the desire to provide surprises in his lessons: surprise is useful and necessary in all aspects of life. But I do not sympathize with his desire to prevent learners from making the fullest possible use of their resources for staying in touch with the language. The chance to look ahead to future lessons and spend time preparing oneself for them is welcome to many learners. This is particularly so when the learner is having trouble staying in touch with the average level of the group he or she is in. In any case, if textbooks are used for the purpose for which they are best suited—that of providing a core framework, but not everything that happens within it—there are many other ways of providing the useful element of surprise and suspense. This is not to argue that textbooks themselves cannot and should not be designed so that at least one part of the book relies on 'unseen' material. For example, in a book of twenty-six-page units, one page could be devoted to a continuous story running through the book. This text could be designed to reinforce the language presented in the other five pages of the unit. However, the story need not actually appear on the sixth page. That page could instead be used for questions and exercises based on material provided only in the teacher's book. The teacher could read out or play a tape of the story when and as necessary, and the class would never see the full text of the story in their books.

The third reason for using the textbooks we had selected for the course was their appearance and the quality of their presentation. This is still one of the least discussed reasons for using textbooks. I do not mean that textbooks should be glossy, glittering products in full colour, packaged and sold like deodorants or American automobiles. But neither should they, simply because they must be functional in several senses of the word, look like one of those catalogues you sometimes see in funeral parlours advertising coffins or cremation urns. Home-made materials tend to get shabby very quickly and, even in these days of high-quality photocopiers and word-processors, cause enormous production and storage problems. Even though we had access at the shipyard to excellent photocopying and duplication facilities, we found we could not use them as often as we needed to without causing problems and tension with other people in the yard who needed the same facilities for purposes which they saw as far more pressing and immediate than ours. Even after a certain time had been set aside each day for us, we ran into the simple problem of expense. It costs far more to photocopy 100 pages of your own material than it does to buy 200 pages bound together in a book. This has been discovered not only in places where such copying facilities are scarce or under great pressure from other users, but in language schools on the south coast of England for example, which have generously provided such facilities and practically unlimited access to them for teachers. The cost has often turned out to be staggering, not only in paper and other direct copying costs but in service calls each time the copier breaks down. Books are good value for money simply in terms of paper alone. The fact that they are bound means they are easy to carry and to look at where and when the learner wants to, on buses, at meal times, in parks, while waiting for appointments, etc. No other medium is as easy to use as a book.

There is beyond this something enormously valuable and important about the feel and size and shape of a book. It can be argued that my sentiments here are hardly objective, since I depend largely for my income upon other people sharing my views. But I had these sentiments about books long before I got involved in writing or producing them. Sheets of paper, particularly A4 paper, issued in batches to learners throughout a course have a terrible habit of getting lost and confused, and are difficult to carry about.

The fourth and final reason has been hinted at earlier. But it needs greater elaboration. In my opinion it is important that textbooks should be so designed and organized that a great deal of improvisation and adaptation by both teacher and class is possible. Below I shall give an example of such improvisation and adaptation, and I shall try to explain why it is necessary. But before I do so, I want to consider why such a statement, on the surface unsurprising and unexceptional, runs counter to at least one concept of language teaching that is still dominant and informs both teacher-training and coursebook-design in various places. I shall call this concept or view of language-teaching and coursebook-design the 'grand-master' school of thought. According to this view the teacher must know exactly what will happen in the lesson and have planned for it. Anything that occurs in the lesson does so because it is part of the teacher's plan (or perhaps the plan of some other person or body, such as a textbook author or the teacher's employer). Objectives are clearly stated and adhered to. Although certain alternative possibilities of attaining them may have been envisaged in the 'plan', they are still foreseen and calculated.

There are many examples of this school of thought, although it is not always articulated so explicitly. There are concepts of teacher-training which begin with an idealized model of the 'good teacher' (the teacher that will carry out the aims of a particular methodology, organization, or textbook), and then attempt to mould all trainees to this model. There are language institutes. some of them very prestigious, which issue elaborate materials to their teachers with carefully detailed goals and sub-goals for each lesson. Each lesson moves from carefully planned 'input' stages to equally carefully planned 'output' phases (the computer terms are no accident), such as pre-planned drill or exercise. Such lesson plans may even allow for 'free' stages, but usually strict time limits are set and these 'outputs' are 'free' only in the sense that they are slightly less pre-planned than the other phases of the lesson.

What, however, do I propose as an alternative model of coursebook-design, teacher-training, and language-teaching? Put briefly, perhaps even simplistically, the alternative view begins with the simple belief that there can be no model of an ideal teacher, or lesson, or learner (or textbook). Since people are diverse in their personalities, inherent learning strategies and rhythms, such a thing as a teacher-training programme must seek not to mould all teachers according to a preconceived notion of what teachers should be, but must try to build on the individual and differing strengths of each teacher so as to make the maximum effective use of that teacher's qualities. This clearly has implications for both textbook-design and teaching methodology. No textbook can expect to appeal to all teachers or learners at a particular level. There is a basic need for choice and variety, not only in teaching-style and learning opportunity but also in the style and approach of materials available. Teachers have not 'failed' because they get on well with one group of learners but not another. Neither is a textbook necessarily unsuccessful if its style and content do not please some learners at the level at which it is aimed.

However, there are many ways of designing textbooks so that they can be used by a variety of learners with a variety of ultimate goals, and so they can be taught by a variety of teachers with a variety of teaching styles. For example, units of material can be designed so that they allow a choice of basic objectives. There might be for instance a choice of at least three such objectives for the unit. Although different, they can be related.

1 Eliciting opinions through questions like 'What do you think we should do?' 'How do you think we can do it?' 'What do you think will happen if we do it this way?'
2 Analysis of indirect questions in other contexts: 'Do you know if we can . . . ?' 'Can you tell me what is the best way to . . . ?' etc.
3 Meaning and use of contrasting stress patterns as in 'What do YOU think we should do?' and 'What do you think we should DO?'

The unit designed around these objectives might include, for example, a short dialogue, a text, and a series of structure and intonation exercises. In the dialogue two people might propose and discuss solutions to problems. The strongly functional elements of the materials—eliciting someone else's opinion—occurs in the dialogue. The text narrates the results of their decision and what they did, as well as an alternative problem for the class to discuss and try to solve. These first two components would contain other points of focus and activity as well as those mentioned above. For example, the dialogue would not only present the kinds of questions used to elicit other people's opinions; it would also be suitable for stylistic transformation: a very informal style may be used by the speakers (who seem to be very friendly with each other); then changes can be made to introduce a more formal style (such as the style one would use at an official meeting or with one's superior at work). The short text could be used for reading comprehension as well as for discussion. The exercises in intonation and in transforming direct into indirect questions would serve two functions: besides practising features of intonation and grammar, they could be done independently by the class while the teacher reflected during the lesson on how best to continue and perhaps found other material, either in the textbook or from some other source, which would be relevant continuation. There are objectives in the lesson. The teacher's notes would suggest various ways of using the material. But it would be recognized from the outset that the lesson might develop in a number of ways which could not be predicted exactly beforehand.

Such ideas are by no means novel or original. It is possible to execute them even with many conventional textbooks. Indeed, the very form of a book makes this possible. No other medium is quite as easily handled in this way as is a book. You can jump from one part of a book to another, glancing first at one page then at another as you remind yourself of what is in it (assuming you are familiar with it, as teachers should be with the textbooks they use) in a way you cannot with a video cassette or with a set of loose materials given out in dribs and drabs but never fully surveyed by the class. What is more, if the group using the book is introduced to it in outline and briefly taken through it before the material is formally taught, they can influence selection and development of the material far more than they can with heavily media-dependent materials. Certainly, whatever the other advantages of more modern ways of presenting material, such as video, it is impossible to carry them around in your pocket, look at them as you go home or to work in a bus or train, and difficult to leaf backwards and forwards in them to see what has been or will be done.

This is not an argument against using such modern aids as video or audio recordings. It is an argument for the textbook, which may be supplemented by these modern aids but not supplanted by them. If that happens, I suspect it will not be long before the textbook is re-invented. We need such creative tools because language learning itself is nothing if it is not creative. Unless learners learn how to say what only they want to say in lessons, unless they begin to acquire the generative tools of language to do this, and unless teachers are able to deal with the unexpected, the unpredictable, and the at times irrelevant turns of spontaneous interaction in the classroom, what is taught will be not language but language-like behaviour.[1] We need objectives in our lessons and materials, and we also need flexibility and improvisation so that we can use the creative accidents that occur regularly in lessons and not smother them with exhaustive (and exhausting) pre-determined plans.

It might also seem from what I have said that those materials put together by teachers or authors outside the commercial process of publication have no place in teaching. I am thinking of all the different kinds of materials teachers write or assemble in direct response to the needs of a class. My argument is not that these have no place. On the contrary, they are an essential part of the process through which new textbooks and published materials get written. It is a process that often begins with a nibble, which becomes a bite and then a gulp. At first the user of a textbook—the teacher—becomes dissatisfied with some aspect of it and replaces parts of it with his or her own material. It may be one or two reading texts, or the questions in the book about a text, or some of the drills. Gradually, however, more and more of the published textbook is abandoned and replaced by materials the teacher devises or finds elsewhere and regards as more suitable or relevant. This is how I started writing textbooks. Sometimes, of course, the process is more radical and less gradual. A teacher or a group of teachers set out to create what is in essence a new textbook because nothing on the market seems suitable. In both cases what one usually ends up with is a new textbook. It is the classic process described by Kuhn in *The Structure of Scientific Revolutions*, the paradigmatic process through which one theory or concept replaces another.

My colleague in the German shipyard was scornful of any materials not written directly for a group by someone with direct knowledge of that group. The assumption is that each group is so unique that its needs cannot possibly be met by material developed to meet the needs of another group. I believe this is a false assumption for two major reasons. First, the differences tend to obscure the similarities, which are great. These similarities, include such things as the common need to possess enough of the generative equipment of a language to use that language as an independent, creative tool and the fact that the basic functional needs of one group often differ from those of another only in their specific applications, and these can hardly ever be foreseen or predicted by anyone. They arise spontaneously and must be met spontaneously by the learner and the learner alone. By this I mean that although we can predict that a learner will have to request things, explain how things work, make time and tense distinctions, offer and refuse to do things, understand deictic meaning, etc., we cannot predict the exact utterances the learner will have to generate, and we should never pretend that we can, except in certain very limited cases.[2] The second reason is that, particularly today, with the great and growing variety of materials devised all over the world to teach English to different groups, there is usually *something* we can find to provide the core teaching material for the group we regard as so unique and utterly different from any other. I have referred to both these things earlier and I shall end by repeating them. Textbooks can at best provide only a base or a core of materials. They are the jumping-off point for teacher and class. They should not aim to be more than that. A great deal of the most important work in a class may start with the textbook but end outside it, an improvisation and adaptation, in spontaneous interaction in the class, and development from that interaction. Textbooks, if they are to provide anything at all, can only provide the props or framework within which much of this activity occurs. Textbooks, like any other medium, have inherent limitations. The authors of textbooks must make it clear what those limitations are; for example, whether or not the textbook is intended as a self-study tool or aid, or for classroom use by a teacher and a group of learners. Most of all, the authors and creators of textbooks must abandon any claim that their products are anything more than the basic tools I have spoken of. Since language is an instrument for generating what people need and want to say spontaneously, a great deal must depend on spontaneous, creative interaction in the classroom. Textbooks can help to bring this about, and a great deal in their design can be improved in order to do this. If that creative interaction does not occur, textbooks are simply pages of dead, inert written symbols and teaching is no more than a symbolic ritual, devoid of any real significance for what is going on outside the classroom.

Notes

1 The term 'language-like behaviour' has been used by David Wilkins and others to describe what occurs when the learner of a language never acquires the basic tools of grammar.
2 There are of course examples of very stereotyped language, such as that used by Air Traffic Controllers or computer instructions.

(*Originally published in Volume 36/2, 1982*)

O'Neill's paper concludes with a plea to textbook writers to be honest about the limitations of their materials, a plea which could also be directed, with some justification, at the writers and publishers of computer software packages and video language courses. The outlay on both hardware and software is great in these fields, and the dangers of failure even greater when one considers the problems which inevitably arise whenever education concerns itself with technology. The lesson of language laboratories has not been lost on teachers and administrators.

It is appropriate, then, ten years after the appearance of the first 'blockbuster' video courses, that Iain MacWilliam should question the value of video as a medium in such a thoroughgoing way in his article. In a field which is particularly susceptible to technique-level articles, he has chosen to raise fundamental questions about the value of video as an aid to language learning. His conclusions about, for example, the optimum effective length of time for viewing and learning, will surprise all but the most experienced and well-read exponents of educational television.

Video and language comprehension
Iain MacWilliam

There is currently a lot being written about video in the language classroom, but most of it seems anecdotal or takes the form of generalized observation. Doubtless the '1,001 Uses of Video' compendium will always need updating, but there can be very few practising (and journal-reading) teachers with access to video who still need to be told that 'video places language in context' or who are as yet unaware of the virtues of the freeze-frame button. With one or two notable exceptions, no one appears to be considering one of the main questions arising from the widespread adoption of video as a language teaching aid, namely: *How effective is the video medium as a source of language input to the foreign-language learner?*

The question 'how effective', of course, presupposes a qualitative measure of some sort, and one of the more obvious explanations of the omission noted here is that there has been practically no recorded research into language learning from video. It may be that the extensive use of off-air broadcasts has inhibited would-be investigators; copyright law makes no concession even to the most altruistic pirates. On the other hand, the ELT profession, and in particular its British branch, has tended to eschew empirical research into the effectiveness of approaches and methodologies, preferring instead to rely on the solipsism known as 'construct validity' for its measure of pedagogical approval. The absence of data, then, is hardly a novel phenomenon in English language teaching.

Fortunately, the use of video for educational purposes has not been confined to those working in language teaching, and the purpose of this article is to consider some of the relevant research findings and observations from other fields, notably educational broadcasting and communication studies. The fact that these largely derive from first-language contexts need not wholly detract from their importance to the domain of second-language learning. The principal concern is with the use of 'authentic' video material—in the main, recorded television—rather than with materials specially contrived for language-teaching purposes or with the use of video for the recording and monitoring of student and teacher performance.

Central to any consideration of language input is the notion of *comprehensibility*. In the sense that Krashen and others have used the term, comprehensibility of input is usually seen to depend on various language-based criteria such as communicative complexity, discourse type, and so forth. The concept of 'relative difficulty' for the learner is usually described in linguistic terms, quite rightly if language is the goal of the learner. But the question arises: *Does video, particularly in its authentic form, introduce any additional factors which may, in some way, inhibit its usefulness as a language-teaching aid?* There is some reason to believe that this indeed may be so.

In a recent article, Eunice Fisher of the Open University called into question some of the assumptions made about television as a pedagogical aid to the (first) language development of young children. In particular, she focused on the relationship between the kinds of information presented simultaneously through the aural and visual channels, posing the following question:

> ... let us imagine a small child who, for reasons which may be social, cognitive or a combination of both, is not a competent language user. If such a child watches a programme in which the speech is largely redundant ... will this child
> (i) process the visual and linguistic information, achieve some sort of cognitive matching and strengthen any shortcomings in the linguistic mode by using visual information, or
> (ii) avoid the effort of processing linguistically ... and concentrate on making sense of the visual information?
>
> (Fisher 1984:88)

Fisher, who labels these 'complement' and 'conflict' processing models respectively, goes on to cite a number of authorities who tend to support the view that younger children, i.e. less competent language users, do find conflict between information presented in linguistic and visual modes. Donaldson's view that 'it is the linguistic mode which is ignored where a choice must be made' (Donaldson 1976) is one that finds resonances in the work of others working in educational television research both in Britain and the USA (see Vernon 1953; Mielke and Chen in Howe 1983).

The similarity implied here between adult second-language learning and first-language acquisition among young children is, of course, open to question, but the analogy is one frequently invoked (or implied) by those working in other areas of linguistic analysis, notably interlanguage studies and second-language acquisition. However, the problem of competing aural and visual channels does not appear to be one confined to young children.

In a series of experiments on comprehension across different media (Trenaman 1967), some evidence emerged that increased visual movement on television programmes had a detrimental effect on the comprehension scores of test subjects classed in the 'unskilled' job category (for which, perhaps, read 'restricted code user'?). More recently, in a series of experiments at North-East London Polytechnic (Gunter 1980), an attempt was made to measure the retention of information presented in three types of television news broadcast.[1] In these experiments, three different visual formats were compared:

—'talking head'—newsreader only
—'talking head' interspersed with still pictures
—'talking head' introduction followed by motion pictures.

In all formats the spoken commentary remained the same. The research finding was that there was a greater loss of information by test subjects from news stories accompanied by picture materials than from those presented by the newsreader alone. A similar conclusion, that the visible presence of a speaker enhanced aural comprehension, had also been reached by the psychologist M. D. Vernon in a series of experiments conducted in the early 1950s (Vernon 1953).

The preoccupation of all of the researchers quoted here has been with the loss of information presented via the aural channel, i.e. spoken language, when accompanied by visual information of a non-linguistic nature. There is no suggestion that paralinguistic features, for example, or subtitling[2] are anything but supportive of speech comprehension. The general position taken here is the one taken by Severin in what he termed 'Cue Summation Theory', which states:

> Irrelevant cues in the audio or visual channels will cause a loss of learning from either channel, but additional cues in either channel will lead to greater overall learning.
>
> (Severin 1968)

More or less the same conclusion was reached by those engaged in the Schools Television Research Project (reported on in Kemelfield 1969).

What are the implications of such research for the use of video in foreign-language teaching? Certainly it will make one approach with caution some of the larger claims made on behalf of the medium, such as 'The video stimulus also greatly improves the level of retention of teaching items in the students' memories' (RSA 1980:41–2). More particularly, it might prompt a re-examination of the use of certain types of video, especially those deriving from off-air sources. For example, widespread use is made of documentary-style programmes in which voice-over commentary is often the major auditory input. Indeed, probably on account of their topic-relatedness and generally 'serious' content, it may well be that such programmes represent a high proportion of video stock in current use. It is true that this kind of material is often valued for its 'information' content rather than linguistic content, or as a stimulus to post-viewing discussion activities and the like, but very often it is presented as listening or 'viewing comprehension' input. For all but the more advanced learners this may result in a lot of viewing and little comprehension—at a linguistic level, at least. On the other hand, the more convergent audio and visual strands of something like the soap opera *Coronation Street*, though less obviously 'respectable' in terms of content, may prove more supportive to the English language learner.[3]

A problem related to that which has been described above concerns video text length. In a fairly recent survey of video use in EFL establishments (McKnight 1981), it was found that the average length of classroom viewing sessions was between thirty and forty minutes, and that hardly any were less than twenty minutes in length, even for elementary-level groups. Since broadcast television itself rarely works in units of less than half an hour, these figures are hardly surprising. More recently, there have been calls for shorter units for language-teaching exploitation (Potter 1982; Pilbeam 1984) and, increasingly, ELT-specific materials have reflected this need (see Macmillan's *Video English*, for example). The main reason for this appears to have been a desire for material which could be more intensively exploited. But there is another good reason for working with shorter video texts.

In an earlier series of experiments on the retention of information from broadcast television (Vernon 1953), it was found that there was a steep decline in the amount of aural information retained during the course of a half-hour transmission, and, from this research, it was felt that between six and seven minutes was the optimal maximum for native-speaking viewers. One can only assume that, if the main aim in using a video text in the foreign-language classroom is language comprehension (and it may not be, of course), anything longer that this will be a relatively less efficient use of the resource by the learner.

If the research and observation noted here do have relevance for foreign-language learning, then clearly the video resources presently available are far from adequate. The current choice of 'authentic' television or simplified series leaves a very large gap, especially for the intermediate range of learners. In the same way that management-training interests have devised materials specifically to meet their training needs—and have not, say, relied on scenes from *Dallas* to illustrate boardroom communication strategies—it should be possible for the language-teaching profession to create video which is both authentic, in the sense that the language is not artificially constrained, and, at the same time, amenable to exploitation for language-teaching purposes. Quite apart from the practical advantages to be won, it would go some way to dispelling the notion that anything appearing on a video screen must be 'good television'. However, if alternative criteria of design and use are to be adopted, they should be based on an understanding of the salient characteristics of the medium and of the learner's response to it, and little progress will be made towards either of these aims without a more rigorous, research-based approach to its use.

Notes

1 It may be that television news presents a special problem for viewers. In a study by Nordstreng (quoted in Glasgow Media Group 1976), just under half of a sample of Finnish viewers questioned about the content of television news programmes immediately after they had

been transmitted could not remember a single item of news, even when given helpful prompts by the questioners!
2 An interesting account of a study concerning one particular use of subtitles is to be found in Lambert *et al.* (1981).
3 For some fascinating insight into the relationship between sound and vision in British soap operas, see Watt (1983).

(Originally published in Volume 40/2, 1986)

Once again, there are messages in this paper for publishers and materials writers. One sign that not all messages of this sort fall on stony ground is the increased interest in *learner-training*, (cf. Allwright above) displayed in textbooks and supplementary materials published during the eighties. The term itself is relatively new, and there is some evidence that it means different things to different people. At one extreme, it may simply mean the process of training learners to make more effective use of the tools they use to learn with. Seen in this sense, Underhill's *Use Your Dictionary* and Shepherd *et al.*'s *Ways to Grammar* are early examples of study skills-related training for learners. At the other end of the spectrum are tasks and exercises which increase learners' understanding of the processes by which they learn, thereby encouraging them to reflect more on their own learning practices. Both types of learner-training have evolved in response to calls for more learner-centredness in our classrooms, but it is the latter type which Anita Wenden writes about in her paper. The 'metacognitive strategies' which she describes are certainly of interest to teacher trainers as well as teachers.

Helping language learners think about learning

Anita Wenden

Introduction

'. . . Talking and reading English are the key. I took two courses in business—micro-economics and accounting. That was a very good experience. I read, studied, listened to lectures and took notes in English. I thought about the meaning of the subject. I did not think about the language. I was trying to learn English the natural way . . .' *Miguel*

'. . . In Korea, I studied English ten years . . . We learned a lot of grammar, so when I came to the United States, I knew grammar and I could read, but I couldn't speak easily. But grammar background is important. Without it, you will be limited. You should also take a class. You are pushed to learn and it's systematic . . .' *Eun Jin*

'. . . I think the improvement of language is due to some inheritance . . . the most important thing is our personal ability to learn English. In my case, I have no personal ablility, so I think it will take a long time . . . there is no good way to speed up my learning . . .' *Ryuichi*

'. . . My theory was similar to the theory I had working with adults. They become like children when they're in school . . . they regress. I decided when it happened to me I wouldn't worry. But still it wasn't easy to endure and live through it . . .' *Cida*

The above statements are representative of the beliefs of a group of 34 language learners, who were interviewed about how they 'self-directed' their language learning. Most of the learners interviewed held one or a mix of the following beliefs:

Learn the natural way

This is Miguel's belief. He believes that language is best learned by using it to communicate in the social contexts in which he finds himself. In these situations, he does not usually think about language form or the purposes of learning. His emphasis is on communication. Moreover, he feels he should avail himself of every opportunity to practise and not care about making mistakes. As much as possible, he avoids thinking in his native language. For Miguel and other learners like him, language learning is an unconscious process.

Learn systematically

This is Eun Jin's belief. She believes language should be learned 'step by step . . . from easy to hard', and so advises taking formal language courses. Learning step by step also means starting with grammar and vocabulary— the building blocks of the language. In other words, to learn a language means to learn about it—to understand how it works. Using the language to communicate is secondary. Of course, she does not discount the importance of practice, but her emphasis is on learning— practising will help her to remember the grammar and vocabulary she has learned. Finally Eun Jin, and other learners like her, believe that language learning is a conscious process. Therefore they advise always being open to 'receive' information about the language. They emphasize the importance of being mentally active— manipulating or transforming in some way new words, sounds, structures in order to understand and remember them.

Personal factors are important

Both Ryuichi and Cida hold this belief. It is their view that certain personal characteristics can facilitate or inhibit language learning. Ryuichi points to the influence of language aptitude and Cida to self-concept. Other learners referred to their feelings, preferred way of learning, personality, or social role.

The interviews also indicated that these beliefs were reflected in the learners' approach to language learning, that is (1) the kinds of strategies[1] they used; (2) what they attended to; (3) the criteria they used to evaluate the effectiveness of learning activities and social context which gave them the opportunity to use/practise the language; and (4) where they concentrated the use of their strategies (Wenden 1984). In other words, in the case of these learners, their beliefs seemed to work as a sort of logic determining—consciously or unconsciously —what they did to help themselves learn English.

Assuming that these learners are typical, we may expect that most language learners will hold some beliefs about language learning, although they may not always be explicit or easily available to awareness. If this is so, teachers should try to discover what their students' beliefs are and how they may influence their approach to language learning. It is also important that the students themselves be given opportunities to 'think about their learning process' so that they may become aware of their own beliefs and how these beliefs can influence what they do to learn. Finally, they should be exposed to alternative views.

The purpose of this article is to describe a unit of eight modules designed with these general objectives in mind. The modules are also intended to provide students with opportunities to develop facility in their aural/oral skills. In other words, they illustrate how helping our students learn how to *learn* a second language can be integrated with helping them learn how to *use* it. The objectives, resources, and procedures that constitute each module will be described. Then, the potential value of such activities for second-language students will be discussed.

Module (1)

Beliefs (an oral activity)

Objectives

– Students consider the origins and function of beliefs.
– They examine their beliefs about succeeding in college.

Procedure

1 Divide students into groups of three.
2 Students discuss and reach agreement on how to complete one of the following statements:

    a *To succeed in college, you have to* ....
    b *If you want to succeed in college, you* ....

3 As groups report their opinions, list them on the board.
4 Have students identify similarities and differences among opinions.
5 Ask students how they formed these opinions (e.g. from personal experience or the opinions of respected persons) and how these opinions influence them (e.g. do they predict and guide behaviour?).
6 Give them the 'technical' term for what they have been discussing: these opinions which are based on experience and opinions of respected others, which influence the way they act, can be called *beliefs*.
7 Tell them that in subsequent classes they will be discussing their beliefs about language learning.

Special notes

- Caution students to complete the statement in step 2 with an opinion that represents a *strong* belief.
- Other topics can be selected from the sentence completion. However, they should represent a goal that is familiar and common to your group of students.

Module (2)

Bicycle riding and the art of language learning (listening/writing)

Objective

Students discuss their beliefs about learning.

Resources

- Excerpt from *Bicycle riding and the art of learning* (see Appendix 1). (Any article about learning may be used, but it should be provocative.)
- Listening guide based on the excerpt.

Procedure

1 Introduce any unfamiliar vocabulary items in the passage.
2 Recount the event in the passage. (Do not read it. Tell it.)
3 Students take notes and, after the first account, answer the questions in the listening guide as completely as possible.
4 Recount the event in the passage a second time.
5 Students listen for information that they did not get the first time.
6 They complete their answers and compare them with those of another classmate.
7 Referring to the answers, initiate a discussion of what students consider important to successful learning.
8 Students use their answers to write a short summary of the event.

Module (3)

Bicycle riding and the art of language learning (discussion/writing)

Objective

Students compare language learning with other kinds of learning.

Procedure

1 Divide students into pairs and have them determine whether they agree or disagree with the following statements and why:

   Learning a second language is just like
   a learning to ride a bicycle
   b learning to use a computer
   c making friends.

2 Results of the small-group discussion are reported and serve as a basis for determining what is common to all learning and what is unique to language learning.
3 Students write a letter to a friend in their country describing their language learning experience, their problems, what they do to help themselves improve, how they feel about it, etc.

Special notes

- Again, the topics listed in step 1 are suggestions. Teachers may choose any that will be of special relevance to their students.
- Keep the students' letters on file as they will be used in subsequent modules.
- Students who are preparing for a trip abroad and have not yet had the experience of language learning 'on the spot' could be asked to write a plan of action indicating how they will approach their language learning (instead of writing the letter).

Module (4)

To learn a language you should . . .? (reading/discussion)

Objectives

- Students examine the beliefs of other language learners.
- They relate beliefs to approach.

Resources

Student accounts of how they learned English (see Appendix 2). Miguel's illustrates the principle 'learn the natural way'. Eun Jin's illustrates the principle 'learn systematically'.

Procedure

1 Students read the two accounts at home.

2 In class, they are divided into groups and asked to state the advice each student gives about language learning, and to compare the two learners.
3 These discussions can be summarized under the following headings, which should be written on the board:
    a general principles or guidelines
    b strategies for learning vocabulary
    c pays attention to (i) . . . language   (ii) . . . meaning
    d language problems are . . .
    e strategies for practice.
4 Students consider each learner's principles or guidelines and try to synthesize them into a statement that represents each one's beliefs.
5 Students compare how each belief influences strategies, attention pattern, and assessment of problems.

Module (5)

Personal factors are important

Objective

Students will consider the importance of personal factors in language learning.

Resource

A short questionnaire on the importance of personal facors (see below).

Procedure

1 Students express their opinions on each of the statements below by writing (a) *yes;* (b) *no;* (c) *maybe;* or (d) *sometimes.*

    You can't learn English very well if you

    . . . feel frustrated
    . . . feel bored
    . . . don't have an ability for language learning
    . . . are not a child
    . . . don't understand the culture
    . . . have a teacher who doesn't understand your way of learning
    . . . don't have the right personality
    . . . are not ambitious
    . . . are not interested in the culture
    . . . have no confidence in yourself
    . . . are not a full-time student
    . . . have other responsibilities (e.g. a job, a family)
    . . . are treated like a child by the teacher.

2 After completing the survey, students compare their responses with those of one or two other classmates and explain the reasons for their opinions.
3 The outcomes of these small-group discussions are shared with the whole class to determine which of the above factors are considered detrimental to the learning process by the majority.
4 Class discussion on these factors leads to the formulation of a third set of beliefs, namely that personal factors are important.

Special note

The questionnaire is intended to highlight the following personal factors: feelings, language aptitude, age, cultural background, learning style, personality, motivation, social role, and self concept.

Module (6)

My belief is . . . (reading/discussion)

Objective

Students determine what their beliefs are.

Resources

Students' letters describing their approach to language learning (from module 2).

Procedure

Students read their letters to determine what their beliefs are or whether they have any at all. They compare their approach to the approach of the two learners discussed in the previous module. They also note whether they have emphasized any personal factors.

Special note

In the discussion of their students' beliefs, teachers should be alert to beliefs not brought out in the previous material or to other beliefs that may be specific to their students. They should also note whether their students, in fact, adhere to more than one belief.

Module (7)

Definition of a good language learner (reading/discussion)

Objectives

— Students analyse the beliefs of successful language learners.
— They note that good language learners are guided by more than one belief.
— They note the relationship between beliefs and approach.

Resources

- Definition of the good language learner (see Appendix 3).
- Reading comprehension guide based on the definition of the good language learner.

Procedure

1 Students read the passage and complete the comprehension guide before class.
2 In class, they compare their answers to the guide with those of a classmate and determine which of the three beliefs discussed in the previous modules good language learners use. (In fact, they appear to be guided by all three.)
3 Class discussion following the group work should focus on (a) whether one set of beliefs is better than another; (b) whether beliefs are related to purposes or learning styles; (c) whether beliefs can and should be changed; (d) which beliefs they prefer; and (c) how beliefs can influence approach to language learning.

Special notes

- The definition can be used as a reading exercise or as the basis for a listening exercise. In either case, teachers should adapt it to the level of proficiency of their students. The various strategies referred to in the definition can be made more concrete by adding examples.
- The strategies of the good language learner are most easily implemented in a setting where English is the language of the country. It is important, therefore, that students learning English in their native countries (i.e. as a foreign language) should be led to examine resources in their communities that would allow them to follow the example of the good language learner.

Module (8)

Am I a good language learner? (reading/writing)

Objectives

- Students compare their approach with the approach of the good language learner.
- They determine whether and how they will modify their approach.

Resources

A questionnaire about good language learners, based on the reading used in module 6.

Procedure

1 Students complete the questionnaire.
2 They determine whether and how they should expand their present repertoire of language learning behaviours.

3 They write an essay comparing themselves to the good language learner, and indicate how they plan to change their approach if they plan to do so, and if not, why not.

Special notes

- Each of the behavioural descriptions of the good language learner can become one item on the questionnaire. Next to each item, students indicate whether they do this often, sometimes, rarely, or never.
- They can complete the questionnaire on their own or administer it to each other.
- A guided outline is useful for focusing the composition.
- Instead of a composition, a teacher can choose to discuss the questionnaire during student conferences.

Target groups

The modules can be used with different student groups and sequenced in a variety of ways. I have used them during the first two weeks of a fifteen-week semester course with students who are enrolled part-time in an ESL programme (9 hours) and part-time in college. Alternatively, the activities could be sequenced throughout a semester, one or two classes a week being set aside for this purpose. Language institutes and immersion programmes that provide intensive language training for college-bound students, new immigrants, and tourists could use the modules in the same way. They could also be used as part of an orientation programme for foreign language majors who are planning a stay in the country where their target language is spoken, whether on their own or as part of an exchange programme. This kind of language orientation should also be beneficial for people who travel for professional purposes.

Educational value

The value of activities in which younger and older adults reflect upon their beliefs about language learning lies in the fact that such activities can surface for examination, evaluation, and possible change and/or modification of the expectations that adult learners bring to their language learning. Based on their previous educational experiences, some approach the learning of a language as they would biology or history, for example. In other words, they view it as a content course, and when their language course does not provide them with new information about the language, they may become impatient and bored. They do not always realize that learning a language means being able to use it as well as knowing about it, and that at a certain point it is no longer a matter of knowledge but of meaningful practice.

Moreover, many tend to view their progress in terms of the time units set out by the length of a course. If there are four courses in the programme they are enrolled in and if these courses represent 48 weeks of work, they expect to have 'learned' English in that allotted amount of time, and may consider themselves as having little language aptitude if they have not. Certainly, students have the right to expect progress after a given period of time, but they should also appreciate the fact that learning a language takes time, and that time frames will vary from individual to individual.

Students may also have definite views about the function of the classroom and of the social environment outside the classroom in language learning. They may not always view the social environment outside the classroom as an opportunity to learn about the language. Rather the classroom and the social environment outside it are often assigned mutually exclusive roles: the former for learning about language and the latter for practising it.

Finally, students also bring to their language learning experience certain views about their role and the teacher's role. Ordinarily, they expect that the teacher will make learning happen, and they do not see themselves as taking a very active or autonomous role in the endeavour. Nor do they have confidence in their ability to do so.

These are examples of expectations that groups of students I have worked with over the years have brought to the task of language learning. They are not intended to be a comprehensive description of what all groups of students may expect. The point is, however, that adult students will come into the classroom conditioned by their previous educational experiences, and that these experiences should be taken into account if one wishes the language learning/teaching task to be a co-operative endeavour.

In *The Modern Practice of Adult Education* (1970:45), Malcolm Knowles suggests that an 'unfreezing' experience built into the early phase of a course, workshop, or other sequential educational activity is one way of helping adult students 'look at themselves more objectively and free their minds from preconceptions'. In other words, it is one way of taking their experience into account. The assumption underlying this activity is that learners will become more receptive to approaches to learning that are different from their own. It is further assumed that such receptivity is a precondition to effective learning. A unit which encourages language students to reflect upon and evaluate their beliefs about language learning is an example of such an 'unfreezing' experience.

Thinking about learning in this way by reflecting on our beliefs has been referred to as 'metacognition' by cognitive psychologists. While the parameters of this concept are still under dispute (cf. Brown *et al.* 1982), it is agreed that the phenomenon to which it points is important. The absence of metacognitive skills is considered to be one reason for learning disabilities in mildly retarded children (Brown and Palinscar 1982). Moreover, studies have demonstrated that training in the use of learning strategies was more enduring when students were informed about the significance of the strategies and given reasons for their potential effectiveness (Brown *et al.* 1982).

As experience will have demonstrated to most of us, some language learners come to the task of language learning with highly refined metacognitive skills. In their case, thinking about their beliefs might help them to further clarify and label what they already know. Many others, however, have developed their metacognitive abilities to a much lesser degree. Activities that help them reflect on their learning and articulate their unstated beliefs should help develop these important metacognitive skills and, consequently, allow them to assume more control over their learning.

Finally, the sequence of modules lays the foundation for teachers who wish to engage further in the development of activities for the refinement of their students' learning competence. Reading about and discussing the strategies of the good language learner will give students an initial acquaintance with the notions of learning strategy and learning style. It will introduce them to the importance of diagnosing their language problems, evaluating the outcome of their learning activities, setting forth objectives, and learning to deal with their feelings (other metacognitive skills). In other words, the modules can be useful in raising students' awareness about the learning skills necessary to help them become more active and diversified learners. At the same time, these activities could serve as a diagnostic tool for classroom teachers. They will provide them with valuable insights into their students' beliefs about learning and their preferred learning strategies. Such data could serve as a guide in the choice of activities they devise for further helping their students 'learn how to learn' a second language.

Notes

1 There are two kinds of strategies: learning strategies and communication strategies. Learning strategies are defined as steps or mental operations used in learning or problem-solving that require direct analysis, transformation, or synthesis of learning materials in order to store, retrieve, and use knowledge. Communication strategies refer to techniques learners use when there is a gap between their knowledge of the language and their communicative intent.

Appendix 1

Bicycle riding and the art of learning

The following is adapted from Robert Kraft's article by the same name.

I sometimes ride a bike to school. When and how did I learn? When I think of how I learned to ride, I remember a heavy green and white girl's bike my mother had bought me. I was seven. I was the youngest in my family and too small to reach the pedals on my brother's bike. My dad's store, with candy cookies, was three blocks away. I went there several times a day, and I was tired of walking. Besides, smaller kids could ride two-wheelers.

I straddled the bike and came down hard on the top pedal. I tipped over. I got back on and tipped again. The bike fell on top of me and I scraped a thigh on the sidewalk. But I had to learn, so I kept at it. In a week I could ride pretty well. Today I can also read, write, ski and even fix the clothes-dryer in my home. I learned them all the same way. There is something very simple in this way of learning. I needed to know or do something, so I went after it. It was hard and hurt sometimes, but it worked.

But learning in the classroom was not like learning to ride a bicycle. Often I sat passive, waiting for class to be over. Sometimes I got interested in something and read up on it. I did well on tests and everyone thought I was a good student, but I have forgotten many of the things that I learned in school.

Appendix 2

Miguel was majoring in economics in Spain. He had not studied English in high school or in college, so he did not know any English previous to his visit to London.

' I spent ten weeks in the south of England with a British family. I didn't want to live with other foreign students. I think that's the best way, especially if you're accepted as part of the family. I had a close relationship with the family. We spoke at dinner time and while watching TV, we talked about what we saw. Everything was natural. I could practise what I learned in school. That was good because my problem was using and understanding English outside the classroom. Sometimes I tried to make sentences using words the landlord used. I also read the papers every day. I read news about Spain. I decided I would not use a Spanish-English dictionary. I guessed the meaning by looking at the words I knew. I didn't think about grammar. I tried to catch the meaning. Everything was natural. When I went into a restaurant, I had to order. So I looked at the menu and learned words that way.

'In the summer of 1978, I decided to go to Berkeley. The class was a disaster. It was not organized by the university. There were only Spanish students; they did not divide the students according to their levels, and the teachers had little method. After one month, I enrolled as an auditor in a university course and attended two seminars. The summer in California was very satisfying. My English was much better than it was in England. I understood more and I talked more easily. I had made progress, but I couldn't measure it. It was all unconscious. But I was always trying to get information in a conscious way. I read the ads, listened to radio commercials, and watched TV.

'I still had a problem using words, so I took every opportunity I had to practise. That's the secret. In a conversation your partner speaks to you and you have to answer. You become very interested in the subject and you remember words you learned. You learn new ones. In this way you understand better. Of course, I did not like making mistakes, especially in the seminars. But if you don't speak and if you don't write because of your mistakes, you'll have to wait twenty years before you say something. It's better to talk.

'I returned to the United States the next spring and spent 16 weeks at a university in Connecticut. The problem was that the campus was far from the city and after the first semester, all the American students left. There was no opportunity to practise. I didn't like that. So I decided to come to New York and to enrol in courses at the university. In that way I could discuss with American classmates and read books in my field. You have to practise English. Talking and reading English are the key. I took two courses in business—micro-economics and accounting. That was a very good experience. I read, studied, listened to lectures, and took notes in English. I thought about the meaning of the subject. I did not think about the language. I was trying to learn English the natural way . . .'

Eun Jin came to the United States from Korea with her husband, who was enrolled in a graduate programme. She had studied English in high school and college in Korea and, after receiving her BA degree, she had continued learning English in language institutes and on her own.

'In Korea I studied English ten years in high school and in college. We learned a lot of grammar, so when I came to the United States, I knew grammar and I could read, but I couldn't speak easily. But grammar background is important. Without it, you can't improve. You will be limited.

'Before coming to the United States, I studied on my own. I bought a grammar book and attended classes at a private institute. I took a course in listening. It was awful. I couldn't understand. They spoke fast and their pronunciation was different. We had learned British pronunciation. After one month, I quit and read short stories in my grammar book. I consulted my dictionary and my grammar books to understand. I have studied many grammar books.

'Later I took a reading course. We used *Time* and *Newsweek* magazines. I found it very difficult. The articles were heavy. I could not understand what I read. I spent three hours and could only read half a page. That class was very frustrating. I realized it was important to learn grammar and vocabulary first. It was the turning point. I quit the class and studied grammar and vocabulary on my own.

'When I first came to the United States, I took an English course in a community language programme. I had time, and Americans were closed to foreigners if they did not speak fluently. I also decided to take the TOEFL test to push myself to learn grammar and vocabulary. During that time, it was very hard to understand what people said. I guessed the meaning by using the vocabulary I knew. Now I understand more easily, and so I try to catch the grammar. When I read, I also pay attention to the grammar. I feel uncomfortable if I can't get it exactly. Learning grammar is fundamental. If you concentrate only on the meaning, you can't improve.

'Vocabulary is also important. When I was in Korea, I looked up all the words I didn't know and made a notebook. I tried to memorize ten words a day. But you can't remember the words if you don't use them. Now, when I watch TV and listen to the news, I concentrate on vocabulary. I try to figure out the words from the pronunciation. Then I look them up in the dictionary or ask my husband to explain.

'I've made some progress. I have no problem understanding and talking to people in ordinary situations. But I'm not satisfied. I want to understand English exactly. I want to conquer English. I'm ambitious. I must make more effort. It's important to study step by step—from easy to hard. In the beginning I was too confident. I thought I knew a lot and did not pay attention to basic English. Taking a class is also important. You are pushed to learn and it's sympathetic . . .'

Appendix 3

A definition of a good language learner

The following definition is based on the research of Naiman, Fröhlich, Stern and Todesco (*The Good Language Learner*; Ontario Institute for Studies in Education, 1978). They interviewed adults who had learned a second, third, and sometimes a fourth language successfully. The following is a list of the strategies that good language learners reported using.

Good language learners find a style of learning that suits them: When they are in a learning situation that they do not like, they are able to adapt it to their personal needs. They believe they can always learn something, whatever the situation. They also know how they prefer to learn and choose learning situations that are suited to their way of learning.

Good language learners are actively involved in the language learning process: Besides regular language classes, they plan activities that give them a chance to use and learn the language. They know practice is very important. Sometimes they choose an activity because they are already familiar with the ideas. Sometimes they choose activities that help them with their special problems. They also often do things they don't usually do to gain more information about their second language.

Good language learners try to figure out how the language works: They pay attention to pronunciation, grammar, and vocabulary. They develop good techniques for improving their pronunciation, learning grammar and vocabulary. For example, some learners try to imitate the sounds of the language without using real words. When learning new words, other learners make a picture of the object in their minds. They compare the words in their native language to see how they are different.

Good language learners know that language is used to communicate: They have good techniques to practise listening, speaking, reading, and writing. In the early stages of their language learning, they do not worry about making mistakes. They speak and try to become fluent. They look for opportunities to speak with native speakers.

Good language learners are like good detectives: They are always looking for clues that will help them understand how the language works. They make guesses and ask people to correct them if they are wrong. They compare what they say with what others say. They keep a record of what they have learned and think about it.

Good language learners learn to think in the language.

Good language learners realize that language learning is not easy. They try to overcome their feelings of frustration and their lack of confidence.

(*Originally published in Volume 40/1, 1986*)

The move towards 'learner-centredness' in the mainstream of language teaching during the late seventies and eighties must have caused a wry smile on the face of the late Caleb Gattegno during his final (but still professionally active) years. After all, his 'Silent Way' is based on the oft-quoted principle of the 'subordination of teaching to learning'. Catching him in a break during a typically active and controversial seminar in the UK in 1981, Richard Rossner interviewed him for *ELT Journal*, and the resultant 'Talking Shop' includes Gattegno's observation on that fundamental principle.

Talking shop

A conversation with Caleb Gattegno, inventor of The Silent Way

In recent years language has been influenced by a number of methodologies which, their authors and supporters claim, represent radical breaks with the established traditions of the field. These so called 'fringe methodologies'—a term some adherents find objectionable—include Suggestopoedia (developed by Lozanov and his followers in Bulgaria), Community Language Learning (which arises out of the work of Charles Curran and his followers in the U.S.A.), and—perhaps the best known of all—the Silent Way.

In spite of the fact that they are often 'loosely grouped together in discussion, these methodologies (and others such as Total Physical Response) have very different origins. While Community Language Learning (CLL) has its roots in the counselling techniques of psychotherapy, the Silent Way is derived from an assertively individualistic view of learning, for example. It relies on the teacher's ability to exploit each student's previous experiences with language, his or her imagination and intuition, rather than solely memory or intellect. Devices such as the colour coded pronunciation charts and pointer are used to assist the teacher to develop students' sensitivities to the new language via its sounds without the traditional techniques of 'modelling' pronunciation and correcting errors. Indeed, those who use the method claim that it is unnecessary for the teacher to intervene verbally at all since students can be guided and student production can be elicited much more effectively by the use of gesture, facial expression, and (on the teacher's part) silent routines using the materials.

The inventor of this method and the special materials that go with it was Dr Caleb Gattegno. In fact, Gattegno started out in the sciences in Egypt. He became involved in the training of teachers (principally of mathematics) during his time at the University of Liverpool and the London University Institute of Education between 1945 and 1957. (1954 saw the publication of *Numbers in Colour*, which Gattegno wrote with Georges Cuisenaire, inventor of the rods of the same name that are widely used in mathematics teaching as well as in language teaching by the Silent Way.)

While working with UNESCO in Ethiopia Gattegno, who is a polyglot, developed a new approach to the teaching of the reading and writing of Amharic to native speakers of that language. As the approach evolved it was applied to more and more languages, and in 1962 *Words in Colour*, a scheme for the teaching of reading and writing to primary school native speakers of English, appeared. The Silent Way, a methodology for the teaching of foreign languages, was a natural development of this, which has since resulted in the setting up of companies[1] in the USA to produce and market materials world-wide.

On 7 November 1981 Dr Gattegno was giving a seminar[2] on the Silent Way and the view (his own) of the learning process that gave rise to it. The participants were either teachers who were already using the Silent Way in their teaching of English at various schools in the UK, or people whose interest in the method had been aroused by what they had heard about it. The sometimes rather stormy seminar, which included demonstrations of the teaching of Arabic by the method, lasted for two days and was led by Gattegno single-handed—no mean achievement for a man of seventy. The conversation which appears below in edited form was recorded during a lunch break.

Richard Rossner: Dr Gattegno, you seem in your seminars to be absolutely convinced, and many of those using the Silent Way seem absolutely convinced, that it is the 'right way' to teach languages. Why is it the 'right way'?

Caleb Gattegno: I cannot say that it is the right way as a political statement, and the fact that I am the author of it weakens my position. I can tell you only what I know: I looked at the field and found that nobody was making a study of the learning of foreign languages, so I began to make a study of my own. As a result, I had ideas that didn't occur to others, and I practised and experimented in 48 countries in a dozen languages, with people from all sorts of backgrounds, and I succeeded in making all of them work. I was able to get all of them to read a script which they were seeing for the first time. So my feedback was that my method was working.

Richard Rossner: So basically it's the right way according to your empirical evidence.

Caleb Gattegno: Yes. Now, I don't say it's the right way for everybody. But if teaching is to be subordinated to learning, there is no other method to turn to.

Richard Rossner: What do you mean precisely by 'the subordination of teaching to learning'?

Caleb Gattegno: To explain that, I have to go back a bit: in education we started historically by teaching the classics to the *élite*, and the way in which they were taught was the only appropriate way to teach them, especially as people did not want to use Greek and Latin for spoken communication. So when, in the sixteenth century, the Jesuits wanted to develop their schools, they took what was there and they developed schools which were typical of what goes on in education today. 1564, 1964—four hundred years of doing the same things with the chalkboard, the teacher, students, homework, corrections, and so on. So there is a long tradition, a long-standing belief in this way of working, because many generations learnt in no other way. So who can say it doesn't work? It works very well; it has produced so many great people. But when society wanted changes in teaching, first by allowing a wide variety of other subjects (not just the classics) to be taught, and when around the end of the last century education was opened to everybody, then it was found that the 'classical' methods didn't work. Before that, nobody worried whether they worked or not, because they weren't intended to produce the legions of people whose support governments need. In the last hundred years we have found out that opening education to all means problems which had not been foreseen. So you had reformists everywhere. I learnt all I could about the reformists, but what they were proposing only made a difference in *me*, not in my students. It didn't make a difference to the learners' 'yield'. So the notion of yield, the economics of education became my preoccupation. And I found that the greatest yield is to be found in babies. So I tried to learn from babies how *they* learn. Since they teach themselves, and since I have been self-taught all my life, I realized that my privileged position (which I had seen as a hindrance in my recognition of my own place in the world) as a person who was his own teacher places me far ahead of myself. I worked with pupils from where *they* were, as I had worked with myself, and I found that they could do remarkable things. I worked with the blind, the spastic, the learning-disabled, the mentally retarded, the old who had never been to school, the illiterate, and so on, and everywhere I found that I could work on what *they* were able to do successfully.

Richard Rossner: So you adopted an evolutionary approach. How would you compare your work with, say, Montessori's?

Caleb Gattegno: She was mainly concerned with very young children, and her psychology, which was right for her time, was too narrow for me. We have learnt a lot since her time. Therefore, although I studied all her work and applied it and worked in Montessori schools, and although she had the view, now shared by many, that children can do a lot more than we assume they can, she didn't know *what* they can do and *why*.

Richard Rossner: You mentioned just now that babies are able to learn much more and in a much shorter time than 'non-babies', shall we say.

Caleb Gattegno: Only if we teach (the non-babies) in a manner which hinders their learning.

Richard Rossner: So the first step in your approach is to locate these learning abilities of the baby that are still within us.

Caleb Gattegno: That's right, and they are in everybody, except those who erect barriers and don't allow anything to go through them. And there are some.

Richard Rossner: What can the language teacher, for example, do in order to help his or her students find the baby in them?

Caleb Gattegno: He (or she) doesn't have to help them find the baby in them: he can give them exercises which are immediately accessible, and the baby comes out. I work with rectangles and discipline them to make the sounds (of the L2). If they agree to remember a very few items, say a dozen, the rest follows naturally because they are intelligent learners. And then I put up a chart of the written forms, which they have never seen before, and ask them to locate the words (we have been practising). The charts are coloured so that there is a clue to allow them to overcome the difficulties of different scripts (and spelling systems). I do several things to free students from having to remember, which is not what we do at school. All the time (at school) memory is stressed, and, since people forget, we are in trouble!

Richard Rossner: And how does the concept of 'surrender', another key word in your vocabulary, relate to this 'baby in us'?

Caleb Gattegno: Babies know that language is not theirs. It belongs to others. What surrender does is to put you where you belong. You have power, but you don't know the language; you have powers that you have cultivated in one language—call them discrimination, sense of generalization, recognition through analogy, recognition of alterations—but it's not memory. All this is available to you only if you 'surrender', and you respond because it's in you, not because you make analogies.

Richard Rossner: So it's getting rid of the intellectual games that students and teachers play?

Caleb Gattegno: If they were intellectual, I wouldn't get rid of them, because the intellect is a power. We have not asked students to use their intelligence while learning, and they become stultified, paralysed.

Richard Rossner: Another term you use is 'the spirit of a language'. What to you is the spirit of a language, say English? What does it include?

Caleb Gattegno: The spirit of a language is subconscious. In every language there are things that are transmitted from generation to generation, that correspond to what people thought was 'right'. Now the British, the people who invented and developed the English language, were not generally people who operated vertically, by becoming more and more 'egg-headed'. Instead, they preferred to work in a broad area, and the fact that they lived on an island and became used to resisting invasion means that you can begin by saying that this community is (likely to be) enclosed, turned in on itself and has developed a particular set of behaviours, and an outlook on life. Of course, this has changed since the Second World War, but this particular outlook persisted for a long time. How is it reflected in the language? Well, the British prefer verbs: when I arrived here at the very end of the War, I heard words like 'to camouflage' and 'to torpedo' for the first time; all the things that are nouns in France had become verbs here. And you (the British) do that automatically, because that is where your spirit is. You are 'in motion'. The British sense the evolution of language.

Richard Rossner: To return to language learning and 'the baby in us', another key concept in your approach is that of the 'temporal hierarchy'. As I understand it, you are implying that there is a certain order in which growing and learning take place. How can this be exploited in the language-learning situation?

Caleb Gattegno: It is exploited in my method and my demonstrations: I make students make noises; they can see and concatenate sounds; I work entirely at a level of perception and action. But when students have a developed intelligence (as the participants at this seminar have), they can make inferences, and I can exploit that too. So the hierarchy works like this: as babies, we handle what is brought to us through the senses and integrate this with the sensitivities we have accumulated since birth and since before birth. But there is a universe of perception, which takes a number of years to explore. Then we take the next step: we use what we have gained through perception to explore the world of action. If you look at very young children, they are in the 'absolute of perception'; if you look at boys and girls of primary school age, they are in the 'absolute of action'. This means that any action gets hold of them, but it doesn't eliminate what has been gained previously. It simply puts stress on the quality of learning.

Richard Rossner: How does your view of child development match Piaget's view?

Caleb Gattegno: In no way. His stages don't have anything to do with mine: mine are concerned with the universes that have to be conquered by people who know how to conquer them. Piaget says 'What we have to do is make you like me' (i.e. work out how you get from babyhood to adulthood). He say things from his schema down, and did experiments to confirm his vision, not to find out what people are like. For instance he found that very young children don't have conversation.[3] I say: it's the other way round; young children don't need conservation, so they don't develop it. When they need it, they develop it. I would like to study each baby, everything they do, from the moment I first come into contact with them until I leave them. That's the ideal. But if I go into primary schools to look at children, I can only observe them during their recess breaks. How can I claim to know all there is to know about children, if I only observe them for 15 minutes in the morning and 15 minutes in the afternoon? But no researcher is able to be with his subjects from beginning to end. Only parents can do this, and they could contribute a lot, but they don't.

Richard Rossner: What areas do you think researchers should be concentrating on? Where do we really lack knowledge, which we could, maybe, get?

Caleb Gattegno: We *do* get more all the time as we abandon the view that we have to base research on the existing literature. We have to start on new challenges, and the greatest number of new challenges is to be found in learning. Every researcher in education asks for more time to allow for its continuation, or asks other people to do the research again, so marking time is characteristic of this type of research, and therefore very little is discovered. Every researcher says 'This is not final'. No-one says 'I found this, and you'll find the same thing, whatever you do'.

Richard Rossner: But that's the nature of research, isn't it?

Caleb Gattegno: No, not at all. Physics, mathematics, biology, and so on don't work that way. Why should education work that way? I am preparing a treatise 'The Science of Education', in which I am summarizing all that I have learnt in this life. There are nineteen chapters which summarize my findings. Part One provides the answer to the question 'Where do we find ways of generating subjects for research?', and the second part applies the answers to this question to twelve disciplines. I concern myself with finding out which sensitivities a person needs to develop in order to be able to say, for example, 'I am a biologist', and which sensitivities he (or she) hasn't developed, so that he can't say 'I'm a mathematician' or 'I'm a limerick-writer because of my training'.

Richard Rossner: Do you have any views on another approach to language teaching that has been grouped with the Silent Way, Community Language Learning (CLL), which seeks to implement some of the ideas of Charles Curran and Carl Rogers in the language classroom?

Caleb Gattegno: Well, I can tell you something that has been reported to me by people working with it: they have adopted the (Cuisenaire) rods; they have adopted my charts and my pointer, so they are using my techniques, because they haven't invented techniques of their own.

Richard Rossner: But their emphasis is on relations in the classroom rather than on technique, isn't it?

Caleb Gattegno: Yes, because Curran was a counsellor. But, if you give me a class of twenty people who can't talk to each other, I can teach them English. You can't do that unless you have twenty teachers in CLL. As to Suggestopoedia, it's probably a good method for developing memory. But there aren't sufficient people doing the sort of research I'm doing, either among CLL or among Suggestopoedia experts. And I do research, not to please people or to be in the limelight, but because there is no other way.

Richard Rossner: I think the final question has to be this: you have many roles: researcher, teacher, teacher-trainer, materials developer, president of two corporations (in the USA). Which of these is the most important to you?

Caleb Gattegno: The one that I haven't talked about, which is to *understand*. I want to understand why I am around and why others are around, and why we come into contact.

Notes

1 Notably Educational Solutions Inc., New York.
2 Organized by David Berrington-Davies, Principal of the Abon School, Bristol, under the auspices of ARELS.
3 *Conservation*: a psychological term for the ability to understand that the quantity, weight, and volume of matter do not change when its shape (or the shape of its container) is changed; e.g. a litre of liquid in a tall thin bottle equals a litre of liquid in a rectangular carton.

(*Originally published in Volume 36/4, 1982*)

Gattegno's reference to Curran's work is hardly complimentary, and there is more than a hint of the ideologue in this edited interview, just as there was in his seminars. Yet Gattegno's overriding concern with the *quality* of an educational experience shines through as a reminder to those in the profession whose focus is narrower and, for all sorts of reasons such as cost-effectiveness, more goal-oriented. The contributions of Gattegno and Curran, despite attempts to dismiss them as 'fringe methodologists', have had their different and important effects on our views of both teaching and learning. For many teachers, the experience gained as learners or 'clients' in Community Language Learning has led to important insights into both acquisition and learning, as well as into teaching and learning styles. The tradition of counselling and psychotherapy, from which Curran's work derives, has much relevance to education, and Carl Rogers (1985) draws the two areas together in a memorable way. Rogerian counselling has become established in many walks of life in Britain as well as the U.S., and the profession of counsellor is emerging in its own right alongside those of psychologist, psychiatrist, and psychotherapist. In the short and thoughtful article which follows, David King describes the activity of counselling in Rogerian terms and explores its relevance in teaching and, particularly, teacher training.

Counselling for teachers

David King

The term 'counselling' is much used in English language teaching today and has come to be used as a blanket label covering a wide range of activities inside the classroom and out. The fact that it is used in such a general way leaves it open to the dangers of abuse, misconception, and the dilution of its true meaning, from a highly-developed skill that requires a great deal of training into any kind of advice-giving that might be needed.

In this article I should like to clarify some of the confusion surrounding the term and suggest that the introduction of counselling to teachers and teacher-trainers can be of real benefit to institutions in our field. I shall be concerned not so much with language teaching methods based on counselling techniques (i.e. Counselling-learning, Community Language Learning) as with attempting to describe and illustrate how the acquisition of such skills can contribute to teacher development. More specifically, two vital areas in which they could have immediate application are, first, in teacher-training, getting the teacher to understand why things have gone wrong, accept responsibility for them and adjust his/her behaviour in the future to avoid such situations recurring; and second, in the classroom, getting students to recognize realistic aims in terms of their time and ability, to accept the limitations of their individual aptitudes, and to understand their personal balance of strengths and weaknesses.

What is counselling?

At its most potent, it is about putting counsellees in touch with their true feelings so that they may be receptive to the kinds of insight that will enable them to work towards greater self-knowledge and an understanding of how the conduct of their lives causes their problems.

The ability to counsel is within every one of us, but before we can reach other people we have to be in touch with ourselves. We have to learn to recognize our own inhibitions and anxieties, 'blocks' and prejudices, 'safe' and 'unsafe' areas, and how far we are prepared to listen to other people's feelings. To do this we must first recognize our own motivations as teachers: 'A teacher cannot make much headway in understanding others or in helping others to understand themselves unless he is endeavouring to understand himself. If he is not engaged in this endeavour, he will continue to see those whom he teaches through the bias and distortion of his unrecognized needs, fears, desires, anxieties and hostile impulses' (Jersild 1955:14). Unfortunately however, no one of us can set about achieving this greater self-knowledge, which in turn can be used to facilitate insight in others, just by reading a couple of books by Stevick. It is a long and often painful business, and requires the guidance of those trained in psychotherapy and the support of a group of similarly intentioned people over a period of time. This is what a good counselling course should provide.

Counselling in teacher-training

The training of teachers has much to gain from observing the training of counsellors, and one of the most essential areas which is rarely questioned in teacher-training is the basic 'operational philosophy' of the individual. How many of us in teaching have searchingly asked ourselves or are aware of the issues raised by the questions in this checklist of Carl Rogers:

> The primary point of importance here is the attitude held by the counsellor towards the worth and the significance of the individual. How do we look upon others? Do we see each person as having dignity in his own right? If we do hold this point of view at the verbal level, to what extent is it operationally evident at the behavioural level? Do we tend to treat individuals as persons of worth, or do we subtly devaluate them by our attitudes and behaviour? Is our philosophy one in which respect for the individual is uppermost? Do we respect his right to self-direction, or do we basically believe that his life would best be guided by us? To what extent do we have a need and a desire to dominate others? Are we willing for the individual to select and choose his own values or are our actions guided by the conviction (usually unspoken) that he would be happiest is he permitted us to select for him his values and standards and goals? (Rogers 1951:20)

Part of the problem of being involved in education is that most of us have a desire to 'educate'; that is, to change or influence other people for what we believe to be the better. It tends to give us 'tunnel vision' and to make us dismissive of people who do not see things in the same way as ourselves. Our normal professional position is that of instructor, imparter of knowledge, priding ourselves on our ability to 'weld' groups and to control and to direct. Even if, to help us feel more at ease, we use more 'humanistic' terms to describe our activity (e.g. 'the knower', the 'learning facilitator', 'the guide'), we cannot disguise the fact that our work makes us anxious to influence, anxious to provide input.

We and our students have been conditioned to think that this is what teaching is about, and so it is to a certain extent. But these very skills and attributes which enable us to stand up in front of a class and 'perform' can block our way when the need arises to reach people (including ourselves) at a personal level.

It is important to understand that 'both counselling and teaching are deeply concerned with human relationships . . . learning and learning processes are at the heart of counselling. It is therefore a particularly proper activity for a teacher, provided that he/she is able to allow pupils to learn and not simply instruct them in a rigid way' (Hamblin 1974:3)

How, then, do the learning processes explored through counselling differ from, yet supplement and nourish the basic skills learnt in teacher training? As I have already suggested, the essential ingredient is self-exploration which is guided and directed to enable the individual to understand and come to terms with those elements in his/her personality which have formed blocks and blind spots and prevented further growth. These are present in every one of us and are at the root of our everyday anxieties and the way we conduct relationships. Unless they are reached, the same kind of problem will occur again and again. An example is the teacher whom students of a certain personality type invariably complain about but who is successful with everyone else.

As soon as the process of self-analysis is under way, the individual can begin to get in touch with his/her own qualities as a listener, as an understander and as a facilitator of others. The process, however, must derive from within.

The qualities needed in counselling

Truax and Carkhuff state that, apart from respect for the worth and dignity of others, the factors which are most 'facilitative' in the initial stage of counselling are empathy, concreteness, and genuineness.

One may feel that empathy is a natural gift—something one either has or has not. Although it is true that some people seem to be born with more empathy than others, it is also something which can be developed. Empathy is often defined as the ability to put oneself in another's shoes. This English word lacks much of the power of the German 'Einfühlung' (literally 'in-feeling'), which was coined as a psychological term from the original Greek, and for which the English equivalent would perhaps be 'gut-feeling'. Empathy is 'the power of projecting one's personality into, and so fully understanding, the object of contemplation' (*Shorter Oxford English Dictionary*), and it is an emotion to be experienced deep inside oneself. It implies the ability to cut through the sentiment, the thoughts welling up, the memories of a similar experience aroused, the day-to-day concerns filling our minds, and to feel the depth of the counsellee's trouble.

The ability to be silent, with ourselves and with others, is an important constituent of empathy. In modern society, silence is often interpreted as hostility, and most of us feel awkward and embarrassed when silence falls in a social situation, and lost and anxious when we have nothing to do. Few Westerners feel at ease when there are no diversions to fill the spaces, and even our teacher-training conditions us to fill our lessons with sometimes frantic 'busyness'. We must come to recognize and to overcome this anxiety, because it prevents us from getting in touch with our own well-being. Silence provides necessary space for people to explore their feelings, search for the right words to express what they want and digest what has been said. So 'empathic' identification is to be aimed at, in which the counsellor becomes a sort of 'alternate self' perceiving, even living, the emotions, feelings, and attitudes of the counsellee but at the same time remaining emotionally whole and outside; 'the greatest intimacy at infinite distance'.

Another quality is concreteness. This is involved with the skills of putting individuals in touch with their feelings and keeping them in touch. It is the ability to get the counsellees to be more precise in what they are saying, to search within themselves for more accurate definitions of what they are feeling, to cut through the posturing, the camouflage, and the vagueness in order to try and pinpoint the problem. On the part of the counsellor it requires patience and silence, and the skills of concentrating hard, and of timing any intervention with great sensitivity. In a teacher-training situation it might go something like the following:

> A teacher is having problems with a class: they have complained that he treats them like children. He retorts that they are uninterested in the work; they just want to play about and they deserve to be treated like children.
> The teacher is sitting with legs crossed and arms folded, staring past the trainer out of the window in silence . . .
>
> *Trainer:* . . . how are you feeling . . . right now?
> *Teacher*: Well, I think it's a cheek. What right have they got to complain about me? I've been teaching for five years and all my classes have been perfectly satisfied.
> *Trainer:* So . . . you're feeling angry?
> *Teacher*: Well, you remember that class I had in the summer . . . best teacher they'd ever had . . . they all keep sending me postcards . . .
> *Trainer*: . . . so . . . you're feeling angry?
> *Teacher*: Well, yes . . . you know how much work I put into my lessons . . . There are some other people on the staff who never open a book as soon as they walk out of the door.
> *Trainer*: . . . and hurt? . . . Are you feeling hurt? . . .
> *Teacher*: Hurt? . . . No, it doesn't *hurt* me, it's their future, not mine . . . If they want to waste their time and money acting the fool that's their look-out . . .
> *Trainer*: So you don't feel let-down at all?
> *Teacher*: Well, I think they've let me down, yes . . .
> *Trainer*: In what way?
> *Teacher*: It's like being betrayed—people you try to help . . . bash your head against a brick wall all day trying to teach them something . . . they turn round and stab you in the back . . .
> *Trainer*: Do you think they don't like you?

etc., etc. The trainer continues painstakingly to get the teacher to confront the problem, to verbalize his feelings more and more precisely and to work towards a position where he starts to be honest with himself. They work from vagueness to specifics, but slowly and gently. Apart from taking the class away from the teacher, there is no short-cut to dealing with such a training problem.

Then, there is genuineness. The counsellor must come to the session as an open human being. We must have no axe to grind, no points to score, no poses to maintain. For teachers who see themselves as 'a character' or 'colourful', this can be more difficult, but usually genuineness shines through any surface eccentricity. Genuineness is a necessary requisite for trust. It involves eye contact, but above all it involves just being natural, just being oneself.

These four basic factors are a necessary foundation for the skills of counselling, as well as being necessary requirements for good teaching. They are also disciplines (empathy, respect, and concreteness, at least) which can be largely trained and developed, and they are all vital ingredients for successful intrapersonal and interpersonal relationships. Once people have worked on these elements in themselves, they will feel more confident about their own strengths and weaknesses, less inhibited when confronted with feelings, and less open to manipulation.

(*Originally published in Volume 37/4, 1983*)

Tensions abound on teacher-training courses, and it is not surprising that King should identify a need for a counselling approach in one-to-one situations when problems need to be addressed. Such problems, particularly during pre-service training, are often to do with sensitive personal issues such as self-confidence or self-awareness. Time is usually available for individual tutorial guidance on courses of this sort.

The problems encountered on larger scale in-service training programmes are different in nature. Though many experienced teachers may face personal difficulties, too, the problems which are articulated by practising teachers, in response to attempts to introduce change, are usually objectified and externalized in some way. The main thrust of the paper by Rob Nolasco and Lois Arthur is towards practical means of overcoming understandable objections by teachers (in this case in the Moroccan secondary system) to the introduction into their classroom of pair work, group work, and other techniques related to communicative teaching. Whilst acknowledging the value of counselling as an approch to *teachers*, they remind the reader of the paramount need to work on and with the *learners* on new classroom approaches. It is, they argue, important to acknowledge the power of educational tradition, and to start by respecting and valuing learners' present beliefs and past experiences [cf. King]. Only by starting with this acknowledgement can any concrete progress towards innovation be made.

You try doing it with a class of forty!
Rob Nolasco and Lois Arthur

Introduction

Teacher trainer: Why don't you try doing an information-gap exercise?
Teacher: You try doing it with a class of forty!

When we are exposed to new methodological proposals, our first reaction is often a feeling that what is being suggested would not work in our teaching situation. Consequently many proposals for new techniques are either not tried or are discarded after they have been tried only once. This was certainly the case of the majority of the 115 British teachers recruited by The Centre for British Teachers Ltd[1] for service in the final three years of the Moroccan secondary system. As these teachers were faced with a difficult teaching situation, it was natural that many of them felt there was a considerable gap between the theory of communicative methodology and the realities of teaching in classes of forty or more learners. But it was the hostility that these teachers showed towards suggestions which the authors knew from experience would work that led to an examination of the problem of how to introduce methodological change into the large classes that are common to much secondary teaching. The problems and suggested solutions form the basis of this article, and while they grew out of work with secondary teachers, it is possible that the principles outlined would apply in any foreign-language teaching situation.

The starting point

Seventy-five per cent of the British teachers for whom we were responsible were new to TEFL. One of our basic aims as trainers was to make them aware of techniques, procedures, and classroom activities which would offer a chance for student/student interaction independent of the teacher, and for students to determine what they wanted to say. This was counter to norms, widely accepted by teachers, inspectors, and learners alike, which derived from audio-lingual principles of language teaching where the emphasis was on repetition, teacher control, and grammatical manipulation. However, our aim was thought to be valid in order to try to overcome the strong sense of failure experienced by the majority of the students of English.[2]

The rationale

Bearing in mind the methodological maxim 'If it is a phenomenon it must be in the interaction' (Sacks 1963, quoted in Mehan 1979:24), we started by looking at teacher/student interaction in a variety of classes taught by both British and Moroccan teachers, and found that in almost all cases the style of teaching was 'lock-step'. Regardless of the focus of the lesson, the pattern of interaction typically consisted of:

Teacher initiation: Was the train early or late?
Student reply: Late.
Teacher evaluation: Full sentence, please.

The greater proportion of questions were 'display' questions (e.g. *What's the opposite of 'big' in English?*), designed to elicit information already known to the questioner (a situation similar to the one reported by Long and Sato, see Gaies 1983:208). Where the teacher had an awareness of language and the ability to control language and direction and pace, then student participation and involvement were good. Many of these teachers agreed that the 'lock-step' style of teaching denied the students any opportunity to use the language.
—for a purpose (so that mistakes matter)
—in real time (not where someone waits for the right answer)
—to express their own attitudes, feelings, emotions, fears, etc. (not what someone else tells them to say).

But despite this, and despite the fact that many had demonstrated an interest in more communicative techniques through voluntary attendance at seminars and conferences, the ideas put to them were not being tried. The question was, why?

Initial assumption

In 1984–85 the new intake of teachers began with an 18-day Orientation Course, aimed at providing an introduction to living and working in Morocco. The course covered the following areas:
1 background to the Moroccan education system, and guidelines on the official syllabus and administrative procedures expected of teachers in schools;
2 background to TEFL, including language analysis and introduction to methodology;
3 information on TEFL in Morocco, including:
    —a guide to common problems such as starting the school year, discipline, etc. with a view to presenting tried solutions
    —standard lessons taught in the Moroccan *lycée*
    —assessment procedures
    —planning the year;
4 background to living in Morocco, including a visit to the town and in some cases the school of their posting;
5 practice lessons with special classes of volunteer students in a *lycée*;
6 lessons in colloquial Moroccan Arabic.

Teaching on the course was a mixture of input sessions and tutorial work, and it was supported by a 130-page Orientation Course Handbook, as well as a guide to living in Morocco. The Handbook and the bulk of the teaching on the course was the responsibility of British teachers who were already at post. It was their role to prepare input sessions, give demonstrations, and run tutorials. Each course also had input in the form of demonstration lessons and tutorial support from selected Moroccan teachers. These colleagues also taught Moroccan Arabic. For these lessons the new teachers were put into groups of forty, so that they were able to experience the problems of beginners in a foreign language, as well as exposure to the high-energy question-and-answer approach characteristic of most Moroccan teachers of English. Orientation Course tutors were prepared for their role through a series of planning meetings which included a management course focusing on communication skills. Briefs were also provided to give tutors guidelines on how to structure sections of the Handbook, input sessions, and tutorials. Within the general framework provided, it was up to the course leaders and their teams to decide on programme balance, detailed timings, etc., and this led to the staff becoming very committed to their course. The inclusion of peers as trainers was an extremely valuable training exercise for the teachers concerned; all the participants were extremely satisfied, and the new teachers were very positive about the strongly practical orientation of the course. This was in complete contrast to the first orientation course, which had relied on outside informants, and we hoped that after a settling-in period teachers would begin to introduce new techniques. Despite the positive start and the practice of a few who showed that change was possible and desirable, the myth that activities such as pairwork and groupwork were impossible within the Moroccan teaching situation persisted, and objections to proposals for more adventurous and pedagogically sound techniques were still the rule rather than the exception. The feeling grew that communicative techniques belonged to an idealized form of TEFL with no relevance to the secondary classroom, and this led to professional frustration for all concerned, as many teachers with future EFL careers in mind wanted to experience these techniques. We decided, therefore, to have a look at these objections to see if we could help.

Objections

The most common objections to the introduction of new ideas and techniques and our analysis of these at the time were as follows:

1 *'The students are not interested when I try things they are unfamiliar with.'* It was certainly the case that new techniques were often met with apparent indifference, lack of participation, or even downright hostility. It seemed reasonable to assume that these new techniques did not match the expectations that students brought with them. We did not have time

to research students' expectations, but all the informal evidence from watching lessons and talking to teachers and learners suggested that Moroccan learners expected the teacher to be an authority figure, and the teacher methods to conform to the 'lock-step' pattern described above. Long (1975:217) suggests that this type of teaching encourages the following assumptions:
—it is the teacher who initiates language exchanges;
—the student's task is to respond to the teacher;
—the teacher judges whether the student's performance is acceptable.

Although our teachers reported that many students felt the need to be able to do something in English rather than repeat paradigms or patterns, they appeared to reject a methodology that would help them to achieve these goals. The reason seemed to be that taking part in classroom life involves taking part in the classroom game. A major part of this game is being able to answer questions, and doing this involves knowledge of the conventions governing a particular type of teaching, as well as an ability to 'read the signs' in the teacher's structuring of the lesson (Jackson 1968). Some of this knowledge is very deep-seated and tacit, and common to all classrooms (Mehan 1979), but the knowledge required to take part in lessons is also classroom-specific (Lancy 1978). It seemed that students often apparently rejected new ideas or complained that the teacher was not teaching, because the security and sense of order found in the familiar routines, in which they knew their status and role, had suddenly been violated by something new. They no longer knew the rules of the game.

2 *'Discipline is a problem.'* There was a strong feeling that chaos developed as soon as the teacher moved away from an 'up-front' position.

3 *'There are too many physical constraints.'* The majority of the classrooms had heavy double desks which in some cases were fixed to the floor. The acoustics were generally bad and the rooms large and cold. They were often without electricity. The teacher was expected to stand on a small platform, and the only thing adorning the walls was a blackboard. However, once a week classes had what were known as 'group hours' involving only half the class (i.e. about 20–25 students). These were designated as conversation lessons and designed to allow the teacher more flexibility and an opportunity to offer more individual attention to students. Nevertheless they tended to be used for tests or further 'up-front lock-step' teaching because of the teachers' heartfelt feeling that this was the only source of discipline, control, and order.

4 *'It is virtually impossible to provide the necessary duplicated materials.'* Access to duplicating machines was difficult, and the methods time-consuming and expensive.

5 *'Students prefer grammar and exam practice.'* Particularly in the final

year of secondary school, the students became obsessed by preparing for the Baccalaureate, which usually consists of a narrative-style reading passage with multiple-choice and open-ended questions, a series of grammatical transformation exercises focusing on obscure areas of usage, and a narrative compostion. None of these reflected or promoted the objectives for the system which are stated in the official textbook for English (*Steps to English Book 1*) as: training Moroccan students to use English to 'receive information about the world at large and to communicate to people elsewhere their own reality.' While the educationalists are aware of this inconsistency, administrative reform has been slow, and the consequence is a constant tension between the short-term felt needs of the students to pass the exam and longer-term objectives set by the system and favoured by the great majority of teachers. It is therefore up to the individual teacher to resolve the dilemma in his or her own classroom, (a situation which Professor Abutalib of the Faculty of Letters in Rabat described as 'creative chaos' when he gave an account of the state of language teaching in Morocco in 1985).

6 *'The school "administration" does not like noise when all the students talk at the same time.'* Moroccan headmasters are administrators, and they prefer teachers who are seen and not heard! But this attitude did not in fact result in interference with teachers who did try more communicative methodology and were perceived as successful by their students: there were no complaints. Teachers actually have a great deal of autonomy in their classrooms.

7 *'The students will not use English when put into pairs.'* Although this was true of some students, there was no evidence that it was universally the case.

8 *'The students complain that I am not teaching them if I ask them to work in pairs or groups.'* As many of the students were aged 18 or over, they were articulate in formulating what they expected or wanted.

9 *'Once motivated by more interesting classroom activities, the students become over-enthusiastic and difficult to control.'* A genuine problem.

All of these are important factors and not dissimilar to objections reported in secondary teaching situations elsewhere (see Bolitho and Early 1981). However, we felt that these were constraints rather than impediments. As the influence of official instuctions on the teaching was relatively weak, and as some teachers showed they were able to use 'high risk' activities and overcome the shortage of recent materials designed for communicative activities (for example, through the creative use of blackboard flaps or large sheets of paper visible only to part of the class for the creation of an information gap), we felt it was the students' perceived 'wants' (Allwright 1982:28) which were responsible for the continued dominance of 'lock-step' in the classrooms of British teachers. Conscious of the problems which can occur when a teacher does not meet the

Week	Aim	Means
1	To extend responsibility for initiating short responses to the learner.	Teacher-controlled open and adjacent pair work on question-and-answer exercises.
2	Consolidation plus introduction of dialogue exchange in pairs.	Dialogue reading: learner takes one part. Move from Teacher reading A and learners B through open and adjacent pairs to whole class work in closed pairs.
3	Consolidation plus introduction of learners to the habit of choosing the content of communication in oral work.	Longer read dialogues, followed by the introduction of cued dialogues.
4	Consolidation plus introduction of the idea of working together in English.	Introduce discourse chains to prompt recall of known dialogues; get learners to work on comprehension exercises in English.
5	To introduce the idea of guided role play, as well as simple problem solving.	Introduce role cards on the basis of familiar material; a short period in closed pairs; work on problems of grammar.
6	Consolidation plus introduction of 'information-gap' exercises.	Longer guided role plays; practice in moving quickly into pair work exercises; information gap in which half the class sees the picture; teacher controls questions and answers.
7	Consolidation and extension.	Information gap similar to (6), but done in closed pairs; jigsaw reading.
8	Consolidation and extension.	Introduce free role-play activities in pairs, then threes and fours; small group essay preparation for the final stage of guided composition lesson.
9	Consolidation and extension.	Introduce ranking activities.
10	Consolidation and extension.	Group preparation of ideas and structure for essay.

Table 1: A ten-week plan for introducing students to and training them in the use of pair and group work[3]

sociocultural expectations of a student (Ben Bechir 1980), we decided it was worth outlining a strategy whereby teachers could work on student expectations even in large classes.

Towards a solution

We realized that if our methodological proposals were to succeed, we needed to consider how to implement the systematic learner training that was fundamental to change. We felt that such training had to cover the *how* and the *why*. The *how* involves the gradual introduction of techniques so as to proceed from the known to the unknown. The *why* had to cover the rationale behind the activities. Such proposals are not new (see, for example, Candlin and Breen 1980), and our interest was to see how they might be applied in large classes.

Introducing pair and group work

If the main reason for 'lock-step' was the need for control, then freedom from control implied responsibility. Therefore, as our principle in dealing with *how* was to proceed from the known to the unknown, a reasonable first step in the introduction of pair and group work was to gradually widen the 'turn allocation' procedures used in the classroom by extending from the teacher to the learners the responsibility of deciding who should speak. In a situation such as that in Morocco, we felt it could easily take up to ten weeks to introduce and establish pair work as a routine, and the plan in Table 1 offers an illustration of what might be involved. This could of course vary from class to class.

The principle of proceeding from the known to the unknown is a powerful one, and it is perhaps the trainer's responsibility to suggest ways in which a staged and gradual introduction of new techniques is possible. We also discovered through observing our teachers that an ability to use students' names, give clear instructions, and check and facilitate understanding through questions and demonstration were crucial factors in the introduction of new techniques in a situation where repair of misunderstanding is very difficult once the activity is under way. Dealing with the rationale of activities in a large class involves appealing to common sense, and some of our teachers found questionnaires and ranking activities very profitable ways of bringing to the surface discussion of the language teaching and learning process.

Conclusion

It has been common practice to regard teachers as the source of resistance to change, and some observers have suggested counselling as one of the ways forward (Early and Bolitho 1981, Rinvolucri 1981). While there is a lot in this, we seem to have forgotten the learner. In the secondary system, learners may be particularly resistant to change if the change that is required of them runs counter to what is taking place elsewhere within the system. The creation of a fresh set of expectations is, therefore, essential to the acceptance of change by learners, who in turn have a great deal of influence on teachers' behaviour. It may be that learners new to language-school situations are more willing to accept something new because they are in a slightly different learning environment from what they have been used to, and therefore the introduction of change is less of a problem. Our contention is that, while taking a student's current needs and expectations as a starting point is second-nature to good teachers, not all teachers do it automatically. It is therefore the responsibility of trainers to focus on and develop this skill by formulating suggestions for new methodological practices in terms of practical procedures. When this is done, our observation is that teachers will try doing it with a class of forty.

Notes

1 The Centre for British Teachers Ltd, a registered educational charity based in London, recruits British teachers for service overseas. CBT schemes are paid for by the host government, and the British teachers usually work alongside colleagues in the national educational system of the host country. CBT currently operates within the state system in Brunei, Malaysia, Morocco, and Oman.
2 Separate statistics for the pass rate in English in the Baccalaureate do not exist, but a senior inspector of English estimated in a presentation to a conference of the Moroccan Association of Teachers of English in 1985 that only 25 per cent of the students pass.
3 *Open pairs:* Teacher-nominated pair work involving two students in different parts of the class.
Adjacent pairs: Teacher-nominated pair work involving two students sitting next to each other.
Closed pairs: All students work in pairs at the same time. The teacher monitors the activity.
Discourse chains: Students are given an outline of a dialogue in functional terms, e.g. greet, apologize, etc. They have to find the words to express the function and build up a dialogue using the clues.
Jigsaw reading: Students are given a text which has been cut up in some way (e.g. at the end of each paragraph) and have to reconstruct it.

(*Originally published in Volume 40/2, 1986*)

This last paper, like those of Wenden and Allwright, contains some illustrative samples of data in the form of worksheets, questionnaires, etc. Any approach to teachers on in-service courses is likely to be more successful if it has a firm basis in the reality of the classroom, and there is no doubt that data of the sort used by Nolasco and Arthur, Wenden, and Allwright can help to 'bring the classroom into the training room' in a way which will help teachers to feel that they are on familiar territory and that their views will be listened to and valued. The articles by Esther Ramani and Jeremy Harmer follow this trend. Ramani argues forcefully that teachers will approach theory willingly enough if allowed to reach out for it as needed from their present positions. She describes a procedure for building on teachers' existing constructs, helping them to identify related theoretical issues and pointing them towards selected background reading. Her 'familiar' point of departure was a video-recorded lesson and her context a seminar in Bangalore. But her message surely has relevance for anyone who trains teachers.

Theorizing from the classroom
Esther Ramani

Introduction

The integration of theory and practice has been seen as one of the most crucial issues in teaching training. In a recent article in *ELT Journal*, Widdowson makes a plea for greater attention to the development of a spirit of enquiry among teachers, and stresses the need for teachers to understand the relationship between theoretical principle and practical technique and 'to test one out against the other in a continual process of experimentation' (1984:86). In another article in *ELT Journal*, Allwright discusses the need for teachers to adopt 'more of a research attitude to their ordinary lives as teachers' (1983:132), and Brumfit (1984) devotes an entire book to the exploration and evolution of a teacher's conceptual framework for integrating research and theory with teaching. Theory is therefore seen as playing a central role in the *practice* of teaching. Yet in most teacher-training and orientation programmes, theory and practice are kept apart and are even listed as separate components of the training curriculum! Trainees are 'exposed' (through lectures or reading assignments) to various theoretical models of language learning, primarily to provide them with an historical overview. Teaching practice sessions are often marked by a heavy reliance on procedures, and participants are trained to use particular techniques without being required to understand the theoretical assumptions underlying them. As a result, teachers often see themselves as 'practitioners' who have little or nothing to do with theory.

This article attempts to describe a possible methodology for raising the theoretical awareness of teachers by encouraging them to conceptualize their practices and thus to narrow the gap between theory and practice in their everyday lives.

The methodology

Stern says 'No language teacher—however strenuously he may deny his interest in theory—can teach a language without a theory of language teaching, even if it is only implicit in value judgements, decisions, and actions, or in the organizational pattern within which he operates. However, it is an important function of theory formation to advance from a "naïve" and unreflecting "realism" to a more conscious understanding of the principles and concepts underlying one's actions' (1983:27). The methodology I outline here is based on a range of procedures to recover and make explicit this 'hidden theory' and then to examine it in the light of current understanding as it is set out in the literature on language learning, applied linguistics, and allied disciplines.

The starting point of the methodology is an item of classroom data in the form of a live or video-taped lesson, an audio-recording, or a lesson transcript. Teachers' subjective responses to these data are used to raise questions, both specific and general, which can be linked to current theoretical issues. These questions will suggest the areas which need to be discussed, read up on, or investigated. Greater clarity and understanding of these issues could then form the basis for exploring changes in practice. The actual procedures I used are described in the following section.

Illustration of the methodology

I tried out these procedures in a two-hour session with a group of twenty-five in-service teachers of English, who were participating in a two-day workshop held in Bangalore, South India in July 1985. Nine of them had received ELT training. The classroom data I used comprised a video-taped demonstration lesson taught by a specialist to a vernacular-medium group of school leavers who had joined a vocational course of study. The thirty-minute video-taped lesson may be characterized as a communicative ESP lesson (a label I did not provide the participants with).

I began with a brief introduction stressing that theory was implicit in everything we did as teachers, and then outlined the aim of the session and the activities planned. The exercise of theorizing was then conducted in the following stages.

Stage 1

I invited the participants to discuss this question in groups: 'What three things would you be interested in looking at while viewing the video-taped lesson?' This pre-viewing exercise was meant to elicit from them their usually hidden criteria for evaluating the teaching that they observe. These implicit criteria are also likely to be the ones that subconsciously influence their own teaching. We can therefore see these criteria as a teacher's unformalized 'pre-theoretical' map, because they reveal what the teacher considers important in the teaching–learning process. I could have given them a pre-determined list of observation criteria, but that would have pre-empted their own perceptions and would have robbed my approach of any credibility.

Stage 2

Each group's views were then elicited and written up on the blackboard. None of the criteria were discussed, except to eliminate repetition or overlap. There were the things that the teachers wanted to look at in the video-taped lesson:

1. the 'social' organization of the class;
2. the relationship between the teacher and the pupils;
3. the teacher's questions;
4. the materials used;
5. the pupils' participation;
6. aspects of language taught;
7. the relevance of the lesson to real-life needs;
8. student activities in the lesson;
9. the creativity of the teacher;
10. the ratio of teacher talk to pupil talk;
11. the teacher's handling of learners' errors.

We can readily see that these criteria cover almost the entire range of things which happen in a classroom, several of which, such as teacher–pupil interaction, error management, pupil involvement, real-life relevance, and language pre-selection, are the focus of current research, debate, and discussion. Clearly, teachers can perceive and articulate the potentially interesting areas in the teaching–learning process. My own role at this stage of the exercise was to clarify and re-state the teachers' contributions.

Stage 3

I then provided some minimal information about the video-taped lesson as a background for viewing it. No information about the methodology used in the lesson was given.

Stage 4

The participants viewed the lesson, and several of them took notes.

Stage 5

I then asked the participants to discuss two questions in groups:

1. Which parts of the lesson did they consider most satisfactory, and why?
2. Which parts did they consider least satisfactory, and why?

This exercise was meant to elicit the participants' real and subjective responses to the lesson. A time limit of ten minutes was enforced, to prevent revision of their spontaneous responses. To aid recall of the video-taped lesson, handouts containing information on the stages in the lesson, the dialogue on which the lesson was based, and the true/false exercise used in the lesson were supplied. (See Appendices A, B and C.) I expected that their subjective responses would reveal favoured, not favoured or untried ways of doing things. Asking for reasons for their responses would force them to reflect on them, and thus deepen their understanding of why they reacted as they did.

Stage 6

Each group then presented its impressions of what were the most satisfactory and the least satisfactory parts of the lesson for them. I did not at this stage comment on their responses; I simply wrote them up on the blackboard. I list these impressions below, using the teachers' own words, where possible.

The most satisfactory parts of the lesson were seen to be:

1. The variety of activities, because they 'maintained student interest'. They were also felt to 'reinforce the dialogue'.
2. The re-ordering task (stage 2 in Appendix A), because it 'demanded a lot from the students'.
3. The group activities, because they ensured the participation of all the students.
4. The way the teacher elicited responses from the students because 'he forced them to think'.
5. The different questioning techniques used by the teacher because he 'modified his questions' to enable students to handle them.
6. The different teaching aids (tape recorder, strips of dialogue) because they 'provided variety'.

The least satisfactory parts of the lesson were seen to be:

1. The dialogue used, because it was 'artificial' and contained unfamiliar cultural ideas such as 'full board' and 'bed and breakfast'.
2. The activities chosen, because they could be done 'without real involvement'.
3. The repetition of lines of the dialogue (stages 4, 8 and 9 in Appendix A), because this was artificial and the purpose of the repetition and recall was not clear.
4. The use of the same dialogue for *all* the activities, because it was 'tedious' and the 'material was overworked'.
5. The role-play exercise, because it was 'weak and uninteresting and its purpose was not clear'.
6. Listening to the dialogue again at the end of the lesson, because it was 'irrelevant when they had already done all the exercises based on it'.

An overall comment made was that it was difficult to assess whether any learning had taken place.

Stage 7

I then pointed out that in their subjective evaluations the teachers had implicitly applied some of their own criteria, which they had articulated in Stage 2 of the exercise. I suggested that we collectively discuss only two of the criteria (due to lack of time). We focused first on the student activities in the lesson. I pointed out that, in their subjective responses, the variety of activities was seen as both one of the most satisfactory and one of the least satisfactory parts of the lesson. Starting from this contradiction, we had a long discussion, at the end of which some teachers observed that, although the variety of activities had seemed attractive at first, in actual fact the use of the same dialogue in all the activities had led to a gradual decrease in the interest and challenge of each task, culminating at the end of the lesson in simple role play and repetition. From this observation a perceptive generalization was made: although variety was important, it was much more important to ensure that the activities were genuinely challenging. Several specific suggestions were made as to how this could be achieved, such as using different but parallel dialogue for some of the activities. This whole discussion showed how the teachers found themselves revising an assumption that they had held, namely that variey for its own sake is always desirable in the classroom.

The second aspect that we focused on was the teacher's question. I asked them to look at the transcript of the lesson (Appendix D), while listening simultaneously to an audio-recording of it. The aim of this exercise was to find out if their favourable impressions about the questioning procedures were borne out by a closer look at the classroom interaction. This too turned out to be an interesting exercise, from which several insights emerged. The largest generalization made was that the teacher's questioning procedures involved giving up his maximal expectations and opting for minimal success in the light of on-going evidence of what the learners could reasonably handle.

The actual techniques they discovered were:

1. starting with wh- questions and moving on to yes/no questions and back (lines 6,13,14, and 18 in Appendix D);
2. repeating the question (lines 1–2, 21–23, lines 27–32);
3. reformulating the questions by breaking them up into smaller information-seeking units (lines 17–18; 27–32);
4. providing time for the students to think (pauses in the audio-recording).

A general observation was made about the dogged persistence of the teacher: 'He just did not give up and provide the answers himself, though he must have felt tempted to do so'. An incidental observation was made on the teacher's handling of learners' errors. The participants felt that the teacher had rejected out-of-hand some of the learners' responses (lines 40 and 44). He could instead have explained why the responses were unacceptable, and could thus have converted the errors into learning opportunities. The whole of Stage 7 represented a crucial point in the process of theorizing: examining subjective responses more critically.

I suggested that the other criteria which we had listed in Stage 2 (but which we had had no time to look at) could be similarly examined by placing their subjective responses against a more sustained analysis of the classroom data.

I think that my own role during this stage was that of a reformulator and focuser. I helped the participants to reformulate their own insights in more specific terms, and suggested what might be interesting to focus on in the light of my own awareness of current theoretical issues.

Stage 8 (to be read after reading Appendix E)

The next day I provided a follow-up handout (Appendix E) summarizing the participants' insights, listing the general theoretical questions raised by these and suggesting relevant reading materials. The handout (which could not be discussed at the workshop) serves the following purposes:

1 It gave back to the participants in explicit and permanent form their own perceptions. I hope that it implicitly showed them that their perceptions are worth preserving, and that they should themselves articulate and write down their responses as a way of discovering and clarifying their own thinking.

2 It served to demonstrate that the issues underlying their perceptions are in fact some of the critical issues in second-language acquisition studies, and that a 'metalanguage' for discussing these issues is available. Further, this metalanguage supplies the terms for the concepts that the teachers are *already* partially opening with and thus helps them 'to name the world' (Frière 1972).

3 The handout might demonstrate how to read selectively from the vast literature on language training. For a start, participants need to read only the items that are relevant to the questions that their own perceptions have generated. The readings can confirm, disconfirm, or simply clarify their own ideas, and thus encourage them to examine their own 'theory' against current theoretical understanding.

4 The handout could be used for planning follow-up activity such as group reading projects, practice teaching, classroom observation and data analysis, and further discussion of ideas.

The feedback I received at the end of the workshop was overwhelmingly positive; the teachers said that they had enjoyed the exercise and felt that 'theory' was not so intimidating after all!

Implications for teacher training

In this section, I would like to suggest how this methodology could fit into a teacher-training programme, particularly for in-service teachers, who, given the constraints they work within, are the least inclined to look at 'theory'. In my experience, teachers always enjoy looking at actual lessons (live, filmed, or video-taped), so this could be the starting point for several activities, all of which could enhance their theoretical understanding.

Updating teachers' familiarity with current approaches to language teaching

In most teacher-training programmes, updating the teachers' knowledge of various approaches is an important component. Most often, this component is handled through lectures from trainers, and through reading assignments. In such an approach, trainee teachers are passive receivers of information, and their own perceptions are rarely engaged or strengthened. A possible way of 'exposing' teachers to different approaches to language teaching might be to get them to view a lesson, live or recorded, illustrating an approach, and then to ask them to deduce the 'theory' underlying it. When they have identified the central assumptions underpinning the approach in question, they can attempt a critical assessment in the light of their own assumptions and experience. Areas for reading can then be identified. This procedure could demonstrate that competing approaches may share a lot at the level of classroom technique, and understanding is often a matter of deciding what is seen to be the central principle of the approach in question.

Raising teachers' critical awareness of techniques

Given that most teachers have an eclectic approach to teaching in that they do not subscribe to any one 'school of thought', they need to be more critical of the assumptions about learning that underlie the techniques they choose to use. Therefore trainees could be asked to make a close examination of particular techniques used in a lesson. An exercise such as re-ordering strips of dialogue (which the teachers at our workshop found so attractive) could be subjected to the following questions:

—Does it involve just recall from memory?
—What knowledge does it demand of the learner—knowledge of real-life conversations, discourse structure, logical organization?
—What kind of skills might this exercise help to develop?
—Is it more effective for this exercise to be done individually or in groups? Why?
—At what stage in a lesson should such an exercise be done? etc.

Teachers' subjective responses to an item of classroom data will suggest which techniques to take up for examination. To begin with, those techniques which teachers intuitively find satisfying or unsatisfactory would be the obvious choices for closer examination. Such an approach can enhance teachers' understanding of actual techniques and thus provide a critical basis for selection or rejection.

Making reading a meaningful activity for teachers

A major problem in teacher training is that of getting teachers to read. Most training programmes prescribe a list of books for 'compulsory' reading, but very rarely are these books actually read and discussed. I think if trainees are encouraged to see reading as a search for answers to questions that interest *them*, then their reading is likely to be motivated and meaningful. I would like to suggest that the methodology outlined in this article could help teachers to identify areas to read up on, based on their responses to actual classroom data. The trainer's job would be to raise the relevant questions (that is, to generalize the issues from responses to data) and to direct trainees to the appropriate reading material. To begin with, secondary sources (books which summarize and interpret research and which directly address the teacher) may be suggested. Further, not all the trainees on a programme need to read all or even the same books. Reading projects, in which groups research and read up different areas, may be an interesting way of coping with the problem of 'no time for reading'. Trainees could think up ways of reviewing books, and of consolidating, preserving, and distributing the results of their reading projects. The important thing is to keep alive the dynamic link between teachers' intuitions and the ideas preserved in books.

Observing trainee teachers in practice teaching and analysing classroom interaction

A long-standing problem in teacher training has been that of observing trainees in practice and providing adequate feedback. A major source of tension is that observation is seen as a tool for trainee evaluation rather than for understanding the teaching–learning process in a lesson. I think that observation procedures deriving from the methodology described in this article could help to focus on classroom processes rather than on the teacher's performance. These procedures would include collective identification of criteria; observation by fellow trainees; trainees' reports of their feelings during practice session, evoked by a process of recall and introspection; identification of 'golden' and 'leaden' episodes (Gebhard 1984:505); audio-recording; transcribing; and collectively evolving their own frameworks for analysis.

I believe that reflecting, intuitively and impressionistically, on transcripts of their lessons would help trainees to recover the procedures which they think created the positive learning opportunities in their lesson. They could then formalize their intuitive strategies and use them consciously, thus gaining greater control over their classroom behaviour.

Conclusion

I have outlined only some of the ways in which theory can be made interesting and relevant to teachers. I am sure that classroom data can be used in many exciting ways to get teachers to reflect on their experience. I would like to end this article by restating the major premise underlying the process of theorizing described here: teachers' theoretical abilities *can* be engaged and strengthened if their intuitions are accorded value, and if the entry point into theory is close to their experience as practising teachers.

Appendix A

Stages in the video-taped lesson

1 Students listen to a recording of a simulated conversation between a hotel receptionist and a prospective guest, and answer questions orally.
2 Groups of students are given copies of the conversation cut up into strips; they rearrange the strips to find the correct order.
3 Students listen to the taped conversation again to check whether they have got the correct order.
4 Students listen to the taped conversation and repeat each line of the dialogue.
5 Students work in groups on a True/False exercise based on the taped conversation.
6 Answers to the True/False exercise are discussed by the teacher.
7 Students label strips of the conversation (they write R or G to show who is speaking, Receptionist or Guest).
8 Students role-play the conversation, each half of each group taking one part.
9 Students attempt role play without looking at the conversation.
10 Students listen to the tape-recorded conversation one last time.

Appendix B

Script of the taped telephone conversation used in the lesson

(Telephone rings)
R: Good morning. Orient Hotel. Can I help you?
G: Good morning. I'd like to reserve a room for next week.
R: Yes, Sir. Which days next week?
G: Monday to Friday, please.
R: And do you want a single or a double room?
G: A single with attached bath.
R: All our rooms have attached bathrooms, Sir. Do you want full board?
G: No. Just bed and breakfast, please.

R: So—that's a single room, bed and breakfast, for four nights. Can I have your name and address, please?
G: Yes. It's Mr G. N. Jenkins, 14 Prince Street, Colombo.
R: Thank you, Mr Jenkins. Can you confirm the booking in writing before Monday?
G: Yes. I'll confirm it. Can you tell me how much the room will be?
R: 450 rupees a night, bed and breakfast, Sir.
G: Thank you. Goodbye.
R: Goodbye, Sir.

Note:

This dialogue was used in all the activities listed in Appendix A. **R** stands for Receptionist, **G** for Guest.

Appendix C

True/False exercise used in the video-taped lesson in stages 5 and 6, Appendix A

a. Mr Jenkins wants to stay at the Orient Hotel.
b. Mr Jenkins wants a double room.
c. There are no rooms with baths available.
d. Mr Jenkins wants to have lunch and dinner at the hotel.
e. Mr Jenkins lives in Sri Lanka.
f. Full board at the Orient Hotel Costs Rs. 500/-.

Appendix D

Transcript of first part of the lesson

T: I want you to just say where is the conversation taking place: where is it, OK? Check you can hear. (*Plays beginning of tape-recorded conversation. Telephone rings: Voice says:* Good-morning, Orient Hotel. Can I help you?)
T: So, that's it. Where is the conversation taking place? (*Pause*) What did you hear on the tape now? (*Pause*) Anyone wants to answer? What did you hear?
P: Hotel.
T: Hotel. Did you get the name of the hotel?
P: Orient Hotel.
T: Orient Hotel. Right and so. (*Pause*) Do we know anything else about the conversation? (*Pause*) It is two people in the hotel?
P: No.
T: No. No? Why not? (*Pause*) Are there two people in the hotel—talking? (*Pause*). Where is the conversation taking place? It's in a hotel, but we know something more, don't we? What kind of conversation is it? (*Pause*) Listen again. Kind of conversation. (*Teacher replays only the sound of the telephone ringing*) So what kind of conversation?

P: Telephone. (*very faint*)
T: Telephone conversation. Right. Fine. So, it's a conversation in a hotel. What do you think it's about? It's a telephone conversation in a hotel. What do you think the conversation is about? (*Pause*) No ideas? (*Points to a student*) What do you think it's about? (*Pause*) What do you think the conversation is about?
P: I think it's a receptionist. (*very faint*)
T: It's a receptionist in a hotel. Fine. O.K. So one person is the receptionist—and who is the other person? (*Pause*). What do you think?
P: (*incomprehensible*)
T: One of the . . . ?
P: Passenger.
T: Passenger. You don't call it a passenger?
P: May be a lodger. (*very faint*)
T: What do you call somebody who stays in a hotel?
P: Lodger.
T: Not a lodger, no. Hotel—? (*Pause*) Somebody who stays in the hotel. Yes? What do we call that person? Hotel . . . ? Know this word? (*Writes 'g' on the board*)
P: Guest. (*very faint*) Guest.
T: Guest. Right.

Appendix E

This handout summarizes some of the issues that were raised yesterday by the discussion we had about the video-taped lesson, and suggests readings to clarify these issues.

1. *Variety in classroom activities*

Some of us began by stating that the *variety* of activities in the lesson was very satisfying, but others felt that the lesson was monotonous. In the discussion, we discovered that the source of the contradiction was the *use of the same material in all the activities*. With each use of the material, the challenge of the task had diminished, leading, at the end of the lesson, to simple role play and repetition, hence monotomy. This perception raises the following questions.

a. What is the role of variety in language learning?
b. Is there any direct relationship between variety in classroom activities and language acquisition?
c. Does variety have an 'affective' function in creating *motivation* (willingness to engage in learning)?
d. What other ways are there of motivating students?
e. What do you mean by 'activities' in the classroom?
   Two types are distinguished in the literature. (i) Psychomotor activities (*doing* things). (ii) Processing activities (*making meaningful* the language that is encountered). Which, do you think, is more important for language learning?

Reading: Read Hutchinson's paper 'Making Materials Work in the ESP Classroom' in the light of the video-taped lesson you analysed. What aspects of the teacher's theory are upheld by the lesson?

2   *The role of repetition in language learning*

We felt that the different activities in the lesson were used *to reinforce the material*. This perception raises the following questions:

a. Does repetition have any value in language learning?
b. Do learners learn anything from role play?
c. What is more likely to promote language learning, repetition or meaningful use of the language? Think of how a child acquires its first language. Think of your own successful experience of acquiring a second language.

3   *Question techniques*

We found the questioning techniques used in the lesson highly satisfactory and were able to locate specific instances of repetition, reformulation, and grading (moving from *Wh-* questions to *Yes/No* questions and back). The issues we can discuss are:

a. How specific are these questioning techniques to the language classroom?
b. Are you likely to find a subject teacher (of biology, for example) using such techniques?
c. Would you find this kind of repetition and rephrasing in 'natural' communication, such as (i) between a mother and her young child and (ii) between a native speaker of a language and a non-native speaker (who does not know the language well)?
d. What is the purpose of repetition and rephrasing? How is this repetition different from what the learners do in Stage 4 of the lesson?

4   *Learners' errors*

Many of us felt that the learners' errors could have been handled better. We thought that several learning opportunities had been missed.
Exercise: Look at the transcript and locate the places where the learners made 'errors'. How would you have handled these? Think of as many different ways of responding to these 'errors' as you can.
Reading: (i) S. P. Corder: 'The significance of learners' errors' in Jack C. Richards (ed.): *Error Analysis*. London: Longman, 1974. (ii) Chapter VII on errors in H. Dulay, M. Burt and S. Krashen: *Language Two*. New York: Oxford University Press, 1982.

5   *Follow-up activities*

We could raise questions about all the aspects of the lesson that we did have time to discuss yesterday. We could start by verbalizing our subjective impressions of the criteria that we collectively listed, and then look at the classroom data to confirm or disconfirm our impressions.

6 General reading

Chapter 11, 'From research to reality: implictions for the teacher' in Dulay *et al: Language Two*. New York: OUP, 1982.

Note

1 I am grateful to Tom Hutchinson for a copy of the video-taped lesson on which this paper is based. An earlier version of this paper won a special award at the English Speaking Union's Annual English Competition held in the U.K. in 1985.

(Originally published in Volume 41/1, 1987)

Harmer's approach in the activity he describes is resolutely task-based. This type of planning activity can be adapted for use in language work as well as teacher-training and like Ramani's sequence it serves as an excellent example of a way in which the trainer can function as a provider of interesting resources and seminar manager rather than as a lecturer.

Balancing activities: a unit-planning game
Jeremy Harmer

Origin

The game was originally designed for teachers' seminars and teacher training groups in Mexico. Its intention was to show how methodological principles (e.g. the reasons for providing a balance of activities) could be put into practice at the planning stage. It is also a way of dealing with a sequence of lessons, rather than looking at planning lesson by lesson, as all too often happens.

The 'unit'

While 'unit' is often used to mean the chapter of a textbook, here it refers to a sequence of lessons. Teacher and syllabus designers often divide terms or semesters into blocks (or 'units'), so that short-term goals can realistically be set, both for them and for their students. This involves planning in blocks, which is often not very easy to do. Two problems seem to present themselves: one is the thematic relationship (if any) between individual lessons in a unit, and the other is the need to balance activities. Each lesson, in other words, should probably not seem the same as any other, but in thematic terms lessons should probably not seem wildly different, either! Both these two strands, of course, have to be matched to language concerns and skill areas (see 'The pre-plan', below). While the planning of a unit is based on the same principles as the planning of a single lesson, there is more to deal with. Reference has to be made to previous and subsequent lessons in order to come to decisions about activities and thematic content.

Methodological background

Participants in the unit-planning game will probably need to have been exposed to a methodological 'approach' which is worth describing briefly here, although it is certainly 'mainstream', and commonly adhered to. When I have used the game with trainees, it has been played after trainees have discussed the reasons for 'a balanced activities approach'.[1] This is a way of trying to draw together different methodological strands, a kind of principled eclecticism.

A balanced activities approach includes, clearly, both 'input' and 'output'. On the input side, emphasis is laid not just on 'finely-tuned input',[2] where language is adjusted to fit exactly the students' level of proficiency (e.g. during 'presentation' stages), but also 'roughly-tuned input'—in other words, listening and reading materials where language is above the students' productive levels but is still comprehensible to them. Output is divided into two types: practice and communicative. The former is characterized by teacher and language control. The latter implies an emphasis on communication, with choices about language left to the student (see Harmer 1982a).

Motivational background

Planning is intimately related to motivational concerns. Students must, as far as possible, be encouraged to feel positive about language learning. What happens in the classroom may provide this encouragement, and good planning can ensure that it does.

In planning a unit, there must be an emphasis on variety and on the balance of activities that the students are involved in. This, of course, is true when planning a single lesson, and it is relatively easy to ensure a varied and amusing sixty-minute session. Sustaining motivation over such a short time should be within the grasp of most teachers in most normal situations. Sustaining motivation over two, four, or eight weeks is, however, a different matter.

The 'pre-plan'[3]

At some stage, teachers have to take general decisions about what they are going to do in their lesson or lessons. They do this before going into detail and making a final plan. This stage is referred to as the 'pre-plan'; it applies to planning of any kind and has four major components: *Activities, Language Skills, Language Type,* and *Subject and Content.*

When planning, teachers should first decide what activities (in the very broadest sense) will be appropriate for their students, based to a large extent on what they have been doing recently. The art of balancing activities in this way is the fundamental skill of planning.

Clearly, teachers will want to make decisions about which skills and sub-skills they wish to involve students in, and also what language type the students should be receiving or producing. Language type could, of course, be specific (e.g. the past simple), more general (e.g. ways of agreeing and disagreeing, the language of written controversy), or largely unpredictable (as in a genuinely communicative task). Finally, teachers will want to make decisions about the subject and content (apart from the language) to be dealt with in the lesson. They will hope to select topics which will motivate their students.

The use of the 'pre-plan' is shown in summary form in Figure 1. There is nothing particularly revolutionary about the pre-plan, but it does force the teacher to concentrate on activities, subject and content at least as much as on the language syllabus. The suggestion, in other words, is that language concerns should not predominate unreasonably. Teachers should ask themselves what activities, and what subject and content are likely to motivate the students with whom they will have to spend time in the classroom.

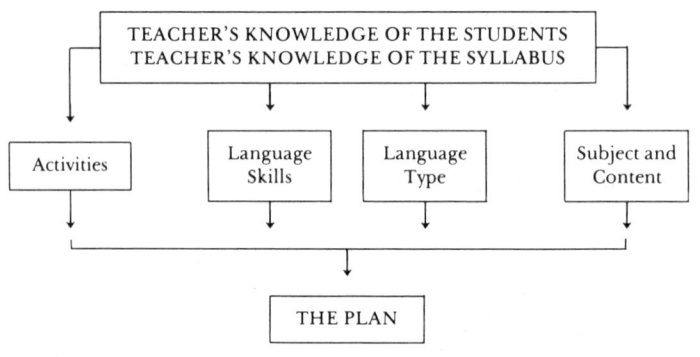

```
           TEACHER'S KNOWLEDGE OF THE STUDENTS
           TEACHER'S KNOWLEDGE OF THE SYLLABUS

    ↓              ↓              ↓              ↓
┌──────────┐  ┌──────────┐  ┌──────────┐  ┌──────────────┐
│Activities│  │ Language │  │ Language │  │ Subject and  │
│          │  │  Skills  │  │   Type   │  │   Content    │
└──────────┘  └──────────┘  └──────────┘  └──────────────┘
    ↓              ↓              ↓              ↓
    └──────────────┴──────┬───────┴──────────────┘
                          ↓
                    ┌──────────┐
                    │ THE PLAN │
                    └──────────┘
```

Fig. 1. The pre-plan

The pre-plan is particularly relevant to the unit-planning game, since it is at this more 'general' stage that decisions are taken by participants. The details of the actual plan are given on the cards; the object of the game, therefore, is for participants to become familiar with handling the four major components of the pre-plan.

The game

The version of the game shown here is designed for trainees working in a non-English-speaking environment (in this case Mexico).

1   The learners for whom the plan is to be made are assumed to be beginning a second semester of English study; thus they have attended

approximately 45 hours of classes so far. Participants are given a 'typical' group to make decisions about, as follows.[4]

Students consist of 21 women and 9 men, aged 16–25:

6	secretaries	1	doctor
5	housewives	2	businessmen
10	university students	4	secondary students
3	teachers		

2   They are told that they will have to plan a sequence of six fifty-minute lessons. Lessons take place three times a week.

3   Participants are told that the students have concentrated on the following language points during their first semester:

who/what/where + verb *to be*	Expressing opinions + agreeing/disagreeing
Present continuous	Asking about location
Present simple	Invitations
Can/can't	Suggestions
Introductions	

This language syllabus is deliberately general and lacking in detail. Its aim is to provide a very general lanaguage context which will not obscure the purpose of the game (the planning of a sequence of activities) by forcing participants to concentrate on a detailed language progression. Nevertheless, the 'syllabus' is similar to that found in many institutions and textbooks.

4   Participants are given a board on which there are columns for each lesson, arranged side by side. They are then given a pack of cards (shown in Figure 2 in no significant order). It should be noticed that each card gives a time limit for the activity in question. Mention should also be made of the 'jokers', for which participants may devise or select activities of their own choosing. The trainer goes through the cards, making sure that the participants understand the activities described on the cards, and giving more details where necessary. He or she explains that participants should choose what activities to use for their 'joker' cards: these should be written on a piece of paper and placed over the joker when the game is played. Participants are told that the total time for all the cards added together is 300 minutes (or six fifty-minute lessons). Participants are then divided into groups (five is the maximum for each). In their groups, participants have to place the cards on the board so that they have six fifty-minute lessons. Each group then does the task, discussing the reasons for their decisions about lesson content, sequencing, etc.

When each group has completed the task, the results are compared and the trainer leads a feedback session in which the different plans are discussed and the reason for the differences investigated.

212 Jeremy Harmer

15 minutes **Dialogue: Offering/requesting** 'I'd like...please' 'Would you like...?'		*15 minutes* **Writing** In pairs: students imagine they are on holiday/a cruise etc. They write postcards to relatives/friends. Focus on present continuous/simple, 'there is/are'.
	20 minutes **Song**[5] Students hear a song, and fill in a sheet with some words missing. They write 'the note' that the girl in the song is supposed to have left. They sing the song.	
10 minutes **Oral Communicative Activity** 'Going to New York' Students are told they're going to New York for 2 weeks. They can take 10 items in their suitcase. They decide individually, then in pairs, then in groups. Everybody has to agree.		*5 minutes* **Game: Noughts and Crosses**
	20 minutes **Presentation** 'Have to do/like to do'	
20 minutes **Parallel Writing**[7] Students read a description of a hotel based on symbols. They have to write about other hotels based on similar symbols. Practice of prepositions, description. 'there is/are', etc.		
	15 minutes **Listening: Interviews** Students hear a tape on which famous people are interviewed. Students have to fill in a chart based on the characters' everyday activities/obligations, etc.	
10 minutes **Listening** Students hear a tape of someone giving directions. They have to follow directions on a map.		*10 minutes* **Describe and Draw**:[6] **Oral Communicative Activity** Pair work: one student has a picture, the other has to draw the same picture without looking at it.
	15 minutes **Reading** Text about different restaurants. Information transferred to a chart comparing restaurants.	*10 minutes* **Reading**[8] Text about the QE2 (luxury cruise liner) True/False questions
20 minutes **Group Writing Activity** In groups, students write part of a tourist brochure for their town/city.		*10 minutes* **Game: Twenty Questions**
	20 minutes **Presentation** 'There is/are'	*15 minutes* **Role Play** A restaurant. In groups, students get a menu. One student is the waiter. A meal is ordered.
		15 minutes **Dialogue: Asking for Directions** 'Excuse me. How do I get to the ...?' 'Take the ... right/left.'
	10 minutes **Oral Activity: Find someone who**[9] Students are given papers with sentences such as 'Find someone who likes to swim'. They have to ask 'Do you like to swim?' and write the name of a person who says yes on their paper.	*5 minutes* **JOKER**
	10 minutes **JOKER**	*5 minutes* **JOKER**
	10 minutes **JOKER**	*15 minutes* **JOKER**

Fig. 2: Cards for the unit-planning game

Comments and reactions

I have used this version with a number of groups, both experienced classroom teachers and trainers on pre-service teacher-training courses. On each occasion, the game has given rise to a great deal of animated discussion and involvement on the part of the participants. When using the game with more experienced teachers, I have not intervened at all (unless asked to): there has been only very general feedback, and there is a lot of interest when the different 'solutions' are compared. Participants have sometimes felt unfairly restricted by the somewhat artificial time limits that the game imposes, and there have been suggestions about how to modify this (see 'Possible modifications' below).

With groups of trainees, there has been more reason for intervention or participation by the trainer. It has often been beneficial to query a group's reasons for the ordering of activities in a lesson (or lessons), and to suggest changes. The feedback session has tended to be rather more formal, with attention being drawn to specific cards and their positioning in the sequence. The game has been successful at this level in preparing trainees for individual project work in which they have to produce a detailed unit plan of their own.

The game seems to work precisely because discussion takes place within each group about why certain activities are appropriate in a certain lesson, and about the sequence that activites might follow. Specifically, participants are asked to make judgements about language and topic sequences and about the balance of activities both within lessons and within the unit. There are, for example, two activities concerned with restaurants, and a dialogue sequence dealing with offers/requests. Are these connected? Obviously they are, but a decision has to be taken about the sequencing of these three activities. Should they all take place within the same lesson, or should they be spread over a sequence of two or three lessons? The same kinds of concern are relevant with the presentation of *there is/are*, the 'hotels' parallel writing activity, and the travel brochure. Where should participants place the postcard-writing activity? Should it necessarily follow on from the text about the QE2? And so on.

Within each lesson what sort of balance should be achieved? It would be possible to include (in terms of time) the 'Describe and Draw' game, the 'Going to New York' card, and the 'Find Someone Who . . .' activity in the same lesson, but would this be appropriate? Such questions form the basis for the discussion that takes place in each group.

Possible modifications

There are various aspects of this version of the game that may not be to everybody's liking, and participants have often commented on some 'design faults'. There is no reason, of course, why modifications should not be made, or why completely new games should not be designed, using the same principle.

One worry may focus on the selection of activities found on the cards. In the version shown here, they reflect techniques and materials that are readily available to the participants. There is no reason, however, why the cards should not be changed to reflect different realities or methodologies—although the game loses a lot of its point if there is not some adherence to a balanced activities approach. Another worry is the artificiality of time constraints, and the mathematical calculations involved in fitting the cards into six fifty-minute sessions. One suggestion has been to provide too many cards, so that part of the participants' job would be to decide what to include and what to leave out.

The game can also be modified to suit different levels and different time-tables. Cards could contain activities suitable for advanced levels or for complete beginners, for adults or for children. Often the decision about what to put on the cards will depend on the main coursebook being used. Many institutions teach more intensively than three fifty-minute classes a week. This would simply mean designing a different board and putting different activities and times on the cards.

There is one situation in which the idea of the unit-planning game would have an immediate practical application, and that is where a group is taught by a team of teachers. This will often be the case on intensive language courses such as those offered by language schools in Britain where students study for four hours every morning. During the morning such groups may be taught by three or even four different teachers, and there are often problems in providing a balanced but coherent programme for such groups. If, however, a group of teachers were to write all the possible classroom activities on cards and then play the unit-planning game, the planning would not only be more enjoyable, it would probably be better.

Conclusions

Planning is of vital importance in successful language teaching, but overworked teachers are often unable to give it the attention it deserves. Teachers in training, of course, are often unaware of the concerns and problems of planning sequences of lessons. For both these groups, the unit-planning game is a way of bringing planning to the forefront and involving participants in balancing activities over a unit—a vital planning skill. The game seems to work, since participants are not only able to discuss planning issues, and therefore come to some conclusions; they are also forced to work out how a variety of given activities might be integrated into a series of lessons.

Notes

1 For a more detailed discussion of a balanced activities approach, see Harmer (1983), Chapter 4.
2 These terms are borrowed form Krashen (1981).

3 The 'pre-plan' is discussed in more detail in Harmer (1982b and 1983).
4 This extremely varied class population is not unusual at the Instituto Anglo-Mexicano de Cultura in Guadalajara.
5 The song is the Beatles' 'She's leaving home'. Charlotte Almsig first used it in this way, as far as I know.
6 This activity is described by Geddes and McAlpin (1978), among others.
7 This activity is from Davies and Whitney (1979).
8 This text can be found in Rossner *et al.* (1979).
9 This is one of the many activities found in Moskowitz (1978).

(*Originally published in Volume 38/2, 1984*)

The role of resource manager, or controller, is familiar enough to those teachers who have run simulations or projects in their classrooms. Too often viewed as 'soft options' for a teacher or as Friday afternoon diversions for learners, both these activity-types, when carefully prepared and structured, have much to offer learners who are working towards fluency and autonomy in the target language. In their attractively titled paper, 'Dear Brown Eyes. . . . .' Graham Carter and Howard Thomas describe a project they ran with young adult learners together with primary school children in Bath. One reason for including this article was its inspiration value. It describes one of those magical experiences, which we all have once or twice in a career, when everything seems to come together. The account of the encounters between the children and their strange visitors from overseas is heartwarming, and shows what can be achieved, albeit in favourable circumstances, by dint of good planning, goodwill, trust, and astute judgement.

'Dear Brown Eyes': Experiential learning in a project-orientated approach[1]

Graham Carter and Howard Thomas

Project work is a familiar feature of teaching programmes in primary, junior, and secondary schools in Britain and elsewhere. It is normally characterized as work which

—takes place outside the classroom
—is cross-curricular
—allows learners to set their own learning targets as they proceed.

However, much of what is carried out under the heading of project work in EFL in Britain would not reflect these criteria, and for good reasons.

Given the constraints of time and lack of familiarity with the new community, foreign learners have fewer resources at their disposal, and require a great deal of assistance from teachers to organize even simple information-gathering exercises outside the classroom (cf. Legutke and Thiel 1982). The role of the teacher is, in general terms, to provide a framework within which 'teacher-independent work' can take place. What this framework consists of, ranging from the germination of the idea for a particular project to the staging of project activities, is the focus of this article.

Background

If the communicative approach has developed towards integrated learning (that is linking, speaking, reading, and writing in various combinations for a variety of communicative purposes), then one could claim for project work that it provides learners with opportunities for practice for 'live' communicative purposes. Moreover, learners who are interacting with the English-speaking community in order to achieve something for the benefit of others are no longer role-playing. At the Bell School in Bath (one of six schools run by the Bell Educational Trust), project work has been part of the curriculum for several years and is the object of increasing attention and development. Earlier projects at Bath included those in which students taught in local schools, wrote a wheelchair guide for the city (see Fried-Booth 1982), and made a video film of the sensitive work of helpers and teachers in a centre for handicapped children. All these projects made a genuine contribution to the host community. In making commitments to others outside their school environment, learners also provided themselves with reasons to be involved in a complex of 'live' communicative activities. Within such frameworks integrated learning gathers its own momentum.

Rationale and aims

The 'Brown Eyes' project arose in 1985 as an attempt to replicate previous experiences with groups of EFL learners in local schools in Bath. It was at the same time an attempt to improve and develop the preparation which the learners underwent before they carried out their 'teaching'. It must also be said that, given contacts in local schools, this type of project is relatively simple to set up: it is much more difficult to find useful roles for students in factories or offices. Local school teachers have recognized the contribution to the work of a school that foreign learners can make, even if it is only in answering children's questions. Colleagues in the local schools instantly recognize the advantages for their children of learning at first hand about other cultures, rather than indirectly from TV or video.

The main rationale for the selection of this project for these learners lay in the need to offer them a language-learning and cultural experience that might bridge the time gap up to their next exam course more effectively than would a conventional textbook-based course. This experience would involve, by means of contact with different types of local people, a need to acquire and use language skills which could be predicted by the group's teacher, 'life skills' such as presentation and organizational abilities, and a knowledge of the English education system and the principles behind it.

It was also important to give learners as active a role as possible. There are several reasons why it was not just ambitious that they should attempt to teach. If learners were to become integrated with the community in some way, they had become involved by *doing* something, rather than functioning just as 'watchers'. A second reason concerns the act of communication itself. The primary classroom would make our learners perform as language users in a way well beyond what they could prepare for by means of a teacher's script. They would have to respond in a host of unprepared situations, stretching their 'strategic competence' to the limit (cf. Tarone 1984). It is a situation where the target language is a means and not the end, and where 'learning-by-doing' is the most important factor.

The choice of age group (8-11 year-olds) was not accidental. Primary-school children are too young and are generally not 'forward' enough in their behaviour, while secondary-school children are often too shy and withdrawn, and beset by the peer-group pressures of puberty. Junior school children in our experience are linguistically sophisticated, confident, challenging, inquisitive, and unaware of any need to make concessions due to imperfect command of the language. Similarly, our choice of project participants was not accidental. The group consisted of upper-intermediate learners at post-FCE but pre-CPE level,[2] so there was a reasonable chance that they would achieve the competence required to perform the task adequately.

Planning the project and course

The amount of teaching that was thought appropriate was set at four days, a figure arrived at from previous experiences, which indicated that involvement in such a project was not only exciting but (after a point) very tiring for learners, if only because of the effort they invested in it. This was a point recognized retrospectively by this group, who were grateful to concentrate their project work into the 'project' part of the week. For teaching weeks for them were not exclusively devoted to the project, but also contained two to three days of normal classroom work, devoted to general language practice. This constituted an important 'recovery' period and helped to avoid staleness.

Having decided that the learners would spend a total of four days teaching in junior schools, it was arranged that the group would be divided into two sub-groups of six, with each sub-group concentrating on two schools, teaching two days in each. It was now necessary to have a clear idea of what they needed to know and what they should be able to do in order to make the experience a successful one, both for themselves and the junior school pupils. This meant 'backwards planning' as outlined below.

Clearly, the learners had to have information about the curricular organization and structure of the schools; the ethos upon which they were based; the educational and social background of the pupils; and the approach to pedagogy and consequent teaching methodology used in the schools, together with a more general introduction to fundamental notions of the psychology of learning.

In addition, the learners needed guidance not only on how but also on what to teach. It was therefore necessary to promote close liaison with the schoolteachers they would be working with, by arranging preliminary visits to the schools. This would also provide an opportunity for first contact with the pupils themselves. The co-operation and first-hand experience gave learners ideas for suitable activities and materials.

With one exception, this was to be the first time any of the learners had been a teacher; for all of them, using English as the teaching medium was a new and potentially frightening experience. Therefore, consideration was given to the development of the necessary language skills, and of a positive group dynamic which would create a co-operative spirit among the members of the group. A readiness to help each other was particularly valuable in the later practical stages of the project, for example during materials preparation, and at moments when emotional support was required.

The analysis of the learners' needs led to the development of a number of activities which included visits from guest speakers, outside visits, 'experiential lessons', group and individual tasks, simulations, and an introduction to the use of classroom media. Subsequently, it was necessary to decide on the order in which these activities should be undertaken, to work out the best way to execute them, and, finally to balance academic needs with the availability of resources. The planning produced a series of stages which are described below:

1   Socialization, group dynamics, procedural tasks.
2   Video familiarization.
3   Introduction to the psychology of learning.
4   Teaching programme and materials.
5   Book and video-film production.

Socialization, group dynamics, procedural tasks

Early in the first week of the course, the group took part in a simulation exercise to encourage the process of socialization and to generate a positive group dynamic. It was felt that if the project were to be successful, then the learners had to share their anxieties and fears as well as their triumphs, to offer a shoulder to cry on as well as ideas and helpful suggestions, and above all, to work efficiently and enthusiastically as a unit with a common aim. The simulation also gave the tutor the opportunity to monitor the learners' free use of language, as a basis for subsequent language sessions introduced at various stages of the course.

The embryonic group dynamic generated in this way was further nourished by a Current Affairs mini-project. The learners, in pairs, and with audio- and/or video-recording equipment, interviewed people in the street, asking questions on a topic of interest with a questionnaire previously worked out in class. This was the first exposure to native speakers outside the school environment. It was interesting to note that the task created some anxiety among the learners: they confessed that they doubted their ability to make themselves understood and to understand the respondents' answers, and that they lacked the confidence to approach strangers in the street and introduce themselves and the questionnaire; many thought that members of the British public would be unwilling to stop and answer questions on political and social issues. A few, however, hid their fears and anxieties behind a display of bravado and flippancy which was strongly criticized by other members of the group. Given such negative expectations, the first part of the feedback phase—to elicit the learners' immediate affective response —was astonishing: fear and anxiety was replaced by self-satisfaction and surprise, together with a new-found confidence in their ability to use English in new, unpredictable situations. The opportunity to express their feelings before the task, together with the feedback phase, enabled the learners to discuss and monitor their own progress. This kind of pre- and post-task discussion was a feature of various stages of the project. The fact that learners themselves were able to recognize the progress they had made generated enthusiasm both for the project and for the continued successful acquisition of English.

Video familiarization

While several learners had had experience of filming members of the public as part of the current affairs mini-project, none of them had, as yet, appeared before the camera. As a video film documenting the progress of the project was to be one of the end-products, it was essential that at an early stage they should all get used to being filmed. Consequently, a series of activities was arranged which required the learners to present themselves to an audience in front of a video camera. Previous experience with pupils of a local comprehensive school[3] had shown that being filmed is, at first, an unnerving, embarrassing experience: many pupils had 'dried up', dissolved into uncontrollable giggles, or hidden their nervousness behind a mask of superciliousness. Seeing themselves on video had been an equally traumatic experience which had reduced all the pupils to a state bordering on hysteria! We were naturally anxious to avoid a recurrence of such a response.

All learners were required to give a prepared talk on a topic of their own choosing to their classmates; this was also filmed on video by learners who had expressed interest in being camera operators for the project. To acquaint both the camera operators and the rest of the group with the basic vocabulary and techniques of film-making, a professional cameraman led a workshop session in which emphasis was given to filming interviews and classroom activities. This had not been a feature of the 1984 Education Project 'Are You Ready, Kids?' (Carter 1984), and the improvement in basic visual and audio quality of the film is evidence of this fresh input.

Our learners were as nervous as the 14/15 year-old pupils in the comprehensive school had been: the prepared talks were dry and largely uninteresting; they behaved unnaturally. It was generally agreed that the activity had been less than successful, but very informative. An opportunity to build on this experience was provided by the next activity, which was a simulation of a television news bulletin. Here the students were required to write and present a news programme to be filmed on video. It not only gave the group more experience of self-presentation and of being filmed, but also exploited and developed the procedural and social tasks, introduced at earlier stages, which are crucial to the successful planning and implementation of project work.

Introduction to the psychology of learning

Another essential component in the preparation for the project was the need to become aware of basic concepts in the psychology of learning and how they affect the junior school classroom. Three sessions were held:

1 A group discussion in which learners were asked to reflect on their own experience of school in general, and of primary school in particular.

2 A 'staged' formal grammar lesson, This 'experiential' session was considered to be more effective than a lecture in making the learners aware of the crucial role that teaching methodology plays in learning. As the basis for project work is learning-by-doing, this session, in a sense, was a microcosm of the whole Education Project. It proved to be highly successful: learners were angered and alienated by the teaching methods used, and unanimously agreed that they had no place in primary schools. The feedback session was followed immediately by a lecture given by a junior school teacher on the teaching methods used in primary schools. The lecture was now a feasible way to introduce some basic notions of the psychology of learning, because it had a basis to it and could involve practical questions, such as what activities would be appropriate for 9–10 year olds.

3 Further insight into how children learn, and an introduction to what techniques and strategies a teacher must use to ensure learning, was provided by an educational psychologist. Enthusiasm for the project was by now running so high that the learners attended the talk on a free evening, and impressed the speaker with their interest and ideas for

classroom activities, which had been extended and clarified by watching two video films made of the previous projects, 'A Class of Your Own' and 'Are You Ready, Kids?'.

Teaching programme and materials

At various stages of the project a number of sessions were held to provide the students with the special training necessary to gain and subsequently hold the children's interest. Clearly, new linguistic and paralinguistic skills had to be learnt. As it had been decided that story-telling would be an integral part of the teaching programme, narrative techniques such as the following were among the skills taught:

—the use of cleft and pseudo-cleft sentences for creating emphasis and suspense; direct and indirect speech for dramatic effect;
—the use of linking words and sequences;
—getting listeners involved by asking them to anticipate subsequent events;
—the use of facial expressions, different voices, and a variable speed of delivery.

By now, all the learners had selected six or more activities and had begun to draw up their teaching programmes. And yet the project remained unreal. In order to make the idea of being teachers real, members of staff from the junior schools were invited one Sunday morning to the Bell School to meet the learners. In this way, the learners had an opportunity to air any worries and to discuss their teaching programmes; at the same time the teachers were able to see what kind of work had been done in the 1984 Education Project and to seek answers to any questions or worries that they or the schools might have had.

It became clear that the learners were confident about the shape and content of their programmes, but their major worry remained their ability to control a small group of children and communicate effectively with them. Consequently, preliminary visits to the schools were arranged.

The learners spent one morning observing their future pupils and later wrote a report based on a check-list which directed their attention to points which they themselves felt to be important. The feedback sessions which followed the visits revealed that much of the self-doubt had evaporated: they could understand and make themselves understood; the children were friendly, interested, and enthusiastic; they were looking forward to being teachers.

Now the preparation of materials acquired a relevance previously missing, and the constraints of the timetable and even pangs of hunger were ignored in a whirlwind of activity. The carefully-nurtured group dynamic generated massive co-operation among members of the group: they made suggestions, helped, reassured, congratulated, shared different skills with one another, all of which involved intense and task-related communication in English. When the materials had been prepared, they were tested in a controlled environment at the Bell School. A microteaching session using other classes was arranged—without the knowledge of 'teachers' or 'pupils'. The aim of the session was not simply to test materials, but also to allow the learners to use newly-acquired teaching techniques and to reassure them of their ability to teach and communicate. This unexpected experience proved enjoyable and instructive for both 'pupils' and 'teachers'. Despite initial reluctance, the former gained in cross-cultural awareness, while the latter confirmed the viability of their materials and methods, as well as their ability to ensure and check comprehension. The 'teachers'' evaluation of their own performance was not limited to a consideration of their language and teaching techniques; they learned obvious but very important practical lessons (for example, do not chew gum or hold your hand in front of your mouth while teaching!). But, once more, it was the affective aspect of the experience which proved remarkable: smiling faces, animated talk, even pride resulted. Not only could they communicate effectively: they could teach too.

Book and video film production

Following the four days' teaching, two weeks of the course remained. It had been decided in the pre-course planning that there should be an end-product over and above the experience of having been a 'teacher'. The 1984 Education Project had had a video film; the 1985 Education Project would have both a video film and a book.

The video film would provide a photographic, documentary record of the project, the making of which generated a number of subsidiary activities: deciding what to film, script-writing, making a storyboard, film editing, production graphics, and a voice-over commentary.

While one half of the group was busy making the film, the other half was putting together a 38-page book conceived, written, designed, typed, collated, and bound by themselves. The book, which has the same title as the film ('Dear Brown Eyes'), contains contributions not only from the learners but also from the Bell School tutors involved with the project, and the teachers and pupils of the junior schools in which they had taught.

Once more, these projects-within-the-project came to dominate the timetable, and the learners' involvement, interest, and enthusiasm overcame the restrictions imposed by normal eating habits and school hours as they missed meals and worked late in the evening in order to finish their tasks.

Conclusions

It is not within the scope of this article to present a detailed description of the teaching materials used or of the lessons themselves, or to attempt to evaluate the learners' performances as teachers. It is sufficient to note in passing that materials included maps, models, and artefacts from their own countries, and that the methodology applied mirrored current practice in British primary and junior schools, in that it encouraged the involvement of the pupils themselves. Of the learners' contribution as 'teachers' we are able to comment that the schools involved in the exercise have invited us back to repeat the experiment with future learners.

Our comments here will be confined to the personal and linguistic developments of the participants, the contact with the community, and some practical considerations.

The students as learners and language users

It would be easy to point to a standard test result and claim that this project could produce a formal language improvement. However, a formal language test before and after the project was not used, because the learners were not preparing for exams, and we felt that it would not measure the kinds of skills they were likely to acquire. Nevertheless there is an abundance of informal observation and feedback on each learner to support the following comments.

Our observations led us to conclude that there had been a substantial growth in the learners' 'strategic competence'[4]—that is, in their ability to convey accurately what they wish to say. The learners themselves report that they feel at ease in 'live' situations with native speakers in most types of discourse and that they are unworried by unpredictable language difficulties or new contexts and situations. This implies that they have developed a range of communication strategies (see Corder 1977, Tarone *et al.* 1976, and Tarone 1977) which compares favourably with or approximates to the range available to native-speaker peers. Several people who met the learners noted, for example, a well-developed ability to paraphrase difficult or unknown words, an ability to develop statements until the 'message' was clear, and a high degree of precision and an absence of circumlocution. Their deployment of appropriate 'turn-taking' procedures and the variety of ways in which they presented information within utterances was also commented on. Above all, however, it was their personal confidence as language users which was most frequently mentioned in the informal feedback. These points were all noted by their teachers, fellow staff at the Bell School, the teachers at the junior schools, and conference participants at IATEFL, Brighton, 1985 who participated in an open forum on project work which included three students from this group.

Cross-cultural learning

A major problem for language learners visiting a country where the target language is spoken is to find an avenue into the culture which allows them some insight into why things are as they are, and why people behave in the way they do, to test our popular notions about a culture, and accumulate their own experiences. Too often prejudices are reinforced rather than being re-evaluated or dissipated. In this exercise, however, learners reported a range of observations which suggested that they had arrived at new and better-informed insights into at least one corner of English society. They gained a better understanding of, among other things, the philosophy and organization of English schools, the prevailing economic conditions and relative levels of prosperity among children, the lack of uniformity in approach to teaching, the different levels of politeness and impoliteness, and the subtleties of the class system in England. As a result, most of the learners revised key ideas and began to look at their host society in a less generalized way. Although they thought, for example, that English society was less egalitarian and organized than they previously believed, they no longer felt that English people were cold and reserved. They were, moreover, very impressed by the friendliness and professionalism of all those they encountered on the experiment.

For the children also it was an opportunity to demolish some of the barriers which their own prejudices and lack of experience had erected. Their drawings, maps, models, and thank-you letters are evidence of the recognition of similarities which emerged. It was an important experience for them to appreciate that people of different appearance and from different cultures are very much like them. (A Danish girl student reported in the 'Are You Ready, Kids?' project that one six-year-old boy would join the others around her to listen to a story only when he had touched her to verify that she was real and that she was like him.) One of the thank-you letters written after the 1985 project, from Darren Gale ('birthday 10 January') suggests the warmth of feeling engendered—and incidentally gave a name to the project:

> *Dear Brown Eyes, Please can I come to Brasil with you because I like Brasil . . .*

Practical considerations

It will be clear from this article that undertaking a project like this requires an approach from the teacher different from a normal classroom-based course. It needs a high level of pre-planning and co-ordination with other teachers regarding school resources, together with an ability to monitor and support learners' motivation, particularly at the beginning. Above all, as this is an exercise involving the community outside the school, great consideration should be given to how one makes approaches to people and institutions in order not to overburden, or indeed alienate, this irreplaceable resource.

Whatever the effort involved, those associated with the 'Brown Eyes' group feel that these language learners developed an unexpected facility with and awareness of language use, in a context which allowed them also to develop as individuals. It is in this wider area of general educational development that we may now begin to see the value of project work in the context of communicative language teaching.

Notes

1 The title of both the book and the video film documenting the project produced by the students was taken from a letter written to a Brazilian student-teacher by one of her pupils in the participating schools. This project was carried out with a group of students taught by Jane Cursiter, with help from Graham Carter, Nick Alt, and Howard Thomas. The success of this work for the students is directly due to the efforts of those involved, in particular Jane Cursiter, whose guidance, care, and energy were indispensable.
2 FCE (First Certificate in English) and CPE (Certificate of Proficiency in English) are examinations offered to intermediate and advanced learners respectively by the University of Cambridge Local Examination Syndicate.
3 'Video Letter' was the result of collaboration between the Bell School, Bath and Ralph Allen School, Bath, in 1985. The aim was to produce a video film which would be exchanged with one produced by a school in Braunschweig, West Germany. The authors and Mick Allen from the Bell School, and Marion Bennett from Ralph Allen School, worked with fourth- and fifth-year pupils on the German and English commentary which covered the City, the School, and a pupil's home (this was performed by the pupils, who also decided what was to be filmed). The idea for the video letter was taken from a similar exchange developed by Klaus Seidler of Biedenkopf, West Germany.
4 'Strategic competence': this is a term used by Elaine Tarone to refer to a part of a learner's performance in the target language. It is not to be confused with 'competence' in the Chomskyan sense of 'competence and performance'. It is (paradoxically) a part of the latter.

(Originally published in Volume 40/3, 1986)

Clearly, once again, the focus here is on individual tasks, leading to the cumulative outcome of a class project. What works in a language classroom ought to work in a training room, too. Put the other way round, there is widespread belief these days that teacher-training practices should, as far as possible, mirror classroom practices. No lectures on group work!

In the context of a plea for more work to be done on the methodology of teacher training, Rod Ellis proposes taxonomies of tasks/activities and procedures for teacher-training and also draws attention to the value of *data* as a basis for many of these activities and procedures. He also lists some different *types* of data. His article is of interest not least because it offers a framework for course planning. Individual sessions can be designed within the framework. This is in contrast to many of the other articles in this section which describe single activities or sequences which are of interest because they can be adapted to other contexts. Ellis's more global view is welcome, and with its forward-pointing conclusion, provides a fitting note on which to end this section.

Activities and procedures for teacher training
Rod Ellis

Introduction

The last few years have seen a number of teachers' manuals for English as a foreign language (EFL) (e.g. Abbott and Wingard 1981; Gower and Walters 1983; Willis 1983; Harmer 1983; Hubbard *et al.* 1983). These manuals vary in their intended audiences and also in their approaches, but, in their different ways, they all provide information about both the theory and practice of English language teaching (ELT). This information is presented in a variety of ways. (1) There are *expositions* of theoretical principles and procedures for carrying out different kinds of lessons. (2) There are *examples* of lesson plans and of teaching materials. (3) There are *activities* for teacher trainees to carry out in order to explore and evaluate different aspects of EFL. These manuals, then, not only inform us about the practice of EFL, but also try to involve trainees actively in the process of taking decisions about what to teach and how to teach it.

The main purpose of this article is to examine in some detail what *teacher-training activities* consists of. I hope that, by providing an analytical framework for describing the various kinds of activities that can be used and the different training procedures for exploiting them, I shall both encourage their use in teacher-training courses and also provide practical information about how to devise and use activities. The framework described in the article is the by-product of a seminar dealing with the 'training of trainers' which was recently held in Thailand with the support of the British Council.[1]

There are three parts to this article. The first consists of a schematic outline of teacher-training practices. This is intended to provide the context for the second part, in which a framework for describing teacher-training activities is presented. This part also includes an example of a training activity. In the third part, a list of training procedures is given, together with a sample of a training plan for exploiting an activity.

An outline of teacher-training practices

Teacher-training practices, in the first instance, can be divided into those that are *experiential* and those that are *awareness raising*.

Experiential practices involve the trainee in actual teaching. This can occur through 'teaching practice', where the trainees are required to teach actual students in real classrooms, or it can occur in 'simulated' practice, as, for instance, when the trainees engage in peer training.

Awareness-raising practices are intended to develop the trainees' conscious understanding of the principles underlying EFL teaching and/or the practical techniques that teachers can use in different kinds of lessons.

Two points need to be made about the distinction between experiential and awareness-raising practices. First, the two types are not mutually exclusive. Teacher training will often involve both kinds, although it is probably true to say that experiential practices are more common in pre-service training, while awareness-raising practices predominate in in-service teacher training. This, however, is perhaps more the result of convenience and tradition than principled decision-making. The second point is that experiential and awareness-raising practices do not need to be separated; they can be combined in a single activity. This occurs, for instance, when teaching practice is used not only to develop the trainees' practical classroom know-how, but also to develop understanding of particular issues through reflection and evaluation. The dotted line in Figure 1 is meant to represent the potential integration of the two types of training practices.

The purpose of this article is not to discuss the relative merits of the two kinds of practices. The assumption that underlies the use of awareness-raising practices, however, is that the practice of actual teaching can be improved by making teachers aware of the options open to them and the principles by which they can evaluate the alternatives. We do not know to what extent this assumption is justified. Do trainers, in fact, really influence what teachers *do* in the classroom by making them *think* about the principles and practice of teaching in training sessions remote from the classroom? It is all too easy to assume that a better-informed teacher will become a better teacher. It would be comforting it there were some clear evidence to support this assumption.

The focus of this article is on awareness-raising practices. These involve the use of training *activities* and training *procedures*.

Training activities consist of the materials that the trainer uses in his or her training; they correspond to ELT materials for use in classroom teaching. Each activity will set the trainee a number of *tasks* to perform. These tasks are likely to be based on some *data*, which constitute the raw material of the activities. It follows that training activities can be described by specifying the different ways in which data can be provided and the different kinds of operations that the trainee is required to carry out in the tasks based on the data. Training procedures constitute the trainer's methodology for using activities in training sessions. Just as the teacher needs to draw up a lesson plan for exploiting teaching materials, so the trainer needs to draw up a training plan incorporating appropriate procedures for exploiting different training activities.

Figure 1 displays in diagrammatic form the various training practices that have been described.

A framework for describing teacher-training activities

In this section a descriptive framework for teacher-training activities is developed. The purpose is not to suggest what 'good' activities consist of (i.e. no evaluative criteria are suggested), but to identify the various options available to the teacher trainer.

Teacher-training activities can be described by detailing (1) the different ways in which data can be provided and (2) the different kinds of operations that the trainees can be asked to perform.

```
                    ┌── experiential (e.g. teaching practice)
                    │              ▲
                    │              │
teacher             │              │
training  ──────────┤              │                        ┌── data
practices           │              │                        │
                    │              ▼       ┌── activities ──┤
                    │                      │                └── tasks
                    └── awareness- ────────┤
                        raising            │
                                           └── procedures
```

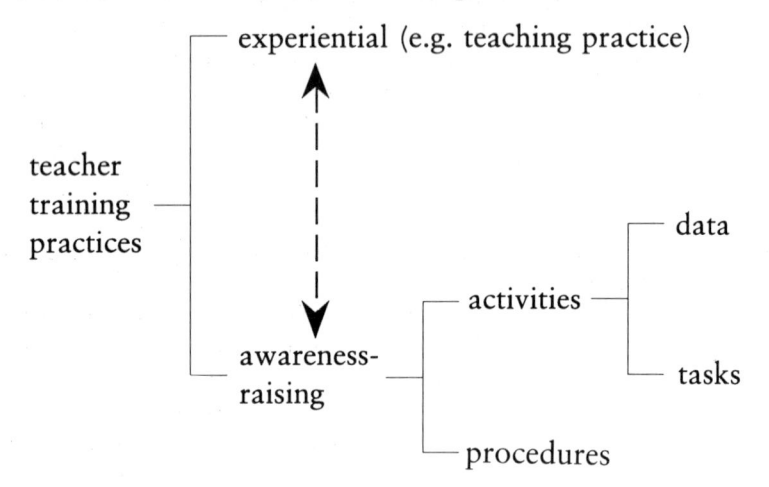

Figure 1: An outline of teacher-training practices

Ways of providing data

1 *Video or audio recordings of actual lessons*: These are potentially rich sources of data, as they can provide samples of real teaching. Ideally the recordings should be made in the classroom contexts in which the trainees will have to teach. There is, however, an excellent collection of video material, covering a variety of teaching contexts, available in the British Council's *Teaching and Learning in Focus*. This consists of a number of edited lessons and also some thematic modules dealing with a number of key issues such as 'class management' and 'dealing with errors'. The video materials are supported by handbooks suggesting a number of ways of using the materials. Trainers who wish to make their own video materials should consider who best to focus the camera on—the teacher, the students, an individual student, or a combination of all of these. The choice will be determined by the particular use for the material that trainers have in mind (i.e. the kinds of tasks they are going to set). Trainers will also need to consider whether the video or audio material is to consist of whole lessons or selected extracts.

2 *Transcripts of lessons*: Another way of presenting classroom data is by preparing transcripts of parts or of whole lessons. One advantage that transcripts have over video or audio material is that they permit detailed

inspection and analysis more easily. There is, of course, nothing to prevent the trainer using video/audio materials in conjunction with transcripts.

3   *Classroom teaching.*

4   *Peer teaching.*

5   *Micro-teaching.*

(3), (4) and (5) are all experiential activities. That is, they can be used to give the trainee direct experience of teaching and do not need to be accompanied by awareness-raising tasks. However, they can also serve as further ways of providing data about teaching for analysis and evaluation.

6   *Reading*: Again, trainees can be provided with readings from articles and books on ELT as ends in themselves. Alternatively, these readings can be used as a basis for a range of interesting tasks.

7   *ELT textbook materials*: Samples of teaching materials —both good and bad, appropriate and inappropriate— can be exploited as data for awareness-raising activities in a variety of ways.

8   *Lesson plans and outlines*: Apart from being invited to prepare complete lesson plans, trainees can be asked to perform various tasks based either on 'authentic' lesson plans or on lesson plans that have been specially designed to illustrate particular training points.

9   *Case studies*: Case studies are another valuable source of data. They can be studies of particular classes, of individual teachers or learners, or of whole courses. Williams (1985) provides two case studies of reading programmes which are good examples of the kind of raw material that can be utilized in training activities.

10   *Samples of students' written work.*

This list is not intended to be exhaustive, but to provide an indication of the breadth and variety of the data that the trainer can use for designing training activities. Any single activity may make use of just one data type or a combination of types.

Different kinds of tasks

The list of tasks below takes the form of a number of 'operations' which the trainee can be asked to perform on whatever raw data are provided. An example of the kind of rubric needed for each operation is given to clarify what is involved in each task.

1   *Comparing*
    e.g. 'Look at the two-lesson plans provided and decide which one you prefer and why.'
2   *Preparing*
    e.g. 'Prepare a marking scheme that you could use to correct the attached sample of students' written work.'
3   *Evaluating*
    e.g. 'After watching the video extracts, evaluate the effectiveness of the teacher's treatment of oral errors, using the criteria supplied.'

4 *Improving*
e.g. 'Read the case study of a reading programme, paying particular attention to the author's own evaluation. What suggestions can you make for improving the programme?'
5 *Adapting*
e.g. 'Adapt the following language exercise in order to introduce an information gap.'
6 *Listing*
e.g. 'Look through the transcript of the lesson provided and make a list of all the different kinds of errors the students make.'
7 *Selecting*
e.g. 'Now that you have listed all the different kinds of errors in the transcript, decide which errors you would choose to correct if you were the teacher and say why.'
8 *Ranking*
e.g. 'Look through the language-teaching materials attached and then rank them according to how 'communicative' you think they are.'
9 *Adding/completing*
e.g. 'Read through the article, listing the principles for the teaching of reading. Are there any additional principles you would like to add?'
10 *Rearranging*
e.g. 'Look at the video recording of a teacher organizing group work. Make a list of the different steps the teacher follows. What changes to the order of these steps would you recommend?'

Other operations are doubtless possible. Once again, the aim has been to illustrate the range of possibilities. Any single training activity can make use of just a single task or a series of tasks.

A sample training activity

Tables 1 and 2 illustrate how data can be combined with operations to devise training materials. The aim of the activity is to increase the trainees' understanding of what communicative ELT activities consist of, and in particular to make them aware that a simple dichotomy between 'communicative' and 'non-communicative' is not possible. The activity consists of the following:

Data: (1) A set of criteria for evaluating communicative ELT materials (based on Harmer 1983).
(2) A selection of ELT activities (mainly from Doff *et al.* 1984).
Tasks: (1) evaluating (i.e. using the criteria to evaluate the ELT activities);
(2) ranking (i.e. ranking the ELT activities according to how communicative the trainees consider them).

Table 1: Sample activity sheet

What is a communicative activity? Below are six criteria that you can use to decide how communicative different classroom activities are. Use these criteria to evaluate the selection of classroom activities attached.

Criteria for evaluating how communicative classroom activities are:

1 *Communicative purpose:* The activity must involve the students in performing a real communicative purpose rather than just practising language for its own sake. In order for this to occur there must be some kind of 'gap' (information or opinion) which the students seek to bridge when they are communicating.

2 *Communicative desire:* The activity must create a desire to communicate in the students. That is, even though speaking is forced on the students, they must feel a real need to communicate.

3 *Content not form:* When the students are doing the activity, they must be concentrating on *what* they are saying not *how* they say it. They must have some 'message' that they want to communicate.

4 *Variety of language:* The activity must involve the students in using a variety of language, not just one specific language form. The students should feel free to improvise, using whatever resources they choose.

5 *No teacher intervention:* The activity must be designed to be done by the students working by themselves rather than with the teacher. The activity should not involve the teacher correcting or evaluating how the students do the activity, although it could involve some evaluation of the final 'product' of the activity when the activity is over. This assessment should be based on whether the students have achieved their communicative purpose, not whether the language they used was correct.

6 *No materials control:* The activity should not be designed to control what language the students should use. The choice about what language to use should rest with the students.

Draw a table like the one below. Put a tick if you think the activities meet the criteria. Put a cross if you think they do not. In some cases you may not be sure, so put a question-mark.

Criteria	Activities					
	1	2	3	4	5	6
1 *Communicative purpose*						
2 *Communicative desire*						
3 *Content not form*						
4 *Variety of language*						
5 *No teacher intervention*						
6 *No materials control*						

When you have finished filling in the table, rank the six teaching activities according to how communicative you think each activity is overall.

1 *(most communicative)*
2
3
4
5
6 *(least communicative)*

Table 2: Selected ELT activities

1 *Group work*
Work in groups of three. Study the example and then continue.

Student A to	**Student B to**	**Student C** (Replies)
Ask Kay to give you her pen.	*Give me your pen, please.*	YES (Here you are.)
Ask Mrs Wright to give us a sandwich.	*Could we have a sandwich, Mrs Wright?*	YES (Certainly.)
1 Ask Jerry if he's got a letter for me.		NO
2 We must do some shopping tomorrow. Ask your boss to give you a day off.		NO
3 Ask Adrian to give you his dictionary.		YES
4 If you want more coffee, ask Mrs Wright.		YES

2 *Communication task*
Practise with your partner:

A Where are you from?
B I'm from (country).
A Which part of (country) are you from?
B (Town).
A What's your address?
B (Address).

3 *Pair work*
Work with your partner and ask each other questions about accommodation in your country. Here are some of the questions:

a What is the cheapest type of accommodation?
b Are meals served in all types of accommodation?
c Does the price of a room always include breakfast?
d What facilities are provided?
e Is advance booking advisable?

4 *Practise accepting and refusing things*
Copy the table below into your exercise book. Put a tick next to each item if you like it. Put a cross if you do not like it.

Item	Like/dislike
1 apples	
2 cabbage	
3 beer	
4 coffee	
5 pork	
6 fish	
7 milk	
8 cakes	

Work with a partner. Offer him each item in the table. He should accept or refuse it and give a reason for his answer. He should then offer you each item.

5 *Communication task*
Draw your family tree. Use it to talk to your partner about your family. Then complete your partner's family tree by asking him/her questions. When you have finished, compare your versions.

(From Doff, Jones, and Mitchell 1984)

Table 3: Sample training plan (based on the sample training activity)

1 *In plenary*
a Explain aim of activity.
b Invite definitions of Harmer's six criteria (with criteria listed on OHP).
c Give out Activity sheet and ask trainees to read through definitions of six criteria.
d Deal with any problems regarding definitions as necessary.
e Check that they understand instructions for first activity and table.
f Individual trainees complete table for ELT Activity (1).
g Call on individual trainees to give their responses in (f), together with their reasoning, and deal with disagreements.

2 *In groups*
a Divide trainees into two groups. Instruct Group A to evaluate the ELT activities starting from Activity (2). Group B likewise, starting from Activity (4).
b Allow groups up to five minutes to begin discussion, and then move from one group to the other.
c Ask both groups to prepare OHP transparency of the results of their discussion.

3 *In plenary*
a Invite secretaries of Groups A and B to display and explain results on OHP.
b General discussion of results.

4 *Pair work*
Trainees work in pairs to prepare an agreed ranking of ELT activities.

5 *In plenary*
a Pairs pass forward note of rankings to trainer, who enters them on transparency. (While this is being done, pairs evaluate ELT Activity (5).)
b Discussion of rankings from (1) to (5).

6 *Individual assignment*
Trainees write an evaluation of Activity (5) in terms of the six criteria and its place in the rank order.

Teacher-training procedures

What procedures for exploiting activities like the one above are available to the teacher trainer? Here is a list of some of the possibilities:

1 *Lectures*: Lectures can be used to provide straight 'input'. Alternatively, they can be used as a way of supplying raw material for the trainees to operate on.
2 *Group/pair discussion*: The trainees work in groups or pairs using activity sheets.
3 *Workshops*: The trainees work individually or in groups to prepare something, such as ELT materials, teaching aids, or lesson plans.
4 *Individual work/assignments*.
5 *Demonstrations*: The trainer demonstrates a particular technique, using either actual students or the trainees themselves.
6 *Elicitation*: The trainer works with the trainees and tries to draw out opinions on specific teacher-training points using a question-and-answer technique.
7 *Plenary discussion*: There is general discussion of ELT issues with all the trainees together.
8 *Panel discussion*: The trainer can make use of panel discussion in several different ways. One way is to invite a number of trainees to form a panel. The other trainees then prepare a number of questions on chosen issues to ask the panel. The trainer acts as the chairperson of the panel.

A single training session may involve just one of these procedures or, as will often be the case, it may involve a combination of several. For training sessions based on activities, the trainer will need to draw up a training plan (on paper or in the head) incorporating appropriate procedures. The training plan in Table 3 has been designed for the sample training activity in the previous section. It is intended to show how selections from the list of procedures can be used to exploit a particular training activity.

Summary and conclusion

The last fifteen years have seen considerable changes in ELT, accompanied by intensive debate about syllabus design, materials, and classroom practice. In contrast, there has been little public discussion of teacher-training practices in ELT (see, though, *ELT Documents 110* (British Council 1981), Holden (1979), and Jordan (1982)). Given the importance of teacher training for ELT, this is a serious deficiency.

The aim of this article has been to develop a schema—obviously not the only one possible—for thinking about the content of teacher training. To this end, I have suggested that it is useful to distinguish between *experiential* and *awareness-raising* practices. In addition, I have outlined a framework for describing different types of training *activities* by listing the various ways in which *data* can be provided, and also the kinds of *tasks* which can be based on the data. Finally, I have described the *procedures* the trainers can use. Together these constitute an embryonic taxonomy of training materials and practices. Such a taxonomy can serve two principal functions. First, it can act as a check-list which trainers can refer to when planning a training programme. Secondly, it can be used for 'training the trainers' by introducing would-be trainers to the range of options that are open to them. It sould be emphasized, however, that the framework is *descriptive*. If we are to develop our understanding of teacher-training practices further, we will need also to decide upon *evaluative* criteria for making principled selections from the range of options, both in devising training activities and drawing up training plans.

Note

1 The seminar was called 'Principles and Practice in ELT In-service Teacher Training'. I am grateful to the following for the various discussions from which the descriptive framework described in the article evolved; Thelma Henderson, Alan Waters, Andy Dunlop, Roger Hawkey, Piers Horey, Barry Hussy, Mike Long, Clarence Shettlesworth, and Julie Tice.

(*Originally published in Volume 40/2, 1985*)

Further reading

Readers may wish to follow up their reading of this section by referring to the following titles:

Brumfit, C. J. 1984. *Communicative Methodology in Language Teaching.* Cambridge: Cambridge University Press.
Gairns, R. and **S. Redman.** 1986. *Working with Words.* Cambridge: Cambridge University Press.
Gower, R. and **S. Walters.** 1983. *A Teaching Practice Handbook.* London: Heinemann.
Grellet, F. 1981. *Developing Reading Skills.* Cambridge: Cambridge University Press.
Grellet F., A. Maley, and **W. Welsing.** 1981. *Quartet 1 (Teacher's Book).* Oxford: Oxford University Press.
Harmer, J. 1983. *The Practice of English Language Teaching.* London: Longman.
Littlewood, W. 1981 *Communicative Language Teaching.* Cambridge: Cambridge University Press.
Nuttall, C. 1982. *Teaching Reading Skills in a Foreign Language.* London: Heinemann.
Willis, J. 1981. *Teaching English through English.* London: Longman.

The following series will also be of interest:

Cambridge Handbooks for Language Teachers (General editors) Michael Swan and Roger Bowers. Cambridge: Cambridge University Press.
Essential Language Teaching Series (General editors) Roger H. Flavell and Monica Vincent. Basingstoke: Macmillan.
Language Teaching: A Scheme for Teacher Education (Series editors) C. N. Candlin and H. G. Widdowson. Oxford: Oxford University Press.
Longman Handbooks for Language Teachers. London: Longman.
Practical Language Teaching (Series editors) Marion Geddes and Gill Sturtridge. Oxford: Heinemann.
Resource Books for Teachers (Series editor) Alan Maley. Oxford: Oxford University Press.

Conclusion

We have attempted, in making our selections for this collection, to reflect the most significant trends in ELT in the eighties. Readers will have their own views on our choice, and may identify issues which they feel we might have covered such as Computer Assisted Language Learning, Language and Literature, or Vocabulary Teaching. However, it is worth noting in passing that the *Journal* in its articles and particularly in its Review section has mirrored these and other developments over the period of this collection.

Where do we go from here?

Some of the articles included, such as Medgyes's, Maley's, and Ellis's have attempted to set 'agendas' in their own field of interest. It is interesting to ponder on the role that journal articles might play in this respect. Many of the most influential books published in ELT over the last twenty-five years, whether textbooks, reference works, or background books of the 'teachers' handbook' variety, have been written by British or American authors. A glance at the 'publications' list in the Chronology (pp. 252–4) in this volume will suffice to confirm this. A journal offers opportunities to a wider cross-section of the profession (teachers as well as academics) from all over the world, to take part in debate on key issues, either through articles, reviews, or letters to the editor. It seems to us that this is a healthy future role for the *Journal* too. Articles such as those by Medgyes and Li Xiaoju in this collection help to remind trendsetters of the responsibility they bear to consider the differing concerns of all branches and outposts of the profession. There can be no global solutions to ELT problems, but they can, and should, be raised in the *ELT Journal*.

A collection like this allows an opportunity to take stock, with the benefit of hindsight, of a period of change and intense activity. It has also offered us, as editors, a rare opportunity to look ahead and to speculate on future directions and priotitites in ELT. What now follows, however, is intended as food for thought rather than as a deliberate attempt to 'set the agenda' for the nineties.

Several of the themes broached in this volume seem likely to remain 'on the boil' for some time to come, not least because the European 'second decade' of communicative language teaching is, in some parts of the world, the first. It would be highly undesirable for generalizations based on insights gained in privileged West European and North American contexts to continue to be peddled as wisdom in Asia, Latin America, and Africa. In our view, this points to a need for a period of consolidation and reflection. Not only do teachers in the rest of the world need time to try out their own versions of these ideas for themselves, but those who wield influence in the profession need to spend more time listening, with an appropriate measure of humility, to those who hitherto have listened so attentively to them.

Publishers have a part to play here, too. So long as teachers and school authorities buy, publishers will continue to produce. Publishing houses have made a significant contribution to innovation, which many of us have had good reason to appreciate, but competition and new technologies have increased the pressure on publishers to come out with 'the newest' and 'the best'. It would be a relief to reflect, in ten years' time, on a period of more careful development in the field of teaching materials. In particular, it would be good to see an end to attempts to sell UK and US produced 'global courses' into totally inappropriate markets. In addition, those publishers who have been particularly successful might look for ways of 'giving something back' to those learners in the more disadvantaged areas of the world and sectors of the profession where imported books are too expensive. This could take the form of low-cost adaptations prepared by local specialists, or guidelines designed to show local teachers how a given global course might be adapted to local needs and used by them *without* each student needing to have sight of a copy (or a photocopy!). Such ventures supported by non-marketing seminars could be of great benefit if designed and run with full local involvement.

Collaborative projects in ELT: Why don't we hear more about them?

A development which has spawned a number of valuable articles over recent years, and which contributes a great deal towards the kind of debate and understanding alluded to above, is the increase in collaborative projects, in ELT and in education generally. Language advisors from most of the main mother-tongue countries are at work throughout the developing world. Educational institutions in Britain, the USA, Canada, Australia, and other countries are being involved in consultancy and advisory work in these projects, many of which promote curriculum change, materials development, and extensive in-service training programmes. So long as power and authority are properly located, this trend can only be positive, offering, as it does, so many opportunities for first-hand contacts between consultants and teachers, and for better understanding in Britain, North America, and Australasia of the constraints which prevail in disadvantaged contexts elsewhere. The materials produced on these projects are largely of local interest, but reports on the nature and extent of the collaboration and on the process of innovation are of widespread concern. It is to be hoped that more and more of those involved in such projects, whether as hosts or visiting consultants, will find time to make their experiences known to a wider audience. In such collaborative ventures, there is an accountability to the profession as a whole and over and beyond that to the paymasters and project managers. Many classroom teachers and teacher trainers have found their voices through an involvement in such work, but their concerns are far too infrequently submitted for publication in journals. These professionals are written about far more often than they write. There are many reasons for their reticence, some of which are familiar enough: lack of time, low self-image, and lack of confidence, unwillingness to commit problems to print for fear of the consequences, and a reluctance to contribute to methodological debate from the limited base of their own classrooms. Yet teachers *do* have views on the innovations they are working with, implying changes of role in the classroom, changes in their view of language, and in the role of teaching materials.

How easy is it to be a 'communicative' teacher?

For many teachers, this has been a period of destabilization and doubt. Their doubts must not simply be swept under the carpet. There have been calls for retraining, and demands on 'professionalism' have increased (though with no visible increase in teachers' status worldwide). There are many who maintain that it takes a better teacher to teach communicatively.

The challenge to policy-makers is to keep the pace of curriculum change in step with in-service training and materials development. The challenge to teachers the world over is to play a more robust role in the decisions which affect their professional lives, to articulate their concerns publicly, and to play a leading part in their own development as teachers.

What about the voice of the learner?

As far as we are aware, *ELTJ* has never published an article by learners who haven't become teachers! This may seem an odd observation, but at a time when we are paying much more attention to learner-centred approaches, to learner autonomy, and to its prerequisite, learner-training, it is perhaps only a matter of time before teachers' periodicals start to include a 'learners' corner'. Taken to its logical conclusion, the communicative approach is bound to increase learners' involvement in their own learning. It would be interesting and illuminating to read more reports from teachers and their students on their reactions to these fresh challenges and to the inevitable tensions (teacher-learner,

learner-home, teacher-learner-institution) which the redefinition of roles and responsibilities engenders.

How should we respond to the spread of ELT?

The voices of young learners of English were 'audible' in Rogers' article in this volume, and the debate he initiated is far from over. The impact of the English language in developing countries extends far beyond the problems which teachers have in implementing the communicative approach. Reasons for recent changes in language policy in countries such as India, Sri Lanka, the Sudan, and Malaysia have to do with deep and broad issues of national identity, religious and cultural heritage, and economic and social realities. Policy shifts of this sort are not always sensitively reported in the mass media, and it is only in the pages of journals such as *ELTJ* that authoritative critical assessments of language policies and their implications are likely to be given. This is an area which it is important for teachers of English to be well informed about, and which would benefit from less emotion and more balanced understanding in the years to come.

How is the ELT curriculum changing?

Increasing acceptance of English as the language of international relations in trade, science and technology, tourism and diplomacy, has brought its own consequences for curriculum development. Many schools are having to 'make room' for ELT, not only in Europe, where the consequences of increasing integration are becoming ever clearer, but further afield, too. One welcome effect has been an upgrading of the status of English as a school subject in many countries and, in many second language contexts, it has brought English teaching into much closer contact with the teaching of other subjects on the curriculum.

One of the results has been a recent preoccupation with 'content teaching' in Canada and the USA particularly. Another has been the development of a language awareness movement with cross-curricular effects in many schools in the UK. Experiments in these areas will be watched with great interest in the nineties, as they promise to help open up new avenues in the quest for more effective classroom approaches.

Do applied linguists have a responsibility to ELT practitioners?

The work of applied linguists has often been closely related, perhaps inadvertently in the first instance, to these curriculum issues. This was the case, for example, with Krashen's Monitor and Input theories, and with the large amount of work done by British applied linguists on the analysis of spoken and written discourse. There often appear to be important classroom implications which language teachers need to concern themselves with, even though the applied linguists' starting point may not have been pedagogic. In other cases, applied linguists have actually said what they feel the implications of their work are for teachers. For example, teachers have been told that they should take quite a different view of 'errors' from that prevalent 15 to 20 years ago, and this has considerable consequences not just for teaching but for testing practices. In the 'Talking shop' in this volume, Pit Corder implies that a task-based approach to language teaching is a necessary consequence of current thinking about second language development. In other cases, the arena for the observation and analysis of second language acquisition has moved directly into the classroom, as researchers try to measure the effects of formal instruction.

Clearly, teachers will take a keen interest both in the underlying principles of the research and in the implications of the findings. In such areas of applied linguistics it is, we feel, the responsibility of applied linguists to help to ensure that all interested parties in the profession, not just other applied linguists, have easy access to their ideas and findings. This means allowing for the fact that a majority of teachers will not have time to go deeply into the background issues or to learn the intricacies of the special register which many applied linguists use. Applied linguists should thus be ready to clarify and debate the issues with teachers and when appropriate to cross the threshold of the 'classroom door'. It may be tempting to say that it is for teachers to draw their own conclusions and work out their own solutions, but applied linguists should make sure first that the conclusions and solutions are reached on the basis of a proper understanding of their ideas and theories. It would be encouraging to say the least, if, in future a greater number of applied linguists spent more time working with teachers both inside and outside the classroom.

ELT Journal and other periodicals in the profession provide important mechanisms for maintaining and strengthening these links and for forging new ones. For it is only by tenaciously pursuing improvements in our understanding of how second language competence develops in classroom settings that the learning and teaching of English as a foreign language can be improved.

In summary, the bridge between theory and practice is one which, like the Forth Railway Bridge in Scotland, needs constant maintenance and attention from both sides.

Appendices

Bibliography

Abbot, G. and **P. Wingard** (eds.) 1981. *The Teaching of English as an International Language.* Glasgow and London: Collins.

Abbot, G. 1984. 'Should we start digging new holes?' *ELT Journal* 38/2: 98–102.

Abutalib, M. 1985. 'Morocco's Journey in ELT.' Talk given to 1985 MATE Conference.

Ake, C. A. 1982. 'Selected sociopsychological attitudes associated with foreign language instruction in high school and post-secondary students'. Doctoral dissertation. Florida Atlantic University.

Alatis, J. E. 1979. 'President's commission receives testimony on ESL'. *TESOL Newsletter* 13/3: 1, 25.

Alexander, L. 1977. Handout for seminar at the British Council, Paris.

Allwright, R. L. 1975. 'Problems in the study of the language teacher's treatment of learner error' in Burt and Dulay (eds.). *New Directions in Second Language Learning. Teaching and Bilingual Education.* TESOL. 96–109.

Allwright, R. L. 1976. 'Putting cognitions on the map: an attempt to model the role of cognitions in language learning' in Povey (ed.). *Workpapers in Teaching English as a Second Language* Vol. X (June): 1–14. UCLA.

Allwright, R. L. 1978. 'Abdication and responsibility in language teaching' in *Studies in Second Language Acquisition* Vol. II/1: 105–121.

Allwright, R. L. 1979. 'ESP and classroom management: the role of teaching materials'. Paper presented at the Second Latin American ESP Regional Conference, Cocoyoc, Mexico.

Allwright, R. L. 1982. 'Perceiving and pursuing learners' needs in M. Geddes and G. Sturtridge (eds.): *Individualisation.* Oxford: MEP.

Allwright, R. L. 1983. 'Talking Shop: The L.A. Tapes.' *ELT Journal* 37/2: 129–36.

Alptekin, C. 1982. 'Cultural dominance and EFL'. *Canadian Modern Language Review* 39/1: 56–62.

Alptekin, C. and **M. Alptekin.** 1984. 'The question of culture: EFL teaching in non-English speaking countries.' *ELT Journal* 38/1: 14–20.

Asher, J. 1969. 'The Total Physical Response approach to second language learning'. *Modern Language Journal* 53: 3–17.

Atkinson, P. 1981. 'Inspecting classroom talk' in C. Adelman (ed.): *Uttering, Muttering.* London: Grant-McIntyre.
Austin, J. L. 1962. *How to Do Things with Words.* Oxford: Clarendon Press.
Barnes, D. 1976. *From Communication to Curriculum.* London: Penguin.
Bartoli, C. 1981. 'Teaching the Silent Way'. *Practical English Teaching.* Vol 2/1: 29, 30.
BBC TV. 1980. 'San Giorgio's Bitter Fruits', *The World About Us.* London.
Ben Bechir, S. 1980. 'The Teacher's Failure to Meet the Learner's Social and Cultural Expectations: A Potential Source of Demotivation.' Unpublished Psycholinguistics Project, University of Lancaster.
Berger, P. O. and T. Luckmann. 1967. *The Social Construction of Reality.* Garden City, New York: Doubleday Anchor.
Berger, P., B. Berger, and H. Kellner. 1974. *The Homeless Mind.* New York: Vintage Books.
Boekaerts, Monique. 1979. 'Towards a Theory of Learning Based on Individual Differences'. Ghent, Belgium: *Communication and Cognition* Monograph.
Bolinger, Dwight. 1975. *Aspects of Language* (second edition) New York: Harcourt, Brace, Jovanovich.
Bolitho, R. and P. Early 1981. 'Reasons to be cheerful: or helping teachers to get problems into perspective.' *ELT Documents 110: Focus on The Teacher.* London: The British Council.
Bowen, J. D. 1977. 'Face validity in TESOL: teaching the spoken language' in Burt, Dulay, Finocchiaro (eds.) *Viewpoints on English as a Second Language.* New York: Regents.
British Council. *Teaching and Learning in Focus.* London: The British Council.
British Council. 1977. *ELT Documents 77/1: Games, Simulations and Role-Playing.*
British Council. 1979. *Communication Games in a Language Programme.* Film and Notes for Teacher Trainers.
British Council. 1981. *ELT Documents 110.* London: The British Council.
Brown, A. L. and A. Palinscar. 1982. 'Inducing strategic learning from texts by means of informed, self-control training.' *Topics in Learning and Learning Disabilities* 2/1: 1–18. (Special issue on metacognition.)
Brown, A. L., J. D. Bransford, R. A. Ferrara, and J. Campione. 1982. *Learning, Remembering and Understanding.* Technical Report No 244. Centre for the Study of Reading, University of Illinois at Urbana-Champaign. Also in J. H. Flavell and E. M.

Markman (eds.) *Carmichael's Manual of Child Psychology, Vol 1*. New York: Wiley and Sons.

Brown, H. D. 1981. 'Affective factors in second language learning' in Alatis, Altman, Alatis (eds.). *The Second Language Classroom: Directions for the 1980s.* New York: Oxford University Press.

Brown, Penelope and **Stephen Levinson.** 1978. 'Universals in language usage: politeness phenomena' in Ester N. Goody (ed.). *Questions and Politeness: Strategies and Social Interaction.* Cambridge: Cambridge University Press (pp. 56–289).

Brumfit, C. J. 1978. Review of D. A. Wilkins' *Notional Syllabuses. ELT Journal* 33/1: 79–82.

Brumfit, C. J. 1980. *Problems and Principles in English Teaching.* Oxford: Pergamon Press.

Brumfit, C. J. 1981. 'Accuracy and fluency.' *Practical English Teaching* 1/3.

Brumfit, C. J. 1984. *Communicative Methodology in Language Teaching.* Cambridge: Cambridge University Press.

Byrne, D. and **S. Rixon.** 1979. *ELT Guides No. 1: Communication Games.* British Council/NFER.

Burstall, Clare. 1975. *Primary French in the Balance.* Windsor: National Foundation for Educational Research.

Candlin, C. N. and **M. Breen.** 1980. 'The essentials of a communicative curriculum in language teaching.' *Applied Linguistics* 1/2: 89–112.

Candlin, C. N. 1981. 'Form, function and strategy' in C. N. Candlin (ed.). *The Communicative Teaching of English.* London: Longman.

Candlin, E. F. 1968. *Present Day English for Foreign Students.* Fourth edition. London: University of London Press.

Carter, G. (ed.) 1984. 'Are You Ready, Kids?'. Unpublished video film, Bell School, Bath.

Cathcart, R. L. and **J. W. B. Olsen.** 1976. 'Teachers' and students' preferences for correction of classroom conversation errors' in Fanselow and Crymes (eds.). *On TESOL 1976.* TESOL.

Clark, Herbert H. and **Eve. V. Clark.** 1977. *Psychology and Language.* New York: Harcourt, Brace, Jovanovich.

Cook, V. J. 1983. 'What should language teaching be about?' *ELT Journal* 37/3: 299–34.

Cooper, H. M. and **T. L. Good.** 1983. *Pygmalion Grows Up: Studies in the Expectation Communication Process.* New York: Longman.

Corder, S. P. 1960. *An Intermediate English Practice Book.* London: Longman.

Corder, S. P. 1960. *English Language Teaching and Television*. London: Longman.
Corder, S. P. 1966. *The Visual Element in Language Teaching*. London: Longman.
Corder, S. P. 1967. 'The significance of learners' errors' in *International Review of Applied Linguistics* 5/4: 161–170.
Corder, S. P. 1973. *Introducing Applied Linguistics*. Harmondsworth: Penguin.
Corder, S. P. 1973–5. *The Edinburgh Course in Applied Linguistics, Vols 1–4* (edited with J. P. B. Allen). London: Oxford University Press.
Corder, S. P. 1977. 'Strategies of Communication.' Unpublished paper.
Corder, S. P. 1979. 'The teacher's contribution to the language learner's linguistic development' in Eichheim and Maley (eds.). *Fremdsprachenunterricht im Spannungsfeld zwischen Gesellschaft, Schule und Wissenschaften*. Munich: Goethe Institut.
Corder, S. P. 1981. *Error Analysis and Interlanguage*. Oxford: Oxford University Press.
Curle, Adam. 1966. *Planning for Education in Pakistan*. London: Tavistock.
Curran, C. A. 1972. *Counseling-Learning: A Whole-Person Model for Education*. Grune and Stratton.
Curran, C. A. 1976. *Counseling-Learning in Second Languages*. Illinois: Apple River Press.
Curtin, J. B. 1979. 'Attitudes to language learning: the adult student'. *ELT Journal* 33/4: 28 1–4.
Dakin, Julian. 1973. *The Language Laboratory and Language Learning*. London: Longman.
Daniel, N. 1975. *The Cultural Barrier*. Edinburgh: Edinburgh University Press.
Davies, E. and N. Whitney. 1979. *Reasons for Reading*. London: Heinemann.
de Bono, Edward. 1967. *The Use of Lateral Thinking*. London: Jonathan Cape.
De Silva, E. 1981. 'Form and Function in Malaysian English'. M. A. thesis, University of Malaya, Kuala Lumpur.
Dittmar, N. 1981. 'On the verbal organization of L2 tense marking in an elicited translation task by Spanish immigrants in Germany.' *Studies in Second Language Acquisition*. 3/2: 136–64.
Doff, A., C. Jones, and K. Mitchell. 1984. *Meanings into Words*: Intermediate Course. Cambridge: Cambridge University Press.
Donaldson, M. 1976. *Children's Minds*. London: Fontana.
Douglass, Edward F. 1976. 'The discovery of commonness—essential for cross-cultural dialogue—based on anthropo-

logical studies in Sierra Leone', *Ideas and Action* 112 (1976/5). Rome: FAO.
Dusek, J. B., and G. Joseph. 1983. 'The bases of teacher expectations: a meta-analysis.' *Journal of Educational Psychology* LXXV/3: 327–46.
Edelhoff, C. 1984. 'Landeskunde zum Anfassen — the Lancaster Outing. Lehrerfortbildung zum Erfahrungenzu machen' in M. Schratz (ed.): *Englischunterricht im Gespräch*. Bochum: Kamp.
Edwards, H., M. Wesche, S. Krashen, R. Clement, and B. Kruidenier. 1984. 'Second-language acquisition through subject-matter learning: a study of sheltered psychology classes at the University of Ottawa.' *Canadian Modern Language Review* XLI/2: 268–82.
Elley, Warwick B. 1980. 'Recent studies of English reading levels in Fiji'. University of the South Pacific: Suva, Fiji. (Mimeographed.)
Elling, B. 1980. 'Special curricula for special needs' in Phillips (ed.) *The New Imperative: Expanding the Horizons of Foreign Language Education*. Skoki, Illinois: National Textbook Company.
Ellis, R. 1985. *Understanding Second Language Acquisition*. Oxford: Oxford University Press.
Ervin-Tripp, S. 1976. 'Is Sybil there? The structure of American English directives.' *Language in Society* 5/1: 25–66.
Evans, D. W. 1980. 'An assessment of the EFL profession in South Korea'. *Teaching English Abroad Newsletter* (September).
Exarchou H., V. Koustsosimou, H. Patereka and E. Sarikoudi. 1983. *Communicative Language Teaching and Teaching Methodology GALA* (Thessaloniki).
Fanselow, J. 1977. 'The treatment of error in oral work' in *Foreign Language Annals*. Vol. 10/4.
Finocchiaro, M. 1982. 'Motivation: its crucial role in language learning' in Hines and Rutherford (eds.). *On TESOL '81*. Washington, D. C.: TESOL.
FIPLV. 1982. Announcement in *ALSED Newsletter,* No. 25. Paris: UNESCO.
Fisher, E. 1984. 'Television and language development.' *Journal of Educational Television* 10/2: 85–90.
Fishman, J. A. 1977. 'English in the context of international societal bilingualism' in Fishman, Cooper, Conrad (eds.) *The Spread of English*. Rowley, Massachusetts: Newbury House.
Flanders, N. 1970. *Analyzing Teacher Behaviour*. Reading, Mass: Addison Wesley.
Freire, Paulo. 1972. *Pedagogy of the Oppressed*. London: Penguin.
Freudenstein, R., J. Beneke and **H. Ponisch** (eds.) 1981. *Language*

Incorporated: Teaching Foreign Languages in Industry. Oxford: Pergamon Press.

Fried-Booth, D. 1982. 'Project work with advanced classes.' *ELT Journal* 36/2: 98–103.

Fried-Booth, D. 1983. 'Bath Handicapped Project.' Unpublished video film, Bell School, Bath.

Gaies, S. 1983. 'The investigation of language classroom processes.' *TESOL Quarterly* 17/2: 205–17.

Gattegno, C. 1963/72. *Teaching Foreign Languages in Schools the Silent Way.* New York: Educational Solutions Inc.

Gattegno, C. 1976. *The Common Sense of Teaching Foreign Languages.* New York: Educational Solutions Inc.

Gebhard, J. G. 1984. 'Models of supervision: choices.' *TESOL Quarterly* 18/3: 501–14.

Geddes, M. and G. Sturtridge (eds.). 1980. *Practical Language Teaching Series.* Hemel Hempstead: Allen and Unwin.

Geddes, M. and J. McAlpin. 1978. 'Communication games–2' in S. Holden (ed.) *Visual Aids for Classroom Interaction.* Oxford: Modern English Publications.

George, H. V. 1981. 'Unhappy professionalism'. *World Language English* 1/1: 9–14.

Giesecke, W. B. 1980. 'Characteristics of English teaching in Japan'. *Teaching English Abroad Newsletter* (September).

Glasgow Media Group. 1976. *Bad News.* London: Routledge and Kegan Paul.

Glasser, Ralph. 1977. *The Net and The Quest: Patterns of Community and How They Can Survive Progress.* London: Temple Smith.

Goke-Pariola, A. 1982. 'A socio-political perspective of English language pedagogy in Nigerian high schools'. Doctoral dissertation. The University of Michigan.

Goody, Esther N. 1978. 'Towards a theory of questions' in Ester N. Goody (ed.) *Questions and Politeness: Strategies in Social Interaction.* Cambridge: Cambridge University Press (pp. 17-43).

Gower, R. and S. Walters. 1983. *Teaching Practice Handbook.* London: Heinemann.

Gunter, B. 1980. 'Remembering televised news: effects of visual format on information gain.' *Journal of Educational Television* 6: 8-11.

Hajjaj, A. S. 1981. 'English language teaching in Kuwait'. *Teaching English Abroad Newsletter* (December).

Halliday, M. and R. Hasan. 1976. *Cohesion in English.* London: Longman.

Hamblin, Douglas. 1974. *The Teacher and Counselling.* Oxford: Blackwell.

Harmer, J. 1982a. 'What is communicative?' *ELT Journal* 36/3: 164–8.

Harmer, J. 1982b. 'Planning, textbooks, syllabuses, and activities'. *Modern English Teacher* 9/3.

Harmer, J. 1983. *The Practice of English Language Teaching*. London: Longman.

Herron, C. A. 1980. 'Second language experiences for everyone' in Phillips (ed.) *The New Imperative: Expanding the Horizons of Foreign Language Education*. Skokie, Illinois: National Textbook Company.

Hill, L. A. 1978. 'Learning a language at the tertiary level through a reading approach'. *ELT Journal* 32/4: 318–22.

Hok, R. 1980. 'Some thoughts on study circles and their potential for language teaching'. *TESOL Quarterly* Vol. 14/1: 117–19.

Holden, S. (ed.) 1979. *Teacher Training*. London: Modern English Publications.

Howe, M. J. (ed.) 1983. *Learning from Television: Psychological and Educational Research*. London: Academic Press.

Hubbard, P., H. Jones, B. Thornton, and R. Wheeler. 1983. *A Training Course for TEFL*. Oxford: Oxford University Press.

Hudson, Liam. 1966. *Contrary Imaginations*. London: Methuen.

Hutchinson, T. 1985. 'Making Materials Work in the ESP Classroom.' Paper presented at the International ESP Conference, Colombo, April 1985.

Hymes, D. 1972. 'On communicative competence' in J. Pride and J. Holmes (eds.) *Sociolinguistics*. London: Penguin (pp. 269–93).

Jackson, P. W. 1968. *Life in Classrooms*. New York: Holt, Rinehart and Winston.

Jersild, Arthur. 1955. *When Teachers Look At Themselves*. New York: Teachers College Press.

Johnson, K. 1981. Introduction to Johnson and Morrow (eds.) 1981.

Johnson, K. and K. Morrow (eds.) 1981. *Communication in the Classroom*. Longman: London.

Jordan, R. (ed.) 1983. *Case Studies in ELT*. Glasgow and London: Collins.

Kachru, B. B. 1977. 'The new Englishes and old models'. *English Teaching Forum* 15/3: 29–35.

Kachru, B. B. (ed.) 1982. *The Other Tongue: English Across Cultures*. Urbana, Illinois: University of Illinois Press.

Kakrides, F. 1986. 'Foreign Languages' (in Greek), to VIMA, Athens, 26th July 1986.

Kehoe, M. 1971. 'Teaching English to speakers of other languages' in Kehoe (ed.). *Applied Linguistics: A Survey for Language Teachers*. New York: Macmillan.

Keller, E. and S. Taba Warner. 1976. *Gambits* (three volumes: *Openers*, *Links* and *Responders and Closers*). Public Service Commission: Ottawa.

Kemelfield, G. 1969. 'Progress report of the Schools Television Research Project.' Part II in *Educational Television International* 3/3.

Kliebard, H. M. 1975. 'The rise of scientific curriculum making and its aftermath.' *Curriculum Theory Network* V/1: 27–38.

Knowles, M. 1970. *The Modern Practice of Adult Education*. New York: Association Press.

Koestler, Arthur. 1966. *The Act of Creation*. London: Pan Books.

Krashen, S. 1977. 'The monitor model for adult second language performance' in M. Burt, H. Dulay and M. Finocchiaro (eds.). *Viewpoints on English as a Second Language*. New York: Regents.

Krashen, S. 1978. 'The monitor model for second language acquisition' in R. C. Gingras (ed.). *Second Language Acquisition and Foreign Language Teaching*. Washington, D. C.: Center for Applied Linguistics.

Krashen, S. 1981. 'The input hypothesis' in J. Alatis (ed.) *The Georgetown Round Table on Language and Linguistics*. Washington, D. C: Georgetown University Press.

Krashen, S. 1981 *Second Language Acquisition and Second Language Learning*. Oxford: Pergamon.

Krasnick, H. 1986. 'The four houses of TESL.' *TESL Reporter*.

Kuhn, Thomas. 1970. *The Structure of Scientific Revolutions*. Chicago: University of Chicago Press.

Ladousse, G. P. 1982. 'From needs to wants: motivation and the language learner'. *System* 10/1: 29–37.

Lambert, W. E., I. Boehler, and N. Sidoti. 1981. 'Choosing the languages of subtitles and spoken dialogues for media presentations: implications for second language education.' *Applied Psycholinguistics* 2:133–48.

Lamendella, John T. 1979. 'The neurofunctional basis of pattern practice'. *TESOL Quarterly* 1:5–19.

Lancy, D. F. 1978. 'The classroom as phenomenon' in D. Bar-Tal and L. Saxe (eds.): *Social Psychology of Education*. New York: John Wiley and Sons.

Legutke, M. and W. Thiel. 1982. '*Airport*': *Ein Projekt für den Englischunterricht in Klasse 6*. Hessisches Institut für Bildungundschulentwicklung.

Littlewood, W. 1981. *Communicative Language Teaching*. Cambridge: Cambridge University Press.

Long, M. 1975. 'Groupwork and communicative competence in the ESOL classroom' in M. Burt and H. Dulay (eds.) *On TESOL '75*. Washington DC: TESOL.

Lozanov, G. 1978. *Suggestology and the Outlines of Suggestopedy*. New York: Gordon and Breach.

Lucas, E. 1975. 'Teachers' Reacting Moves following Errors made by Pupils in Post-primary English-as-a-Second Language Classes in Israel'. Unpublished M.A. Thesis, Tel Aviv University.

Maley, A., F. Grellet and W. Welsing. 1982. *Quartet*. Oxford: Oxford University Press.
McKnight, F. 1981. 'Uses of Video in TEFL', University of Wales. Unpublished M. Ed. thesis.
McTear, M. F. 1975. 'Potential sources of confusion in foreign language lessons: the rules of the game'. Paper presented at the Fourth International Congress of Applied Linguistics, Stuttgart.
Mehan, H. 1979. *Learning Lessons*. Cambridge, MA: Harvard University Press.
Moskowitz, G. 1978. *Caring and Sharing in the Foreign Language Classroom*. Rowley, MA: Newbury House.
Munby, J. 1978. *Communicative Syllabus Design*. Cambridge: Cambridge University Press.
Naiman, N., M. Frolich, H. H. Stern, and A. Todesco. 1977. *The Good Language Learner*. OISE: Toronto.
New Internationalist No. 76. June 1979. 'Children's Voices', Melbourne: New Internationalist Publications Pty. Ltd.
O'Neill, R. 1977. 'The limits of functional/notional syllabuses—or "My guinea pig died with its legs crossed" ' in S. Holden (ed.) *English for Specific Purposes*. London: Modern English Publications.
Paulston, C. B. and M. N. Bruder. 1976. *Teaching English as a Second Language*. Cambridge, Massachusetts: Winthrop.
Pawley, A. and F. Syder. 1984. 'Two puzzles in linguistic theory: nativelike selection and nativelike fluency' in J. C. Richards and R. Schmidt (eds.) *Language and Communication*. London: Longman.
Pillbeam, A. 1984. 'Time ripe for a new type of video.' *EFL Gazette*, October 1984.
Potter, M. 1982. 'Video as a classroom resource.' *EFL Gazette*, September 1982.
Richards, J. C. 1974. *Error Analysis*. London: Longman.
Rinvolucri, M. 1981. 'Resistance to change on in-service teacher training courses.' *Recherches et Echanges* 6/1.
Rivers, W. M. 1968. *Teaching Foreign-language Skills*. Chicago: University of Chicago Press.
Roberts, J. T. 1982. 'State of the art: Recent developments in ELT.' *Language Teaching*. Cambridge: Cambridge University Press.
Rogers, Carl. 1951. *Client-Centred Therapy*. London: Constable.
Rogers, Carl. 1969. *Freedom to Learn*. Colombus, Ohio: Merrill Publishing Co.
Rogers, Carl. 1985. *Freedom to Learn for the Eighties*. Columbus, Ohio: Merrill Publishing Co.
Rogers, John. 1969. 'Why not abandon English teaching in the elementary school?' *Ethiopian Journal of Education* III/1:24–31. Addis Abada: Haile Selassie I University.
Rogers, John. 1982. 'The world for sick proper.' *ELT Journal* 36/3: 144–51.
Rossner, R., P. Shaw, J. Shepherd, and J. Taylor. 1979. *Contemporary English Book 2*. London: Macmillan.

Royal Society of Arts. 1980. *RSA Cert. TEFL Courses: 1980 Conference Report.* London: The Royal Society of Arts.
Rubin, J. 1975. 'What the "good language learner" can teach us'. *TESOL Quarterly* Vol. 9/1: 41–51.
Scott, R. 1981. 'Speaking' in Johnson and Morrow (eds.) 1981.
Seliger, H. W. 1980. 'Second language acquisition: the question of strategies'. Paper presented at the Third Los Angeles Second Language Research Forum.
Severin, W. 1968. *Cue summation in Multiple Channel Communication.* Madison: University of Wisconsin.
Shepherd, J. *et al.*1984. *Ways to Grammar.* London: Macmillan.
Sinclair, J. and M. Coulthard. 1975. *Towards an Analysis of Discourse.* Oxford: Oxford University Press.
Smith, L. E. (ed.) 1981. *English for Cross-cultural Communication.* London: Macmillian.
Soni, Dahel Chandra. 1977. 'The spoken and unspoken word in rural communication: a view-point from India', *Ideas and Action* 115 (1977/2). Rome: FAO.
Stern, H. H. 1983. *Fundamental Concepts of Language Teaching.* Oxford: Oxford University Press.
Stevick, E. W. 1976. *Memory, Meaning and Method.* Rowley, MA: Newbury House.
Stevick, E. W. 1980. *Teaching Languages: A Way and Ways.* Rowley, MA: Newbury House.
Strevens, Peter. 1969. 'Where Has All The Money Gone? The Need for Cost-Effectiveness Studies in the Teaching of Foreign Languages'. Paper delivered to the Technology Section, Second International Congress of Applied Linguistics, Cambridge, September 1969. (Mimeographed.)
Stubbs, M. 1976. *Language, Schools and Classrooms.* London: Methuen.
Swan, M. 1979. *Spectrum.* Cambridge: Cambridge University Press.
Swan, M. 1979. *Kaleidoscope.* Cambridge: Cambridge University Press.
Swan, M. 1985. 'A critical look at the Communicative Approach (1).' *ELT Journal* 39/1: 2–12.
Swan, M. 1985. 'A critical look at the Communicative Approach (2).' *ELT Journal* 39/2: 76–87.
Tarone, E. 1977. 'Conscious communication strategies in interlanguage: a progress report' in H. D. Brown *et al.* (eds.) *On TESOL 1977.* Washington, D. C.: TESOL.
Tarone, E. 1984. 'Teaching strategic competence in the foreign-language classroom' in S. Savignon and M. Berns (eds.) *Initiatives in Communicative Language Teaching.* Reading, MA: Addison-Wesley (1985).
Tarone, E., A. D. Cohen, and D. Dumas. 1976. 'A closer look at some interlanguage terminology.' *Working Papers in Bilingualism No. 4.*
Telatnik, M. A. 1980. 'The intensive journal as a tool to identify and illustrate ESL teacher/teaching variables in the classroom'. Paper

Textbooks Commission. 1983. *Steps to English Book 1*. Rabat: Ministry of National Education, Morocco.

Theroux, Paul. 1977. 'The Flower of Malaya' in *The Consul's File*. London: Hamish Hamilton.

Thomas, H. 1985. 'Cross-Cultural Learning – Three Possible Models for an Investigative Approach to *Landeskunde*.' Unpublished paper.

Toffler, Alvin. 1981. *The Third Wave*. New York: Bantam.

Toukomaa, Pertti. 1982. 'Semilingualism and the education of immigrant children: the Scandinavian research and debate'. Paper presented at the Seventeenth Regional Seminar, RELC, Singapore.

Trenaman, J. M. 1967. *Communication and Comprehension*. London: Longman.

Trifonovitch, G. 1981. 'English as an international language: an attitudinal approach' in Smith (ed.) 1981.

Truax, C. B. and **R. R. Carkhuff.** 1967. *Toward Effective Counseling and Psychotherapy: Training and Practice*. Chicago: Aldine Press.

Underhill, A. 1980. *Use Your Dictionary*. Oxford: Oxford University Press.

Vernon, M. D. 1953. 'Perception and understanding of instructional television'. *British Journal of Psychology* XLIV: 116–26.

Vester, F. 1978. *Denken, Lernen und Vergessen*. Munich: Deutscher Taschenbuch.

Watt, J. 1983. 'British soap.' *Teaching English* 17/1: 26–31.

Wenden, A. 1984. 'Discovering the Theories of Second Language Learners.' Paper presented at the International TESOL convention, Houston, Texas.

Widdowson, H. G. 1972. 'The teaching of English as communication' in C. J. Brumfit and K. Johnson (eds.) 1979. *The Communicative Approach to Language Teaching*. Oxford: Oxford University Press.

Widdowson, H. G. 1978. *Teaching Language as Communication*. Oxford: Oxford University Press.

Widdowson, H. G. 1979. *Explorations in Applied Linguistics*. Oxford: Oxford University Press.

Widdowson, H. G. 1984. 'The incentive value of theory in teacher education.' *ELT Journal* 38/2: 86–90.

Wilkins, David. 1976. *Notional Syllabuses*. Oxford: Oxford University Press.

Wilkins, D. 1983. 'Some issues in communicative language teaching and their relevance to the teaching of languages in secondary schools' in *Perspectives in Communicative Language Teaching*. London: Academic Press.

Williams, E. 1983. 'Communicative reading' in K. Johnson and D. Porter (eds.) *Perspectives in Communicative Language Teaching*. London: Academic Press.

Williams, E. 1985. *Reading in the Language Classroom*. Basingstoke: Macmillan.

English language teaching: a chronology of recent events and publications

(with acknowledgements to A. P. Howatt's *A History of English Language Teaching* (OUP), and thanks to Elizabeth Wilkinson of the British Council ETIC)

DATE	EVENTS	METHODOLOGY, COURSEBOOKS, AND OTHER PUBLICATIONS
1938		*Essential English 1* (Eckersley)
1940	British Council incorporated by Royal Charter; beginning of British Council direct teaching abroad (Lisbon/Alexandria)	
1943	Beginning of BBC English by Radio	
1945		*Teaching and Learning English as a Foreign Language* (Fries)
1946	Professor Bruce Pattison appointed to first Chair with responsibility for EFL (London University)	*ELT Journal* founded
1947		*Living English Structure* (W. Stannard Allen)
1948		*A Learner's Dictionary of Current English* — now *Oxford Advanced Learner's Dictionary* — (A. S. Hornby)
1953		*General Service List of English Words* (Michael West)
1954		*Progressive English 1* (Hornby); *Guide to Patterns and Usage in English* (Hornby)
1957		*Verbal Behaviour* (B. F. Skinner); *Syntactic Structures* (N. Chomsky)
1960	'The Pennsylvania Foreign Language Project'	

1961		CREDIF audio-visual course *Voix et Images de France*
1963	'The Madras Snowball Project'	*Silent Way* (C. Gattegno)
1964	Beginning of TOEFL (Test of English as a Foreign Language)	
1965		*Aspects of the Theory of Syntax* (N. Chomsky)
1966	TESOL founded in USA	'On communicative competence' (D. Hymes)
1967	Association of Teachers of EFL—now IATEFL—founded	*New Concept English* (L. G. Alexander); 'The significance of learners' errors' (S. P. Corder)
1967	Royal Society of Arts (RSA) Certificate in TEFL—now Cambridge/RSA Diploma	
1968	Regional English Language Centre (RELC) Singapore founded	
1969	Conference on Languages for Special Purposes	'The Total Physical Response Approach to Second Language Learning' (J. Asher)
1971		*Kernel Lessons* (R. O'Neill)
1972		'The teaching of English as communication' (H. G. Widdowson); *Grammar of Contemporary English* (R. Quirk *et al.*)
1973	Conference on Communicative Language Teaching (Lancaster)	*Language Laboratory and Language Learning* (J. Dakin); *The Edinburgh Course in Applied Linguistics* (J. P. Allen & S. P. Corder (eds.))
1974	University of Reading Centre of Applied Linguistics (CALS) founded	
1975		*Threshold Level* for English (J. van Ek)
1976		*Memory, Meaning and Method* (E. Stevick); *Counseling-Learning in Second Languages* (C. Curran); *Notional Syllabuses* (D. Wilkins)

1977	Communicative use of English as a foreign language (Cambridge/RSA CUEFL)	*Strategies* (B. Abbs & I. Freebairn); 'The Monitor Model for Adult Second Language Performance' *(S. Krashen)*
1978	*Key English Language Teaching (KELT) Scheme* started	*Teaching Language as Communication* (H. G. Widdowson); *Suggestology and Outlines of Suggestopody* (G. Lozanov); *Communicative Syllabus Design* (J. Munby)
1979	Royal Society of Arts Certificate in the Teaching of English to Adult Immigrants and Preparatory Certificate in TEFL—now Cambridge/RSA Certificate in TEFL; Beginning of 'The Bangalore Project' (Prabhu); English Language Testing Service (ELTS) begun (British Council)	*Follow Me* (BBC English by Television)
1981		*Second Language Acquisition and Second Language Learning* (Krashen)
1983		*Fundamental Concepts of Language Learning* (H. H. Stern)
1984–1987	'Project 12': programme of international workshops for trainers of language teachers (Council of Europe)	
1985	*ELT Journal* Symposium on Teacher Training	*The Story of English* in six parts (BBC Video)

Contributors

Gerry Abbott has been teaching EFL since 1958. After four years of teaching in Thailand and two years as British Council Education Officer in Jordan, he took up a lectureship at Manchester University which he still holds. Short ELT assignments have taken him to Spain, Italy, Algeria, Hungary, Romania, KwaZulu, Malaysia, Pakistan, Cameroon, and Vietnam; but his main secondments have been as Head of the Department of Language Methods, Makerere University, Kampala; UNESCO Expert in English, P.D.R. Yemen; English Language Adviser, Sarawak; and, most recently, as Senior Lecturer in English, University of Mandalay. His articles have appeared in a range of journals and he co-edited and contributed to *The Teaching of English as an International Language* (Collins).

Dick Allwright is Senior Lecturer in the Department of Linguistics and Modern English Language, University of Lancaster. His research interests centre around the relationship between what happens in language classes and what learners get out of them. He is Joint Coordinator (with Hywel Coleman) of the Lancaster/ Leeds Research Project on Language Learning in Large Classes. He also has a special interest in teacher association development, through work on the Executive Board of TESOL, of which he was President in 1988–89.

Cem Alptekin has a Ph.D. from New York University and is Associate Professor of Applied Linguistics and TEFL at Bogazici University, Istanbul, Turkey. His research interests centre around neuro- and socio-psychological aspects of second language acquisition. His principal publications are in the following journals: *The Canadian Modern Language Review*, *TESOL Quarterly*, *ELT Journal*, *British Journal of Language Teaching*, and *ITL Review of Applied Linguistics*.

Margaret Alptekin has an MA from Southern Illinois University and is Director of Research and Curriculum Development at Eyuboglu College in Istanbul, Turkey, where she has been since 1986. Previously she has worked in France, North Cyprus, and the United States. She is particularly involved in teacher training and the promotion of professional development in ELT.

Lois Arthur is Courses Manager for the Bell Educational Trust. She has worked in secondary schools in Germany, in senior posts in language schools in the UK, and was responsible for the overall professional development of teachers working for CBT in Morocco.

Her interests include the training of native speaker teachers of EFL, and the problems involved in teaching young learners.

Graham Carter taught EFL in Italy for four years before returning to teach French and Italian in state schools in England for four years. After a further two years, he started working for the Bell School, Bath in 1981, where he is at present.

Pit Corder who died at his home in Cumbria in January, 1990, retired from the Chair of Applied Linguistics at the University of Edinburgh in September 1983. For over twenty years he had directed the development of applied linguistics studies there, until the Edinburgh department became the most influential in Britain, and probably in the world. Professor Corder's special interest lay in error analysis, and in the early 1970s he combined this with a growing interest in second-language acquisition, thereby establishing 'interlanguage' as a theoretical study. His book *Error Analysis and Interlanguage* (OUP) brought together his papers in this field. He was also elected to the status of Professor Emeritus by Edinburgh University and awarded an Honorary Doctorate from Salonika University.

Rod Ellis is a lecturer at Temple University in Tokyo, Japan. Prior to that he was Head of the Department of English Language Teaching at Ealing College of Higher Education, London. His previous teaching experience includes a ten-year period in Zambia where he worked as a teacher trainer. In the last eight years he has worked on consultancies and short courses in Europe, Africa, South America, and Asia. He has published articles on teacher training and second language acquisition in the following journals: *ELT Journal*, *System*, *Applied Linguistics*, and *Studies in Second Language Acquisition*. He has co-authored a book for teacher training in Africa – *Teaching Secondary English*. In addition he has published a number of textbooks, including a coursebook for use in Southern Africa. His second language acquisition publications include: *Classroom Second Language Development* and *Understanding Second Language Acquisition* (OUP); the latter won the first book prize awarded by the British Association of Applied Linguistics in 1986.

Caleb Gattegno who died in France in July, 1988, was inventor of one of the 'fringe methodologies' called 'The Silent Way'. He started out in the sciences in Egypt and became involved in the training of teachers (principally of mathematics) during his time at the University of Liverpool and the London University Institute of

Education between 1945 and 1957. He co-authored *Numbers in Colour* with George Cuisenaire, inventor of the rods of the same name that are used in mathematics teaching and in language teaching by the Silent Way.

Jeremy Harmer is a freelance teacher trainer and ELT writer. He has taught in Britain and Mexico where he was Director of the Guadalajara branch of the Instituto Anglo-Mexicano de Cultura. His books include the course, *Meridian Plus*, and for teachers, *The Practice of English Language Teaching* (Longman) and *Teaching and Learning Grammar*.

David King is Head of Studies at Eurocentre, Brighton. He has attempted to balance the perceptions gained from many years in teaching, with a continuing experience of the learning process, completing a Diploma in counselling in 1985, and a modular MA in TEFL from Reading in 1987. He has given a number of workshops on counselling skills in the field of TEFL, and, most recently, is co-facilitator on Eurocentre's one-year, part-time course leading to the RSA certificate in 'Counselling Skills in the Development of Learning'.

Harry Krasnick has taught ESL for ten years, in Canada, Hawaii, Guam, and Indonesia. He obtained his doctorate in ESL and his law degree from the University of British Columbia (Canada), and his master's in sociology from UCLA. Besides the *ELT Journal*, he has published in *TESOL Quarterly*, *JALT Journal*, and *RELC Journal*. His area of specialization is academic cross-cultural communication. Since 1988, he has worked with the World University Service of Canada's (WUSC) Canada-Indonesia Pre-departure Program, Universitas Gadjah Mada, Yogjakarta, Indonesia, where he has developed an integrated ESL-and-Sociology of Canada course for advanced-level trainees who will be pursuing post-graduate degrees in Canada.

Iain MacWilliam has been a lecturer in TESOL from 1985 to the present at the Scottish Centre for Education Overseas, Moray House College, Edinburgh. Prior to that he worked at the Institute for Applied Language Studies, University of Edinburgh where he was involved in the development of home-produced video materials for language comprehension purposes. He has taught EFL in Lebanon, Belgium, and the Netherlands, where he served as British Council Director of Studies for three years.

Alan Maley is Director-General of the Bell Educational Trust, Cambridge. He worked for The British Council from 1963–1988 in Yugoslavia, Ghana, Italy, France, China, and India. He has published widely in EFL and Applied Linguistics and is co-author of the following books: *Beyond Words, Learning to Listen, Mind Matters, Poem into Poem, Sounds Interesting, Sounds Intriguing, The Mind's Eye* (all CUP), *Quartet,* and *Literature* (OUP)—to name but a few.

Péter Medgyes is Head of the English Department at Eötvös Loránd University, Budapest where he teaches applied linguistics and methodology. Previously, he was a teacher trainer at a secondary grammar school for more than a decade. He has written several ELT textbooks and articles, which have appeared both in his home country and abroad. At present, he is a Fulbright Fellow at the University of Southern California, Los Angeles.

Rob Nolasco is a self-employed author, teacher trainer and EFL consultant. He was involved in Project Management in Saudi Arabia, Angola, and Morocco where he was Director of The Centre for British Teachers from 1983–85. He also taught EFL to secondary and adult students, at all levels, in the UK, Turkey, France, and Spain. He is the author of many titles for students as well as two methodology books: *Conversation* (OUP) and *Large Classes* (Macmillan) – both with Lois Arthur. Currently his main activity is materials writing but he maintains an interest in management training in educational settings and the problems in setting up the infrastructure for teaching and learning and occasionally runs courses in these areas.

Robert O'Neill is the author of many textbooks, including *Kernel Lessons Intermediate, Kernel Lessons Plus, Viewpoints, Interaction, Kernel One, English in Situations,* and *Business News,* and also co-author of a course for students—*Success at First Certificate* (OUP). He worked first as a teacher and then in the Research and Development Unit of the European Language and Educational Centre in Bournemouth. Since then he has taught extensively in various parts of Europe, and has recently been involved in various intensive courses for industry.

Luke Prodromou is a teacher and teacher trainer at the British Council, Thessaloniki. He has an MA in Shakespeare Studies from the University of Birmingham, and a Postgraduate TEFL Diploma from Leeds University. He is the author of *Medicine* (Pergamon), co-author of *Bits and Pieces* (Collins), and co-author of *On The Move* (OUP).

Esther Ramani has an MA in Applied Linguistics from the University of Lancaster, UK and a Ph.D. in Stylistics from the Indian Institute of Science, Bangalore, where she now teaches scientific communication and supervises research in ethnography and sociology of science. Her interest in teacher development began during her involvement in the Communicational Teaching Project, South India and in the Discourse Analysis Group, Bangalore. Her current interests include classroom interaction analysis, long-term teacher development and the history, philosophy, and sociology of science. She has published in *ELT Journal, English for Specific Purposes, ELT Documents,* and has made several presentations in local and international forums.

Jack Richards is a New Zealander who has worked in many parts of the world, including Canada (where he did his Ph.D.), Indonesia, Singapore, and the US. For the last eight years he has been full professor in the Department of English as a Second Language at the University of Hawaii. At present, he is Professor and Head of the Department of English at the City Polytechnic of Hong Kong where he is setting up a new in-service teacher education program for Hong Kong English teachers, as well as directing a large EAP program. He has written over 100 articles and books. Among his academic books are: *Error Analysis* (Longman), *The Context of Language Teaching* (CUP), and *Longman Dictionary of Applied Linguistics*. Among his books for ESL students are: *Breakthrough, Person to Person,* and *Listen for It* (all OUP).

John Rogers is currently Lecturer in TESOL at the Gold Coast College of Advanced Education, Queensland, Australia. He has previously taught English and trained English teachers in Sweden, Indonesia, Nigeria, Ethiopia, Singapore, New Zealand, and Solomon Islands.

Michael Swan has been involved in English language teaching and teacher training for many years, and is now a full-time writer. He is the author of a number of textbooks and reference books, including *Practical English Usage* (OUP), and *The Cambridge English Course* (with Catherine Walter – CUP). He has also published many articles on aspects of language, language teaching and applied linguistics.

Howard Thomas is Director of Studies at the Bell School, Bath. After graduating in 1969 he worked as a modern languages teacher in Britain and later as an EFL teacher and teacher trainer in Germany. In 1978 he obtained an MSc degree in Applied

Linguistics from the University of Edinburgh. Since then he has worked as a teacher trainer and administrator in EFL in Britain and abroad. He has contributed several articles to EFL journals, and has co-authored textbooks which focus on listening comprehension, video work, and the communicative classroom.

Anita Wenden is Assistant Professor of ESL at York College, City University of New York, where she is ESL faculty specialist in curriculum and faculty development. She held a similar post at Columbia University on the American Language Program and was Instructor in the MA program in TESOL, teaching specialized methodology courses. She also taught at Taiwan University. Her numerous articles and reviews have appeared in *ELT Journal, Language Learning, TESOL Newsletter, Canadian Modern Language Journal*, and *Applied Linguistics*.

Henry Widdowson is Professor of English for Speakers of Other Languages at the University of London Institute of Education. Previously, he was a lecturer at the University of Edinburgh, where he also did his doctorate: before that he had worked for several years with the British Council in Sri Lanka and Bangladesh. He is the author of a number of books, including *Teaching Language as Communication, Explorations in Applied Linguistics, Learning Purpose and Language Use*, and *Aspects of Language Teaching* (all OUP). He was one of the founder editors of *Applied Linguistics*.

Li Xiaoju is Professor of English at the Guangzhou Institute of Foreign Languages in China. She is Director of the Communicative English for Chinese Learners (CECL) project, a project that began propagating the communicative approach in EFL in China in 1979. She is also involved in language testing and is one of the chief designers of several EFL tests used widely in China.

Topic index to volumes 36–42

Activities (focusing on form and communicative outcome): Willis and Willis, 41/1; (communicative and non-communicative): Harmer, 36/3.
Advanced learners (stylistic variations in EFL): Davies, 39/1.
Advanced students (developing their stylistic and lexical awareness): Thomas, 38/3.
Applied linguistics (status in the mid-1980s): Corder, 40/3; (for teacher training): Britten, 42/1.
Authentic listening (using news broadcasts): Zhu, 38/4.
Autonomy (self-directed learning): Bertoldi, Kollar and Ricard, 42/3; (in extended large-scale projects): Woods, 42/3; (in teacher training): Britten, 42/1, Candlin and Fanselow, 42/3.

Class management (integral part of lesson planning): Maclennan, 41/3.
Classroom behaviour (alternative forms): Coleman, 41/2.
Classroom interaction (resembling 'Waiting for Godot'): Dinsmore, 39/4.
Classroom practice (an appreciation of the work of Harold E. Palmer): Tickoo, 36/2.
Classroom procedure (testing current methodological assumptions): Balet, 39/3.
Cloze (new uses – thirty years on): Soudek and Soudek, 37/4.
Communication (pedagogic value of games): Gardner, 41/1.
Communication approach (arguing against Swan's view): Widdowson, 39/3.
Communicational teaching project (evaluation – Bangalore 1984): Beretta and Davies, 39/2; (reluctant complaint – Bangalore, 1984): Greenwood, 39/4.
Communicative approach (conflicting views): Medgyes, 40/2; (theoretical ideas): Swan, 39/1; (a critical look): Swan, 39/2.
Communicative language teaching (intercontinental perspectives – talking shop): Mikulic, Yang, Freive and Kiganda, 39/3; (informal and formal approaches): Ellis, 36/2.
Communicative needs (in foreign language learning): Richards, 37/2.
Communicative performance (focusing on communication strategies): Ellis, 38/1.
Communicative teaching (using texts in the classroom): Morrow and Schocker, 41/4; (in China): Li, 38/1; (in Japan): Sano, Takahashi and Yoneyama, 38/3; (ELT in non-English-speaking countries – talking shop): Bolitho, Gower, Johnson, Murison-Bowie, Rossner and White, 37/3; (with computers): Cook, 42/4.

Communicative techniques (problems of innovation): Nolasco and Arthur, 40/2.
Composition (procedure involving imaginary dialogue with reader): Robinson, 41/4.
Compositions (evaluation): Chimombo, 40/1.
Comprehension questions (improvements to approach and method): Whitaker, 37/4.
Comprehension skills (programme to develop integration of tasks): Lynch, 37/1.
Computer Assisted Language Learning (CALL) (computer-aided English course): Jun, 41/2; (survey review of new handbooks): Carrier, 41/1; (a scoring game for reading skills): Higgins, 38/3; (vocabulary learning): Fox, 38/1; (from failure to success): Kerr, 39/3; (a non-directive approach): Higgins, 39/3; (testing or teaching?): Jones, 37/3; (communicative teaching): Cook, 42/4; (reading comprehension): Nyns, 42/4; (survey review of materials): Scarbrough, 42/4; (vocabulary learning for young learners): Palmberg, 42/4.
Computers (English phonology): Gurney, 41/4.
Continuous writing (different approach to teaching ESL classes): Tomlinson, 37/1.
Correction (errors of accuracy and fluency): Murphy, 40/2; (of mistakes): Johnson, 42/2.
Culture and language learning (culture of native speaker v. culture of learner): Prodromou, 42/2.
Culture shock (and learner training): Pearson, 42/3.
Curricula (multi-dimensional framework for second languages): Ullmann, 36/4.
Curriculum (innovation in difficult circumstances): Kouraogo, 41/3.
Curriculum and syllabus design (talking shop): Candlin and Rodgers, 39/2.
Curriculum development (in Hong Kong's primary schools): Young, 37/3.

Developmental errors (their role in assessing language competence): Ghadessy, 39/4.
Dictation (in need of reappraisal): Morris, 37/2.
Dictionaries (bilingual): Thompson, 41/4; (their use in EFL reading comprehension tests): Bensoussan, 37/4.
Discourse analysis (in ELT classrooms): van Lier, 38/3; (reply to Sopher and Deyes): Barry, 37/1; (for literary interpretation): Deyes, 36/2.

EFL teaching (bilingual and bicultural): Alptekin, 38/1.
ELT (images): Krasnick, 40/3; (pros and cons): Abbott, 38/2; (five

hundred years): Howatt, 37/3; (ideas and techniques – talking shop): Brumfit and Byrne, 36/1; (a better future for the learner?): Rogers, 36/3; (making a videotape): Brennan and Miller, 36/3.
ELT and the British Council (the first 50 years): Lott, 38/4.
ELT Journal (looking back 40 years): Widdowson, 40/4.
English grammar (the notion of restriction): Narayanaswamy, 36/1.
English language examinations (a survey): Simmonds, 39/1.
English phonology (phonemic keyboard): Gurney, 41/4.
English usage (past, present, and future): Ilson, 36/4; (English grammar): Haegeman, 36/4.
Error analysis (differences between native and non-native speaking ESL teachers): Sheorey, 40/4; (counteracting interference): Lott, 37/3; (differing assessment of seriousness): Hughes and Lascaratou, 36/3; (assessment on confidence rating): Yule, 42/2; (why students get things wrong): Johnson, 42/2.
Error evaluation (the importance of viewpoint): Davies, 37/4.
ESL (bilingual folk stories): Baynham, 40/2; (experimental vocational course): Rae, 40/3; (for the unemployed): McLaughlin, 39/2.
ESL teachers (error perceptions of native and non-native speakers): Sheorey, 40/4.
ESP (using translation): Tudor 41/4; (making it more communicative): Hutchinson and Waters, 38/2; (reading for advanced students): Lewin, 38/2; (using logical problems): Dorrity, 37/2; (designing a reading skills course): Frydenberg, 36/3; (reassessment of courses for engineers): Yin, 42/2.

Games (communicative): Gardner, 41/1.
Graded readers (a critique/survey review): Hill and Thomas, 42/1, 42/2.
Grammar (systematic teaching of verbs): Svalberg, 40/2; (simple and continuous forms): Pochiecha, 42/4; (survey review of intermediate-level workbooks): Fortune, 42/3; (survey review of grammar books for teachers): Gower, 36/1.
Grammar books (problems of writing): Chalker, 38/2.
Group work (types): Jacobs, 42/2.

Humanism and harmony (approach to ELT): Stevick, 38/2.
Humanistic activities (sharing of experiences): Cormon, 40/4.

IATEFL (association with ELT Journal): Nolasco and White, 42/3; (TESOL/IATEFL Summer Institute): Candlin and Fanselow, 42/3.
Idioms (difficulties with learning and help with teaching): Irujo, 40/3.
Information gap (procedure to help students with structures): Edge, 38/4.

Interpretative tasks (applied to short stories): Yorke, 40/4.

Language analysis (difficulties in using 'let' and 'let's' in the imperative): Tregidgo, 36/3; (meaning and usage of 'to take for granted'): Chiu-ming, 36/3; (damage caused by restricted conditionals): Maule, 42/2; (hedging – implications for teaching and learning): Skelton, 42/1; (perceptions of teacher talk): Lynch, 42/2; (simple and continuous forms): Pochiecha, 42/4.
Language awareness (for teachers who think they know it all): Gotebiowska, 38/4.
Language learning (non-verbal channels): Soudek and Soudek, 39/2; (positive response to 'phantasy' adverts on T.V.): Lynch, 39/2; (Chinese approaches): Harvey, 39/3.
Language learning and teaching (current underlying issues): Maley, 37/4.
Language study (learner-centred approach): Littlejohn, 39/4.
Language teaching (communicative practices): Nunan, 41/2; (looking back to 1884): Howatt, 38/4; (forms, meanings, and uses): Allison, 37/2; (content): Cook, 37/3; (unusual methodology – sensory deprivation): Swan and Walter, 36/3; (the Silent Way – talking shop): Gattegno, 36/4; (centenary tribute to the work of Wilhelm Vietor): Howatt, 36/4.
Learner autonomy (ESL at university level): Armanet and Obesejecty, 36/1.
Learner training (preparation of short written answers in other subjects): Allison 40/1; (thinking about learning): Wenden, 40/1; (adapting to unfamiliar methods): Bassano, 40/1; (self-directed learning): Bertoldi, Kollar, and Ricard, 42/3; (learner strategies and interviews): Pearson, 42/3; (learning strategies for vocabulary): Porte, 42/3; (for literature courses): Hirvela and Boyle, 42/3.
Learning objectives (specifications for EFL teachers): el Nil el Fadil, 39/2.
Lesson planning (integrated with class management): Maclennan, 41/3; (balanced programme of activities): Harmer, 38/2.
Listening (teaching it effectively): Sheerin, 41/2; (factors affecting comprehension): Boyle, 38/1; (authentic activities): Porter and Roberts, 36/1; (perceptions of teacher talk): Lynch, 42/2.
Listening comprehension (a lecture-based approach): Sally, 39/3.
Literature (courses and student attitudes): Hirvela and Boyle, 42/3.
Literature and ELT (talking shop): Widdowson, 37/1.

Management (innovation in ELT): White, 41/3.
Materials evaluation (textbooks): Sheldon, 42/4.
Microteaching (development of organizational skills): Cripwell and Geddes, 36/4; (in teacher training): Parish and Brown, 42/1; Waters, 42/1.

Moderation (problem-solving through group activities): Purvis, 37/3.
Monolingual dictionaries (the value of etymological information): Ilson, 37/1.
Mother tongue (a classroom resource): Atkinson, 41/4.
Mother tongue materials (for teaching second language literacy): Baynham, 37/4.

Non-native teachers (viewed as learners of English): Medgyes, 37/1.

Oral proficiency (a new comprehensive test): Shohamy, Reves and Bejarano, 40/3.
Oral work (testing in teacher training): Sunderland, Yixing and Barr, 42/1.

Performance (relationship between conversational cloze tests and oral ability): Brown, 37/2.
Performance testing (communicative skills): Allison and Webber, 38/3.
Phonology (redundancy in speech): Abbott, 40/4.
Placement testing (using an 'information gap' exercise): Bowker, 38/4.
Poetry (with mixed ability classes): Tomlinson, 40/1; (in the language classroom): Ramsaran, 37/1.
Pre-beginner phase (extra training for adult students): Haycraft, 37/1.
Prendergast ('Mastery Method' and its impact): Tickoo, 40/1.
Project design (pulling out of extended large-scale projects): Woods, 42/3.
Project work (with advanced classes): Fried-Booth, 36/2.
Pronunciation (testing students' discrimination between different sounds): Hole, 37/2.

Quick writing (to encourage creativity): Jacobs, 40/4.

Reading (English for academic purposes): Walker, 41/1; (improved students' competence): Soulé-Susbielles, 41/3; (using adapted literary texts): Campbell, 41/2; (important teaching principles): Williams, 40/1; (two methods of teaching in Nigerian primary classes): Gbenedio, 40/1; (advanced for ESP students): Lesin, 38/2; (efficient comprehension strategies): Scott, Carioni, Zanetta, Bayer, and Quintanilha, 38/2; (skills assessed by computer): Higgins, 38/3; (problems facing ESL students): Aslanian, 39/1; (activity for developing skills); McGinley, 37/2; (communicational testing): Lukmani, 36/4; (with CALL): Nyns, 42/4; (graded readers): Hill

and Thomas, 42/1; (the work of Michael West): Tickoo, 42/4.
Reference books (coverage of fixed expressions): Alexander, 38/2.
Reform (ELT in Czechoslovakian schools): Repka, 40/3.
Rewriting (helping students to develop this skill): Chenoweth, 41/1.
Role play (use of non-ELT simulations): Crookall, 38/4.
Role reversal (teachers as language learners): Lowe, 41/2.
Roles (teacher and learner): Widdowson, 41/2.

Second language acquisition (The L.A. Tapes – talking shop): Allwright, Eskey, Rutherford, Shaw and Schumann, 37/2.
Self-directed learning (an experiment): Kraus-Srebric, Brakus and Kentric, 36/1; (within an institution): Bertoldi, Kollar, and Ricard, 42/3.
Service English (timetabling): Skeldon and Swales, 37/2; (evaluation of integrated teaching): Siegel and Dube, 36/3.
Skills (strategies for rewriting compositions): Chenoweth, 41/1; (integration and separation): Selinker and Tomlin, 40/3; (writing English script): Ball, 40/4.
Speaking (hedging): Skelton, 42/1; (teacher talk): Lynch, 42/2.
Stress and intonation (problems of teaching with functional materials): Roberts, 37/3.
Structure-based course (making it more communicative in Sri Lanka): Mosback, 38/3.
Stylistic variations (for advanced EFL learners): Davies, 39/1.
Stylistics (impediment to reading): Gower, 40/2.
Syllabus design (an experiment with primary schools in South India): Brumfit, 38/4; (a modular communicative project, parts 1 and 2): Shaw and Estaire, 36/2; (modular approaches): Batstone, 42/3.

Teacher development (innovation strategies): Kennedy, 41/3.
Teacher education (the value of theory): Widdowson, 38/2.
Teacher motivation (resulting from humanistic activities): Cormon, 40/4.
Teacher training (developing reading skills): Jarvis, 41/3; (integrating theory and practice): Ramani, 41/1; (using radio broadcasts): Ahrens and Ghodiwala, 41/3; (activities and procedures): Ellis, 40/2; (peer micro-teaching feedback without embarrassment): Edge, 38/3; (help with understanding TEFL articles for the non-native speaker EFL teacher): Edge, 39/3; (doubts and improvements to well-established techniques): Gotebiowska, 39/4; (counselling): King, 37/4; (hierarchy of decisions for ELT): Brumfit and Rossner, 36/4; (in-service): Kouraogo, 41/3; Parish and Brown, 42/1; Sunderland, Yixing and Barr, 42/1; (course design): Waters, 42/1; (courses emphasizing language improvement): Hundleby and Breet, 42/1; (three stages): Britten, 42/1; (summer institutes):

Candlin and Fanselow, 42/3.
Teaching and learning (a combined operation): Corder, 40/3.
Teaching and researching (using ethnographic methods in ESL writing): Liebman-Kleine, 41/2.
Teaching materials (questioning their value): Allwright, 36/1.
Teletext (using sub-titles): Vanderplank, 42/4.
TESL (in Britain – talking shop): Frame and Nicholls, 37/4.
TESOL (TESOL/IATEFL Summer Institute): Candlin and Fanselow, 42/3.
Testing (oral proficiency): Shohamy, Reves, and Bejavano, 40/3; (error and analysis): Yule, 42/2; (oral work in teacher training): Sunderland, Yixing, and Barr, 42/1.
Tests (communicative oral performance): Fulcher, 41/4.
Textbook evaluation (developing criteria): Williams, 37/3.
Textbooks (arguments for their use): O'Neill, 36/2; (description and evaluation): Sheldon, 42/4.
Texts (communicative use in the classroom): Morrow and Schocker, 41/4.
TOEFL (Test of English as a Foreign Language – an appraisal): Traynor, 39/1.
Total physical response (how to incorporate it into the English programme): Sano, 40/4.
Transactional dialogue (potential practical value in language teaching): Taborn, 37/3.
Translation (interactive methods and communicative procedures): Ege, 40/2; (for advanced learners): Titford, 37/1.

Video (video-aided English course): Jun, 41/1; (language comprehension): MacWilliam, 40/2; (silent viewing): Allan, 38/1; (learning English in a video studio): Charge and Giblin, 42/4.
Vietor, Wilhelm (a centenary tribute): Howatt, 36/4.
Vocabulary (fixed expressions in English): Alexander, 38/2; (role of schemata in teaching and learning): Lindstromberg, 39/4; (ESL proficiency and word frequency counts): Harlech-Jones, 37/1; (practical approach to reinforcement): Stieglitz, 37/1; (learning with the use of grids): Harvey, 37/3; (computers and young learners): Palmberg, 42/4; (learning strategies of poor learners): Porte, 42/3; (the work of Michael West): Tickoo, 42/4.

West, Michael (a centenary tribute): Tickoo, 42/4.
Word-level proficiency (handicap in L2 acquisition): Bullard, 39/1.
Word processor (helping learners to write): Piper, 41/2.
Writing (constructive argument or real issues): Chimombo, 41/3; (comparative study of L1 and L2): Arndt, 41/4; (reshaping ESL students' perceptions of it): Blanton, 41/2; (teaching and researching using ethnographic methods): Liebman Kleine, 41/2; (via the use of a word processor): Piper, 41/2; (English script): Ball, 40/4; (practice for EAP students): McDonough, 39/4; (sources for research purposes): Johnston, 39/4; (correcting devices): Zamel, 37/1; (correspondence with learners): Rinvolucri, 37/1.

Acknowledgements

We wish first and foremost to thank the authors whose papers we have selected for submitting their work to *ELT Journal* originally, for their patience with the vetting procedures and correspondence, and for their permission to reprint the papers here. Without their efforts, there would have been no book.

We also wish to thank the members of the esteemed Editorial Advisory Panel who served between 1980 and 1988. The voluntary work of these people and the time they give up to ensure that the *Journal* maintains a high standard is often overlooked. All the articles included here were originally accepted only after at least two and often up to six other people had read them, thought about them, offered feedback, and perhaps suggested amendments. For the record, the names of those who served on the Panel during that period were: Dick Allwright, Rod Ellis, Marion Geddes, Roger Gower, Elizabeth Hoadley-Maidment, and Alan Moller.

It is also very important to remember the work put into the *Journal* by its OUP custodians, past and present. The period in question spans the jurisdictions of Keith Rose, Simon Murison-Bowie and Cristina Whitecross, who still manages the *Journal*, and has also overseen this volume. We thank them for their interest, advice, and co-operation.

Even more important was the careful and imaginative toil of Catherine Robinson, who had day-to-day responsibility for putting the *Journal* together throughout the period in question. It was thanks to her that the *Journal* actually appeared in its impressive finished form each quarter.

As far as this volume is concerned, we have been grateful for the comments and advice offered by Henry Widdowson. Needless to say, any infelicities and inaccuracies in the introductory, linking, and concluding paragraphs are our responsibility, not his. However, the meticulous preparatory work on the manuscript of the current volume was done by Angela Moar and the designer, Jem Jarman. Without their work, this volume could not have come into being.

Lastly, we wish to offer thanks to our children, Helen and Claire Bolitho and Cathy and Chris Rossner, for putting up with yet another encroachment on time that could have been spent with them, and to our wives, Annick Rossner and Viv Bolitho, for their general long-sufferingness.